PLIGHT OF THE FORTUNE TELLERS

PLIGHT OF THE FORTUNE TELLERS

Why We Need to Manage
Financial Risk Differently

Riccardo Rebonato

PRINCETON UNIVERSITY PRESS

PRINCETON AND OXFORD

Published by Princeton University Press,
41 William Street, Princeton, New Jersey 08540

In the United Kingdom: Princeton University Press,
3 Market Place, Woodstock, Oxfordshire OX20 1SY

ISBN-13: 978-0-691-13361-4 (alk. paper)

Library of Congress Control Number: 2007928672

A catalogue record for this book is
available from the British Library

This book has been composed in Palatino

Typeset by T&T Productions Ltd, London

Printed on acid-free paper ∞

press.princeton.edu

Printed in the United States of America

10 9 8 7 6 5 4 3

To my wife

To my parents

To my newborn son

CONTENTS

PREFACE

[T]here is ... considerable danger in applying the method of exact science to problems ... of political economy; the grace and logical accuracy of the mathematical procedure are apt to so fascinate the descriptive scientist that he seeks for ... explanations which fit his mathematical reasoning and this without first ascertaining whether the basis of his hypothesis is as broad ... as the theory to which the theory is to be applied.

Karl Pearson, 1889, speaking at the Men's and Women's Club*

Financial risk management is in a state of confusion. It has become obsessively focused on measuring risk. At the same time, it is forgetting that managing risk is about making decisions under uncertainty. It also seems to hold on to two dangerous beliefs: first, that our risk metrics can be estimated to five decimal places; second, that once we have done so the results will self-evidently guide our risk management choices. They do not. Even if they did, our risk metrics cannot be anywhere as precise as they are made out to be. This is not because we must "try harder"—say, collect more data, or use cleverer statistical techniques. It is because, given the problem at hand, this degree of precision is intrinsically unattainable.

Given what is at stake, this state of confusion is dangerous. To get out of this impasse we must tackle the task from a radically different angle: we must revisit our ideas about probability in financial risk management, and we must put decision making back at center stage. This is what this book is about.

*Quoted in A. Desrosieres (1998), *The Politics of Large Numbers: A History of Statistical Reasoning* (Cambridge, MA: Harvard University Press).

Given the importance of the topic, I intend to reach both a specialist and a nonspecialist audience. I certainly have professional, and often quantitative, financial risk managers in mind. But I also intend to speak to their managers (and to the managers of their managers), to policy makers, and to regulators, who are unlikely to be as quantitatively inclined as the risk professionals. I want to engage students and academics, but also members of the general public who are interested in matters financial.

Let me elaborate on the thumbnail sketch of what this book is about that I offered in my opening lines. The sound management of financial risk affects not just bankers, traders, and market professionals but the public at large, and more directly so than is often appreciated. Unfortunately, for all its apparent quantitative sophistication, much of the current approach to the management of financial risk rests on conceptually shaky foundations. Many of the questions posed in the quest for control over financial risk are not simply difficult to answer—I believe they are close to meaningless.

In great part this is because in looking at the control and regulation of financial risk we are not even clear what "type of" probability is of relevance or when either type could be used more profitably. This matters because members of the species *homo sapiens* can be surprisingly good at dealing with certain types of uncertain events, but spectacularly bad at dealing with others. Unfortunately, this does not seem to be taken into account by much of current risk management, which, if anything, works "against the grain": it pushes us toward those areas of probability where we make systematically poor decisions, and it neglects the domains where we are, after all, not so bad.

There are more fundamental problems with current financial risk management. These are to be found in its focus on measuring risk and in its scant attention to how we should reach decisions based on this information. Ultimately, managing risk is about making decisions under uncertainty. There are well-established disciplines (e.g., decision theory) devoted to this topic, but these have, by and large, been neglected. To understand whether this neglect is justified or whether we are missing out on some useful tools we will have to look at what utility and prospect theory have to offer. My conclusion will be that a straightforward (and rather old-fashioned) application of these theoretical tools has limited applicability in practical risk management applications. This does not mean, however, that the decisional (as opposed to measurement) problems we are faced with are any less important.

Not all is doom and gloom, though: I will argue in the last part of this book that there *is* a more satisfactory way to look at these matters, an approach that has been successfully employed in many of the physical and social sciences. This approach clearly distinguishes between different types of probability and employs them appropriately to create risk management tools that are cognitively resonant. Probabilities-as-degree-of-belief and probabilities-as-revealed-by-actions will be shown to be the keys to better decision making under financial uncertainty. If these probabilities will seem less "sharp" and precise than those that current risk management appears to offer, it is because they are. They have one great advantage, though: they keep us honest and humble and can save us from the hubris of spurious precision. Not a small achievement if "ignorance is preferable to error and he is less remote from the truth who believes nothing than he who believes what is wrong" (Thomas Jefferson, 1781).

Reading a book involves an investment in time and mental effort probably second only to writing one. Why should the nonspecialist reader find these topics of sufficient relevance to justify this investment? And how can it be that risk-management professionals, students, and academics may find something of relevance in a nonspecialist book? Here is how I can answer these very good questions.

These days, risk management appears to be pervasive in every area of human endeavor. We seem to think, speak, and breathe risk management. In short, we appear to be living in a risk-management culture. Presumably, we should be better at managing risk than we have ever been.

It is true that we have made remarkable progress in recognizing and handling risk. Some current developments in risk-management thinking, however, make me fear that we may have reached an inflection point, and that our attempts at managing risk may be becoming more complex and cumbersome, but less effective.

Let me give a few examples. One of the distinguishing and, from a historical point of view, unprecedented features of the current approach to risk management is its focus on low-probability but potentially catastrophic events. This novel attitude to risk makes us evaluate risky prospects in a very different way than we used to. Take the case of polio and smallpox vaccinations. With the medical knowledge and technology available at the time, administering a vaccine that was too virulent and that could cause a healthy subject to contract the illness it was supposed to prevent had a low, but certainly nonnegligible, probability. Being cautious is obviously commendable, but I sometimes wonder how much longer it would have taken for the polio and smallpox vaccinations to be developed under current safety and risk-avoidance standards—or whether, indeed, they would have been developed at all. This modern attitude to risk is by no means limited to the medical domain: in many other areas, from nuclear energy to nanotechnology to the genetic modification of livestock and crops, we currently display a similar (and, historically speaking, very new) attitude to risk. Whether "new" necessarily equates to "better," however, is debatable.

The examples mentioned above share an important common feature: in a cost–benefit analysis, we currently place much greater weight on unlikely but catastrophic events than we used to. This is neither "right" nor "wrong" per se (in the sense that a mathematical statement can be). It indicates, however, a behavioral response to rare events that is difficult to reconcile with everyday experiences of risk taking. This attitude to risk, called the "precautionary principle," in one of its milder forms states:

> [W]hen an activity raises threat of harm to human health
> or the environment, precautionary measures should be taken

even if some cause and effect relationships are not established scientifically.[*]

A stronger formulation is the following:

[T]he precautionary principle mandates that when there is a risk of significant health or environmental damage ... and when there is scientific uncertainty as to the nature of that damage or the likelihood of the risk, then decisions should be made so as to prevent such activities from being conducted unless and until scientific evidence shows that damage will not occur.[†]

This is not the place to launch into a critique of the precautionary principle.[‡] For the purpose of this discussion the most relevant aspect of this principle is its focus on the occurrence of events whose probability of outcome is either extremely low or so imperfectly known that the most we can say about them is that it is nonzero. Rightly or wrongly, we seem to be increasingly willing to sacrifice tangible and immediate benefits to avoid very remote but seriously negative outcomes. This response to risk *is* historically new, and is spreading to more and more areas. Unsurprisingly, as we shall see, a variant of the precautionary principle has appeared in financial risk management.

Why have we become so preoccupied with managing the risk of very rare but catastrophic events? I venture two explanations. The first is that, throughout the history of the human species, we have always been subject to events of devastating power and consequences: earthquakes, floods, volcanic eruptions, epidemics, etc. In all these instances, *homo sapiens* has, by and large, been at the receiving end of the slings and arrows of outrageous fortune. On an evolutionary scale it has only been in the last five or so minutes of their lives that humans have found themselves

[*]The Wingspread Declaration (1998), quoted in I. Goklany (2001), *The Precautionary Principle* (Washington, DC: Cato Institute).

[†]B. Blackwelder, President of the Friends of the Earth, in a testimony in 2002 before the U.S. Senate.

[‡]For a thorough discussion, see C. Sunstein (2005), *Laws of Fear* (Cambridge University Press).

able to create by their own actions catastrophes of comparable magnitude and import as the natural ones. Nuclear weapons are the most obvious, but not the only, example: think, for instance, of global warming, environmental pollution, antibiotic-resistant bacteria, etc. Indeed, sometimes it seems as though we feel startled by the ability of our actions to have far-reaching consequences— and in some domains we probably attribute to ourselves far more destructive power than we actually have: in Victorian times the "mighty agency ... capable of almost unlimited good or evil"* was nothing more sinister than good old friendly steam; and Mary Shelley's Frankenstein preyed on the then-current fears about that other terrible fiend, electricity. It is plausible to speculate that, given this new-found consciousness of the destructive power of our own actions, we may feel that we have a greater responsibility to control and manage the risks that they have given rise to. Hence, if this view is correct, we can begin to understand our interest in the management of risk in general and of the risk associated with catastrophic events in particular. There is more, though.

There is a second, and probably linked, factor in our current attitude to risk management. As our control over our physical environment, over our biological constraints, over economic events, etc., has increased, we accept less and less that bad things may happen because of "bad luck." Our immediate reaction to a plane disaster, to an unexpected financial crisis, to the spilling of a noxious chemical into a river, or to a train derailment is to set up a fact-finding commission to conduct an enquiry into "who was responsible." In this respect, our attitude to "Fate" has changed beyond recognition in the last one hundred years or so. To convince ourselves, just consider that when life insurance was first introduced in the nineteenth century, many households were reluctant to enter into these contracts because it was felt that doing so would be tantamount to "tempting Fate."[†] We are separated

---

*See Elizabeth Gaskell's *Mary Barton*, quoted in D. Coyle (2007), *The Soulful Science* (Princeton University Press), in which the following example about Frankenstein is also provided.

[†]I. Hacking (1990), *The Taming of Chance* (Cambridge University Press).

from this attitude toward risk of the grandparents of our grandparents by a cognitive gulf that is difficult for us to even compre-
hend. Fate has all but disappeared from our conceptualization of
risk and, indeed, almost from everyday language.* In general, we
appear to be much more willing and inclined to pursue the logical
chain of causal links from a bad outcome to its identifiable causes
than we used to.

I understand that a similar trend toward the "responsibiliza-
tion" of outcomes has occurred in the legal area as well. For
instance, more cases of negligence are currently brought to court
than ever before. And only twenty or thirty years ago the idea
that someone could scald herself with a hot drink purchased at a
fast-food outlet and sue the company would have struck one as
ludicrous. In the legal area, this attitude may be the consequence
of a much wider change: the growth of the tort of negligence
that brought together previously disjointed categories ("pockets") of liability related to negligent conduct inherited from the
nineteenth-century body of English law. The judges active in the
1930s began to organize all these different pockets of liability as
instances of one overarching idea, i.e., that we owe a duty of care
to our "neighbor." Much of the development of the concept of
the tort of negligence has then been the refinement and, by and
large, the extension of the concept of what constitutes our neighbor. But as we begin to think in terms of "neighbors" to whom
a duty of care may be owed, the idea of impersonal "victims of
Fate" recedes in the background: *we,* not the wanton gods, become
responsible.

In sum: there has been a general shift in attitude toward ascrib-
ing a responsibility or a cause of negative outcomes from Fate to
ourselves. We have also come to recognize that, for the first time in
our evolutionary history, we can create our own "man-made catastrophes." Taken together, these two factors go a long way toward
explaining why we are more concerned than we have ever been

---

*For a discussion from an insurance perspective of the links between nat-
ural and economic disasters, see M. L. Landis (1999), Fate, responsibility and
"natural" disasters, *Law and Society Review* 33(2):257–318.

before about risk management in general, and about the management of the risk connected with remote but catastrophic events in particular.

In this book I will deal with these broader topics in passing, but I intend to look mainly at a narrower and more specific aspect of risk management, namely, at the management of financial risk, as practiced by financial institutions and as suggested (or, more often, imposed) by regulators.

This admittedly narrower topic is still very wide-ranging and affects us in ways more direct than we imagine: if we are too lax or ineffective in mandating the minimum standards of financial risk management, the whole globalized economy may be at risk; if these standards are too strict, they may end up stifling innovation and development in one of the most dynamic sectors of the world economy. The financial regulators obviously have a great role to play in this, but, as I will argue, the financial industry and the academic risk-management community share the burden at the very least to a comparable extent.

It is important to understand that regulating and reducing financial risk (as with most instances of regulation and risk reduction) has obvious transparent benefits but also more opaque, yet potentially very great, costs. Excessive regulation or voluntary risk avoidance will, in fact, not only reduce the profitability of financial institutions (the public at large is more likely to display Schadenfreude about this than to shed overabundant tears), it will also curb financial innovation.* This matters deeply, because the benefits of this financial innovation are more widespread and more important for the general public than is generally appreciated. To quote one example out of many, Alan Greenspan marveled in 2004 at the resilience of the banking sector during the

---

*To get a feel for the depth and pace of financial innovation, the bank UBS announced in December 2005 that 50% of its revenue in the fixed-income area came from instruments that did not exist five years ago (*Financial Times*, December 29, 2005)—a statistics of which, as the LEX columnist says, "a drug company could well be proud." By my estimate, the ratio of revenues due to new instruments to revenues due to old instruments would be much higher for other areas, such as credit derivatives.

economic downturn that followed the events of September 11, 2001. This resilience, many have argued, was made possible by the ability afforded to banks by new financial instruments (credit derivatives) to distribute credit risk to a wider section of the economy, thereby reducing the *concentration* of risk that had proved so damaging during previous recessions. As a result, banks were able to minimize the restrictions of credit to the economy that typically occur during economic downturns. This has been quoted as one of the reasons why the 2001 recession was so mild.* And indeed, despite the many high-profile bankruptcies of those years (Enron, WorldCom, Parmalat, etc.), "not one bank got into trouble," as Greenspan famously said.† Interestingly enough, therefore, financial innovation (in this particular case in the form of credit derivatives) has indeed created new types of risk, but has also contributed to the reduction, or at least the diffusion, of other types.

Clearly, it is not just complex derivatives that have brought benefits to the financial sector and to its ultimate users, i.e., the general public: as the International Monetary Fund (IMF) and the Bank for International Settlements recently pointed out, the efficiencies brought about by "deregulation, new financial products and structural changes to the sector" have far outweighed the dangers posed by these developments.‡ What are these broadly felt benefits then? First of all, financial innovation has been useful to redistribute risk, and hence to diffuse its impact. This

---

*"The use of a growing array of derivatives and the related application of more-sophisticated approaches to measuring and managing risk are key factors underpinning the greater resilience of our largest financial institutions, which was so evident during the credit cycle of 2001–02 and which seems to have persisted. Derivatives have permitted the unbundling of financial risks. Because risks can be unbundled, individual financial instruments now can be analyzed in terms of their common underlying risk factors, and risks can be managed on a portfolio basis," Alan Greenspan, Risk transfer and financial stability, *Federal Reserve Bank of Chicago's 41st Annual Conference on Bank Structure, Chicago, IL, May 5, 2005.*

†Greenspan answering questions after a lecture in Berlin, January 13, 2004.

‡J. D'Arista (October 2005), *Capital Flows Monitor* (Financial Markets Center Publication): see www.fmcenter.org/site/.

is, of course, extremely important, but still somewhat "intangible." Financial innovation, however, has also brought about benefits directly felt by the man in the street, as new liquid financial instruments have offered new opportunities to the public at large. New types of mortgages in the United States, for instance, have allowed homeowners to access finance more efficiently and with smaller frictions and transaction costs than ever before in human history. More generally, "Innovation and deregulation have vastly expanded credit availability to virtually all income classes" (Greenspan, April 2005). This has clearly been advantageous for borrowers and, probably, for the economy as a whole. It also carries risks, however, to the extent that such easy finance may cause, say, a real-estate bubble or, more generally, an overheating of the economy.

The changes run deeper. At a very fundamental level, banks had traditionally always been the main "accumulators" of credit risk. If one had to describe their role on the back of a stamp, one would probably write: "Lend the depositors' money to people who may not pay it back." The newfound ability afforded by financial innovation to relocate an important part of this credit risk outside the banking sector has fundamentally changed the nature of risk transfer in a modern economy. Since, as I explain in chapter 5, banks are delicate and "resiliently fragile" institutions, this is a good thing. However, it is much easier to pass risk around than to make it disappear. It has been pension funds and life insurance companies that have increasingly acquired, thanks to new financial instruments, part of the credit exposure that traditionally "belonged" to banks. Since the ultimate direct beneficiaries of the pensions and of the life insurance policies are what economists call the household sector (i.e., you and me), the public have become the "shock absorber of last resort"* in the financial system. The IMF views this broadening of the risk-absorbing basis as beneficial—risk, in general, becomes less "toxic" the more it can be dispersed. The same organization, however, acknowledges the risks inherent in these developments.

*Ibid., p. 7.

Interestingly enough, even as it acknowledges the existence of these risks, the IMF does not call for re-regulation, but suggests that new financial instruments, such as longevity bonds and inflation-linked bonds, may be created, or enhanced, to mitigate the households' exposure to these risks. As far as one can tell at the time of writing, the philosophy of innovation, risk redistribution, and control of these new risks via further innovation has fully spread from the scientific and technological area to the financial domain.[*]

All these new financial instruments, like powerful new medicines, are potentially risky. Striking a good balance between reaping all the advantages they can afford and containing their "side effects" is a formidable challenge. The outcome of this balancing act will have very deep consequences for the world economy: turn the dials too much in one direction and we will certainly be less well off than we could have been; turn them too much in the other direction and we run a small risk of a serious derailment of the economy. Finding the Goldilocks equilibrium is extremely difficult, especially when the incentives of the regulators and the managers of the financial institutions are imperfectly aligned.

Given the magnitude of the task, one may well ask the questions, "Are the tools at the risk manager's disposal up to scratch?" and "Have the many recent innovations in risk-management techniques made the world a safer place?" Judging by the quantity of articles published in the risk-management literature, by the proliferation of books, journals, and magazines, by the attendance of international conferences, it would seem that this must certainly be the case. Indeed, when it comes to financial risk a new, highly sophisticated, and highly quantitative approach to risk management has become very widespread. Risk mangers employed even for junior positions by many large financial institutions are often required to have PhDs in the hard sciences. So widespread is the

---

[*]For further thoughts along these lines, see the remarks made by Federal Reserve Board Chairman Ben S. Bernanke in his talk "Regulation and Financial Innovation" to the Federal Reserve Bank of Atlanta's 2007 Financial Markets Conference, Sea Island, Georgia (via satellite), May 15, 2007.

confidence placed in this relatively new approach to the management of financial risk that it goes virtually unquestioned.

I will argue in this book that, unfortunately, some central aspects of this approach are conceptually flawed. The questions that are being asked are not hard ones. I will claim that they are ill-posed ones. It is not that the techniques are "wrong," of course, but that often they have been, and are being, applied without any serious thought about their relevance for the problem at hand. We are doing a lot of risk-management engineering as if the pillars of risk-management science were so well-established as not to require much questioning. An aircraft engineer does not question the correctness of the physical laws underpinning the technical prescriptions on how to build safe planes every time he has to redesign the profile of a wing. He just gets on and does it. We are behaving in a similar way in the management of financial risk, developing more and more sophisticated pieces of statistical plumbing without asking ourselves if the foundations are indeed as solid as, ultimately, Newton's laws are for the aircraft engineer. Unfortunately, I think that we risk managers have not thought deeply enough about the foundations of our discipline. We are not even clear about the appropriate meaning, in the risk-management context, of the most central concept of all: that of probability. If I am correct, and given that what is at stake is the good functioning of the world economy, both practitioners and regulators should pause for thought.

How is this possible? How can the scores of hard-science PhDs employed by banks as risk managers be guilty, of all things, of an *unreflective* approach to their discipline? If even they are unable to think deeply enough about these problems, who possibly can? Paradoxically, just there, in their finely honed quantitative skills, lies the heart of the problem. Most of the PhDs employed by banks, some for derivatives pricing, some for risk management, obtained their doctorates at the top U.S., U.K., and European universities, and were excellent in their original field of study—very often, physics or mathematics. Why this choice of subjects? Because their employers find that there is no substitute for the rigorous and demanding technical training that these "hard" sciences par excellence impart. As for these young physicists and mathematicians, many, for a variety of reasons, decide that physics, or mathematics, would not suffer unduly if they were to part ways with it and knock at the door of a bank. When the last interview has been successfully handled, a "quant" is born.

So, very hard, but well-defined, technical problems are relatively easy for these quants: finding an efficient technique to solve a very-high-dimensional integral, combining Fourier transforms with Monte Carlo simulations, employing wavelets for signal decomposition, carrying out complicated contour integrals in the complex plane, etc., is just what they have been trained to do for all those years. Especially in the early years of their new career, however, quants are "ignorant experts": they are experts, because of the bagful of analytic tricks they carry over from their original areas of expertise; they are also ignorant because they know, and understand, very little about how a financial institution works, and about finance in general. They often like to be given well-defined, self-contained, and fiendishly difficult tasks, without concerning themselves too much about the "bigger picture." They tend to be impatient about the nuances, and cannot wait to sit down and write some good C++ code and crack the problem. (Lest I offend anyone, I can safely say that as I write this I am thinking of myself some fifteen to twenty years ago.) The good quants, of course, do make the transition from being mere technicians to building a broader picture of where all their complex calculations "fit in." But all too often the financial dimension of what they are doing remains, if not outside, at least at the boundary of their "comfort zone."

When it comes to financial risk management the results of this are, at best, mixed. Those who do understand well the financial questions that need answering (and who often are the bosses of the bosses of the quants) are often not quantitatively proficient and have to take on faith that the quantitative approach chosen will not only be technically correct, but will also "make sense" for the problem at hand. As for the quants, they love nothing more than having to tackle technically difficult problems—the more difficult, the better. Not only will the pleasure in solving the puzzle be greater, but, at least as importantly, the quants' indispensability to the firm will be further confirmed. So, it is not so surprising after all that the quant suggesting that a simpler, less quantitative approach should be used to solve a problem is only slightly less rare than a turkey voting for Christmas.*

This has had unexpected consequences. In the last decade or so the international regulators have been inspired, in writing their rule books, by what they have perceived to be the current cutting-edge industry practice. This approach to regulation has been innovative, refreshing, and laudable. Unfortunately, it has been difficult for the regulators, who were "looking in from the outside," to appreciate the degree of disconnect that occurred in many banks between the quant departments and senior management. In observing that thousands of quants had been employed around the world to crack tough risk-management problems, the regulators were perfectly justified in concluding that this was indeed the way senior bank managers thought about and managed their risk. As the mantra became that financial regulation should be aligned with best industry practice, who could blame the regulators when they tried to cast their rules using the same language they were hearing being employed by the banks' quants? If, in the case of market risk, estimating the 99th loss percentile seemed to be the way many bank risk managers looked at and managed risk, why should it be so unreasonable to ask for the 99.9th percentile, or even for the 99.99th percentile, for credit risk? What are a couple of nines between friends, after all? Who could criticize these industry-aligned regulators, when some of the banks' own quants claimed that the way of the risk-management future lay in gaining intellectual control over these once-in-ten-thousand-years events. Were these not the smartest kids on the block, after all? And had

---

*It should be added that software vendors and "impartial" management consultants, seeing some of the largest contracts in decades dangled before their eyes, are unlikely voices of dissent in this debate. The quantitative management of risk has long ceased to be pure or applied science—it is now big business.

they not been allowed to play with the most powerful computers available? If this isn't "best practice," what is?

The less-than-perfect result of this combination was transparent in the terse comments made at the Geneva 2005 ICBI risk-management conference by a very senior official of one of the international regulatory bodies. (For once, I will leave the comment unattributed.) In looking over the hundreds of pages of the brand new, highly quantitative, bank regulatory regime (Basel II), he sighed: "It does read a bit as if it has been written without adult supervision." This is just what I was referring to when I mentioned above that in recent risk management, extreme attention has been devoted to the plumbing without worrying too much about whether the structural plan was sound. We have been doing a lot of very sophisticated engineering without asking (or, for the reasons given above, wanting to ask) whether the underlying "physics" warranted such precision. Everybody knows Keynes's dictum that it is better to be approximately right than precisely wrong. Alas, in my opinion, I believe that in quantitative financial risk management some of the answers have at times been precisely meaningless. With this book I intend to explain not only to the quants but also to the nonquantitative bosses of their bosses and, hopefully, to the regulators and policy makers why I believe this is the case.

I also think that a more meaningful, yet still strongly quantitative, way of looking at risk management *is* possible. Hard quantitative skills, and the logical forma mentis that comes with them, are therefore not useless—if anything, the technical challenges for a more meaningful approach to risk management (that takes at its root Bayesian analysis and subjective probabilities) are even greater than for the current, more traditional, probabilistic approach. However, these techniques should be used in a *different* way than they have been so far and we should reason about financial risk management in a *different* way than we often appear to now.

So, the quantitative approach probably remains the high road to financial risk management. I will argue, however, that a lot of very effective risk management can be done with a much simpler approach, and that this approach constitutes a reasonable and meaningful "approximation" to the quantitatively correct answer. This way of looking at risk-management problems should have two advantages: it is congruent and resonant with the way human beings actually do think and feel about risk; and, if my suggestions are found useful and convincing, they can be extended without intellectual break into a precise quantitative treatment. Most importantly, the risk managers (quantitative or not) who find my way of looking at these problems convincing should be able to ask themselves whether or not they are asking a meaningful question. This is no small feat, and, I believe, is not too difficult. It just requires fewer formulae (less plumbing) and more thinking. In this book I have therefore deliberately avoided going over the quantitative aspects of these topics, because I really want to keep company with the senior, nonquantitative manager who has to provide the "adult supervision" that the current risk-management project has sometimes lacked so far. As a consequence, this will be my first book without formulae. Since I will try to show that a particular *quantitative* approach to risk management is flawed, and yet I want to reach a *general*, i.e., not necessarily quantitative, readership, I have set for myself an unusually difficult task. I have tried to tackle it by employing a qualitative and discursive style, while still keeping the reasoning as clear and honest as possible. This is difficult, but should be possible. After all, probability, as Laplace said, "is in the end only common sense reduced to calculation." In trying to pull off this feat, I have religiously kept in mind Stephen Hawking's words: "Someone told me that each equation I included in the book would halve the sales. I therefore resolved not to have any equations at all."* I have followed the same piece of advice.

Writing precisely without using formulae is hard: I have waved my hands, sometimes rather furiously, and I have cut numerous corners, but I have tried not to cheat (too much) while

*From the acknowledgement section of S. Hawking (1988), *A Brief History of Time* (New York: Bantam Books).

doing so.* I have tried to post pointers to more quantitative treatments on the way—usually in footnotes or endnotes. These can be skipped by the impatient or nonquantitative reader without loss of continuity.

Finally, a word about the choice of the picture that graces the cover of this book. It is a detail of a painting by Caravaggio called, in English, *The Cardsharps*.† Readers familiar with the painting will remember that it shows a handsome and probably very naive young man who is engaging in a financially rather risky activity: gambling. We become aware of how risky this game of cards really is when we note that a man is looking over the shoulders of the young player and communicating to his fellow cardsharp the cards in the young man's hands: unfortunately, a lowly "three." And, when our attention is drawn by the action of the playing cardsharp to the dagger concealed in the waist band, we begin to fear that what the young man is risking may be more than a few ducats. There are some obvious parallels between what is happening in the painting and the contents of this book. There is of course a reference to financial risk. A bit more subtly, however, both the painting and the book try to alert us to the dire consequences in miscalculating the odds of a risky activity. The parallels should not be pushed too far, though. I do *not* intend to suggest, for instance, that financial markets are a den of gambling

---

*I feel, however, that I have to come clean at least in three respects. First, I have failed to distinguish clearly in this book among probability as degree of belief, Bayesian probability, and subjective probability. This is in general not correct. It is correct enough, however, in the context of this book.

Second, I am aware that the concept of probability as degree of belief (which I implicitly use in this book) is not uncontroversial. I cannot go into the objections and possible defenses. For an impassioned (and in my opinion convincing) defense of probability as degree of belief see E. T. Jaynes (2003), *Probability: The Logic of Science* (Cambridge University Press). For a critique, see, for example, K. Binmore (1994), *Game Theory and the Social Contract*, volume I (Cambridge, MA: MIT Press).

Third, I do not discuss in this book the Laplacian definition of probability based on symmetry. It can be very powerful, but its domain of applicability is somewhat restricted and is of little relevance to risk management. It is also not without its logical problems.

†The picture can be seen in full on many freely available Web sites.

vice, where unsuspecting young men are fleeced by unscrupulous "cardsharps." I simply find the painting very attractive, and more interesting than the usual covers with bulls, bears, dollar signs, and price charts. I am grateful to the publisher for agreeing to reproduce it.

ACKNOWLEDGMENTS

First and foremost, I would like to thank my wife, Rosamund Scott, for careful and insightful reading of this book, and for precious suggestions and discussions. I also thank the friends and colleagues who were kind enough to read this manuscript at various stages of its writing and to offer their comments. I am grateful to the delegates at various conferences (in Geneva, Boston, and New York) with whom I have discussed some of the topics covered in the text. Their encouragement and comments have been invaluable. Two referees (one of whom was Professor Alex McNeil) helped me greatly with their suggestions and constructive criticism. It has been a pleasure to work with Princeton University Press, and with Richard Baggaley in particular. I have found in Sam Clark, of T&T Productions Ltd, the best editor an author could hope for. Thanks to their efforts this book is much the better. Needless to say, all remaining errors are mine.

PLIGHT OF THE FORTUNE TELLERS

CHAPTER 1

WHY THIS BOOK MATTERS

But what I ... thought altogether unaccountable was the strong disposition I observed in [the mathematicians of Laputa] toward news and politics, perpetually enquiring into public affairs, giving their judgement on matters of state, and passionately disputing every inch of a party opinion. I have indeed observed the same disposition among the mathematicians I have known in Europe, although I could never observe the least analogy between the two sciences, unless those people suppose that because the smallest circle hath as many degrees as the largest, therefore the regulation and management of the world require no more abilities than the handling and turning of a globe.

Jonathan Swift, writing about the mathematicians of Laputa

STATISTICS AND THE STATE

This book is about the quantitative use of statistical data to manage financial risk. It is about the strengths and limitations of this approach. Since we forget the past at our own peril, we could do worse than remind ourselves that the application of statistics to economic, political, and social matters is hardly a new idea. The very word "statistics" shares its root with the word "state," a concept that, under one guise or another, has been with us for at least a few centuries. The closeness of this link, between compilations of numbers, tables of data, and actuarial information on the one hand and the organization and running of a state on the other may today strike us as strange. But it was just when the power of this link became evident that statistics as we know it today was "invented." So, in its early days probability theory may well have been the domain of mathematicians, gamblers, and philosophers. But even when mathematicians did lend a helping hand in bringing it to life, from the very beginning there was always something much more practical and hard-nosed about statistics.

To see how this happened, let us start at least close to the beginning, and go back to the days of the French Revolution. In the first pages of *Italian Journey* (1798), Goethe writes:

> I found that in Germany they were engaged in a species of political enquiry to which they had given the name of *Statistics*. By statistical is meant in Germany an inquiry for the purpose of ascertaining the political strength of a country, or questions concerning matters of state.

By the end of the eighteenth century, when Goethe explained his understanding of the word "statistics," the concept had been around in its "grubby" and practical form for at least a century. It is in fact in 1700 that we find another German, Leibniz, trying to forward the cause of Prince Frederick of Prussia who wanted to become king of the united Brandenburg and Prussia. The interesting point for our discussion is that Leibniz offers his help by deploying a novel tool for his argument: statistics. Prince Frederick of Prussia was at a disadvantage with respect to his political rivals, because the population of Prussia was thought to be far too small compared with that of Brandenburg to command a comparable seat at the high table of power. If at the time the true measure of the power of a country was the size of its population, the ruler could not be a Prussian. What Leibniz set out to prove was that, despite its smaller geographical size, Prussia was nonetheless more populous than was thought, indeed almost as populous as Brandenburg—and hence, by right and might, virtually as important. How did he set out to do so in those pre-census days? By an ingenious extrapolation *based solely on the Prussian* *register of births*, which had been started seventeen years earlier and carefully updated since.*

The details of how the estimate was reached need not concern us here—probably so much the better for Leibniz, because the jump from the birth data collected over seventeen years to the total size of the population was, by modern statistical standards, flawed. What *is* of great current interest is the logical chain employed by Leibniz, i.e., the link between some limited information that we *do* have but that, per se, we may consider of little importance—What do we care about births in Prussia?—to information that we *would* desperately like to have but is currently beyond our reach: for Leibniz and Prince Frederick, ultimately, what is the might of the Prussian army? If anyone were ever to doubt that there is real, tangible power in data and in data collection, this first example of the application of the statistical line of argument to influence practical action should never be forgotten. The modern bank that painstakingly collects information about failures in the clearing of cheques, about minute fraud, about the delinquency of credit card holders and mortgagors (perhaps sorted by age, postcode, income bracket, etc.) employs exactly the same logic today: data give power *to actions and decisions*. To the children of the Internet age it may all seem very obvious. But, at the beginning of the eighteenth century, it was not at all self-evident that, in order to gain control over the running of the state, looking at hard, empirical, and "boring" data might be more useful than creating engaging fictions about "natural man," "noble savages," social contracts between the king and the citizens, etc. The first statisticians were not political philosophers or imaginative myth-makers: they were civil servants.

The parallels between these early beginnings and today's debates about statistics run deeper. As soon as the power of basing decisions on actual data became apparent, two schools of thought quickly developed, one in France (and Britain, Scotland

---

*Hacking, *The Taming of Chance*.

in particular) and one in Prussia. Generalizing greatly,* the French
school advocated an interpretation of the data on the basis of
the "regularities of human nature": deaths, births, illness, etc.,
were, according to the French and British schools of thought, no
less regular, and therefore no less amenable to rigorous quantitative analysis, than, say, floods or other "natural" phenomena.
Ironically, the Prussian school, that had founded the statistics
bureau, failed to reap the full advantage of its head start because
it remained suspicious of the French theoretical notions of "statistical law" when applied to human phenomena—and, predictably,
derided the French statisticians: "What is the meaning of the statement that the average family has 2.33 children? What does a third
of a child look like?"

Perhaps it is not surprising that the country of the fathers
of probability theory (Descartes, Pascal, Bernoulli, Fermat, etc.)
should have been on the quantitative side of the debate. Indeed,
100 years before statistics were born, Bernoulli was already asking
questions such as, "How can a merchant divide his cargo between
ten ships that are to brave the pirate-infested seas so as to minimize his risk?" In so doing, he was not only inventing and making
use of the eponymous probability distribution, he was also discovering risk aversion, and laying the foundations of financial
risk management. Probability and statistics therefore seemed to
be a match made in heaven: probability theory would be the ves-
sel into which the "hard" statistical data could be poured to reach
good decisions on how to run the state. In short, the discipline
of probability, to which these French minds contributed so much,
appeared to offer the first glimpses of an intriguing promise: a
quantitative approach to decision making.

The Prussian–French debate was not much more constructive than many of the present-day debates in finance and risk
management (say, between classical finance theorists and behavioral financiers), with both parties mainly excelling in caricatur-
ing their opponent's position. Looking behind the squabbling, the

*For a more nuanced discussion of the two schools, again see Hacking, *The Taming of Chance.*

arguments about the applicability and usefulness of quantitative techniques to policy decisions have clearly evolved, but reverberations of the 200-year-old Franco-Prussian debate are still relevant today. The French way of looking at statistics (and of using empirical data) has clearly won the day, and rightly so. Perhaps, however, the pendulum has swung too far in the French direction. Perhaps we have come to believe, or assume, that the power of the French recipe (marrying empirical data with a sophisticated theory of probability) is, at least in principle, boundless.

This overconfident extrapolation from early, impressive successes of a new method is a recurrent feature of modern thought. The more elegant the theory, the greater the confidence in this extrapolation. Few inventions of the human mind have been more impressive than Newtonian mechanics. The practical success of its predictions and the beauty of the theory took a hold on Western thought that seemed at times almost impossible to shake off. Yet two cornerstones of the Newtonian edifice, the absolute nature of time and the intrinsically deterministic nature of the universe, were ultimately to be refuted by relativity and quantum mechanics, respectively. Abandoning the Newtonian view of the world was made more difficult, not easier, by its beauty and its successes.

It sounds almost irreverent to shift in one paragraph from Newtonian physics and the absolute nature of time to the management of financial risk. Yet I think that one can recognize a similar case of overconfident extrapolation in the current approach to statistics applied to finance. In particular, I believe that in the field of financial risk management we have become too emboldened by some remarkable successes and have been trying to apply similar techniques to areas of inquiry that are only superficially similar. We have come to conclude that we simply have to do "more of the same" (collect more data, scrub our time series more carefully, discover more powerful statistical theorems, etc.) in order to answer *any* statistical question of interest. We have come to take for granted that while some of the questions may be hard, they are always well-posed.

However, if this is not the case but the practice and the policy to control financial risk remain inspired by the nonsensical answers to ill-posed questions, then we are all in danger. And if the policies and practices in question are of great importance to our well-being (as is, for instance, the stability and prudent control of the financial system), we are all in great danger.

WHAT IS AT STAKE?

Through financial innovations, a marvelously intricate system has developed to match the needs of those who want to borrow money (for investment or immediate consumption) and of those who are willing to lend it. But the modern financial system is far more than a glorified brokerage of funds between borrowers and lenders. The magic of modern financial engineering truly becomes apparent in the way *risk*, not just money, is parceled, repackaged, and distributed to different players in the economy. Rather than presenting tables of numbers and statistics, a simple, homely example can best illustrate the resourcefulness, the reach, and the intricacies of modern applied finance.

Let us look at a young couple who have just taken out their first mortgage on a small house with a local bank on Long Island. Every month, they will pay the interest on the loan plus a (small) part of the money borrowed. Unbeknownst to them, their monthly mortgage payments will undergo transformations that they are unlikely even to imagine. Despite the fact that the couple will continue to make their monthly mortgage payments to their local bank, it is very likely that their mortgage (i.e., the rights to all their payments) will be purchased by one of the large federal mortgage institutions (a so-called "government-sponsored agency") created to oil the wheels of the mortgage market and make housing more affordable to a large portion of the population. Once acquired by this institution, it will be pooled with thousands of other mortgages that have been originated by other small banks around the country to advance money to similar home buyers. All these mortgages together create a single, diversified pool of interest-paying assets (loans). These assets then receive the blessing of the federal agency who bought them in the form of a promise to continue to pay the interest even if the couple of newlyweds (or any of their thousands of fellow co-mortgagors) find themselves unable to do so. Having given its seal of approval (and financial guarantee), the federal institution may create, out of the thousands of small mortgages, new standardized securities that pay interest (the rechanneled mortgage payments) and will ultimately repay the principal (the amount borrowed by the Long Island couple).

These new securities, which have now been made appealing to investors through their standardization and the financial guarantee, can be sold to banks, individuals, mutual funds, etc. Some of these standardized securities may also be chopped into smaller pieces, one piece paying only the interest, the other only the principal when (and if) it arrives, thereby satisfying the needs and the risk appetite of different classes of investors. At every stage of the process, new financial gadgets, new financial instruments, and new market transactions are created: some mortgages are set aside to provide investors with an extra cushion against interruptions in the mortgage payments; additional securities designed to act as "bodyguards" against prepayment risk are generated; modified instruments with more predictable cash flow streams are devised; and so on.

So large is this flow of money that every rivulet has the potential to create a specialized market in itself. Few tasks may appear more mundane than making sure that the interest payments on the mortgages are indeed made on time, keeping track of who has repaid their mortgage early, channeling all the payments where they are due just when they are due, etc. A tiny fraction of the total value of the underlying mortgages is paid in fees for this humble servicing task. Yet so enormous is the river of mortgage payments, that this small fraction of a percent of what it carries along, its flotsam and jetsam, as it were, still constitutes a very large pool of money. And so, even the fees earned for the administration of the various cash flows become tradeable instruments in themselves, for whose ownership investment banks, hedge funds, and investors in general will engage in brisk, and sometimes furious, trading.

The trading of all these mortgage-based securities, ultimately still created from the payments made by the couple on Long Island and their peers, need not even be confined to the country where the mortgage originated. The same securities, ultimately backed by the tens of thousands of individual private mortgage borrowers, may be purchased, say, by the Central Bank of China. This body may choose to do so in order to invest some of the cash originating from the Chinese trade surplus with the United States. But this choice has an effect back in the country where the mortgages were originated. By choosing to invest in these securities, the Central Bank of China contributes to making their price higher. But the interest paid by a security is inversely linked to its price. The international demand for these repackaged mortgages therefore keeps (or, actually, pushes) down U.S. interest rates and borrowing costs. As the borrowing cost to buy a house goes down, more prospective buyers are willing to take out mortgages, new houses are built to meet demand, the house-building sector prospers and employment remains high. The next-door neighbor of the couple on Long Island just happens to be the owner of one small enterprise in the building sector (as it happens, he specializes in roof tiling). The strong order book of his roof tiling business and his optimistic overall job outlook make him feel confident about his prospects. Confident enough, indeed, to take out a mortgage for a larger property. So he walks into the local branch of his Long Island bank. *Au refrain.*

There is nothing special about mortgages: a similarly intricate and multilayered story could be told about insurance products, the funding of small or large businesses, credit cards, investment funds, etc. What all these activities have in common is the redirection, protection from, concentration, or diversification of some form of risk. All the gadgets of modern financial engineering are simply a bag of tricks to reshape the one and only true underlying "entity" that is ultimately being exchanged in modern financial markets: risk.

But there is more. All these pieces of financial wizardry must perform their magic while ensuring that the resulting pieces of paper that are exchanged between borrowers and lenders enjoy an elusive but all-important property: the ability to flow smoothly and without interruptions among the various players in the economy. All the fancy pieces of paper are useful only if they can freely flow, i.e., if they can be readily exchanged into one another (thereby allowing individuals to change their risk profile at will), or, ultimately, into cash. Very aptly, this all-important quality is called "liquidity." By itself, sheer ingenuity in inventing new financial gadgets is therefore not enough: the pieces of paper that are created must not only redirect risk in an ingenious way, they must also continually flow, and flow without hindrance.

As the mortgage example suggests, if an occlusion occurs anywhere in the financial flows that link the payments made to the local Long Island bank to the foreign exchange management reserve office of the Bank of China, the repercussions of this clogging of the financial arteries will be felt a long way from where it happens (be it on Long Island or in Beijing). It is because of this interconnectedness of modern financial instruments that financial risk has the potential to take on a so-called "systemic" dimension.

Fortunately, like most complex interacting systems, the financial system has evolved in such a way that compensating controls and "repair mechanisms" become active automatically (i.e., without regulatory or government intervention) when some perturbation occurs in the orderly functioning of the network. Luckily, the smooth functioning of this complex system does not have to rely on the shocks not happening in the first place:

> [T]he interesting question is not whether or not risk will crystallize, as in one form or another risks crystallize every day. Rather the important question is whether … our capital markets can absorb them.*

*P. Tucker, Executive Director for Markets and member of the Monetary Policy Committee, Bank of England, *Financial Stability Review* December 2005:73.

And indeed, most of the time, surprises are readily and "automatically" absorbed by the system. But if the shock is too big or if, for any reason, some of the adjusting mechanisms are prevented from acting promptly and efficiently, the normal repair mechanisms may not be sufficient to restore the smooth functioning of the financial flows. In some pathological situations, they may even become counterproductive. If this happens, the effects can quickly be felt well beyond the world of the whirling pieces of paper and can begin to affect the "real economy." It is exactly because, in a modern economy, the boundaries between the financial plumbing and the real economy have become so blurred and porous that the management of financial risk is today vitally important—and vitally important to everyone, from Wall Street financiers down to the young couple on Long Island.

One of the salient characteristics of the modern economy is that an amazingly complex web of interactions can develop among agents who barely, if at all, know each other, to produce results that give the impression of a strong and conscious coordination (an "intelligent design"). This is, of course, in essence nothing but Adam Smith's invisible hand in action, but the complexity of modern-day financial arrangements would have been unthinkable when *The Wealth of Nations* was written. Accepting that "no one is in charge" but that an intricate network of transactions will, most of the time, work very well remains to this day difficult to accept from an intuitive point of view. "Please understand that we are keen to move toward a market economy," a senior Soviet official whose responsibility had been to provide bread to the population of Saint Petersburg in its communist days told economist Paul Seabright,* "but we need to understand the fundamental details of how such a system works. Tell me, for example, who is in charge of the supply of bread to the population of London." In the industrialized Western world we may have forgotten how astonishing the reply is ("nobody is in charge"), but

---

*P. Seabright (2004), *The Company of Strangers* (Princeton University Press).

this does not make it any less so. In a similar vein, looking at a small portion of butter offered as part of an in-flight meal, Thomas Schelling (rhetorically) asks:

> How do all the cows know how much milk is needed to make the butter and the cheese and the ice cream that people will buy at a price that covers the cost of maintaining and milking the cow and getting each little piece of butter wrapped in aluminum foil with the airlines's insignia printed on it?*

Of all these complex, resilient, self-organizing systems, the financial industry is probably one of the most astonishing. Nobody was "in charge" to ensure that when the couple from Long Island walked into their local bank branch they would get a competitive quote for their mortgage in hours; nobody was in charge to make sure that the depositor who provided the funds needed by the couple to purchase their house would be forthcoming just at the right moment; nobody was in charge when the same depositor changed his mind a week later and withdrew the money he had deposited; nobody was in charge to ensure that a buyer would be willing to part with his money within hours, or minutes, of the security from the pool of mortgages being created and offered on the market; and when, thousands of miles away, a Bank of China official decided to invest some of the Chinese trade surplus in the purchase of the same security, nobody had communicated his intentions and nobody had arranged for a market maker to buy the security itself from the primary investor and hold it in his inventory. Nobody is in charge and yet, *most of the time*, all of these transactions, and many more, flow without any problems.

There, however, in that innocent "most of the time," is the rub. The financial system is robust, by virtue of literally hundreds of self-organizing corrective mechanisms, but it is not *infinitely* robust. This is not surprising because the cornerstone institution of the financial system, the bank itself, is precariously

*T. Schelling (1978), *Micromotives and Macrobehavior* (New York and London: Norton).

perched on the border of stability: just because nobody is in charge, every day a bank owes its existence to the law of large numbers. How does this happen? The most fundamental activity of a bank is the so-called "maturity transformation": accepting money from depositors who may want it back tomorrow, and lending the "same money" to borrowers who may want to hold on to it for thirty years. This is all well and good unless all of the depositors simultaneously want their money back. In normal conditions, of course, it is virtually impossible for this to happen, and the statistical balance between random withdrawals from depositors and equally random repayments from borrowers requires a surprisingly small safety buffer of "liquid cash." And, by the way, many other arrangements in our nobody-is-in-charge industrialized world rely on a similar (apparently fragile and precarious) statistical balance: from the provision of food to the distribution of electricity, the use of roads, telephone lines, petrol stations, etc. As long as all the users make their decisions close-to-independently, only a relatively small safety margin (of spare electricity, spare phone line capacity, petrol in filling stations, food on supermarket shelves, etc.) has to be kept.

Conditions, however, are not always "normal." For a variety of reasons, unpredictable coordination of actions can occur that break the independence in the decisions and disrupt the apparently most robust systems: in the 1980s, for instance, the simultaneous switching on of millions of kettles during the commercial break of a TV program broadcasting a British royal wedding caused chaos across the electricity grid.* Similarly, fears about the robustness of supply can, in next to no time, empty supermarket shelves and create queues at petrol stations. The rumors at the root of these unusual coordinated behaviors need not be true for the effect to be highly disruptive and, in some circumstances, potentially devastating: in a state of imperfect information a set of rationally calculating agents looking after their self-interest will

*Seabright, *The Company of Strangers*.

all reach the same conclusions, and close-to-simultaneously head for the supermarket or the petrol station.*

The amazing efficiency and resilience of the supply chain in the industrialized world therefore contains a potentially fragile core for many goods and services. Banks, are, however, different, and not in a way that makes a bank regulator sleep any more peacefully. If, a few minutes after midnight on New Year's eve, we find it difficult to make a telephone call to wish a happy new year to our loved ones, we desist from calling for ten minutes and, by doing so, avoid clogging the line even more. We do so spontaneously, not because some regulation tells us to behave this way, and it is rational for us to do so. But if a rumor spreads that a bank is not solvent, the individually rational thing to do is to rush to the head of the queue, not to come back tomorrow when the queue, which currently circles two blocks, will be shorter: by tomorrow the queue may well be shorter, but only because there may be no money left in the vault. This is how runs on banks occur: given the asymmetry of information between insiders and depositors, the same response (run for the till!) applies in the case of the perfectly healthy bank as in the case of the one that really has got itself into financial difficulties.

How can these panics be prevented when the rational behavior is to do what everyone else is trying to do—and when this "rational" behavior exacerbates, rather than alleviates, the problem? In most industrialized societies, governments have stepped in by creating deposit insurance. The soothing promise of the government to depositors that it stands behind the bank's commitment to repay (with the implication that their monies are safe no matter what) can prevent, or stem, the flood of withdrawals. In the case of a healthy bank, this arrangement can prevent the run from occurring in the first place.

---

*For an interesting discussion about the consequences of spontaneously organized collective behaviors, see, for example, C. P. Chamley (2004), *Rational Herds* (Cambridge University Press). A possible explanation of how these collective behaviors may become ordered can be found in D. Watts (1999), *Small Worlds— The Dynamics of Networks between Order and Randomness* (Princeton University Press).

It is important to understand that this underwriting of risk by the government is beneficial for the public but it is also extremely beneficial for the banks. For this reason this insurance is not offered "for free." Via the deposit guarantee the government develops a keen, first-hand financial interest in the good working of banks, but only shares in the downside, not in the profit the bank may make. It therefore imposes another stipulation to this otherwise too-good-to-be-true arrangement: the government, the covenant goes, will indeed step in to guarantee the deposits of the public even if the bank were to fail; but, in exchange for these arrangements, which are extremely useful for the public *and for the banks*, it will acquire a supervisory role over banking operations. (Of course it is well within the remit of the government to care about systemic financial risk even in the absence of deposit insurance, but this commitment certainly focuses its mind.)

The management of financial risk therefore acutely matters, not only to the financial institutions in the long chain from the small Long Island bank to the Bank of China, but to the public at large and, as the agent of the public and the underwriter of deposit insurance, to the government. So, the long chain of financial institutions that sell, buy, and repackage risk care intensely about controlling financial risk—if for no other reason, then simply as an exercise in self-preservation. But the national and international regulators who have been appointed to take a broader, system-wide, view of financial risk also strongly care and justifiably see themselves as the ultimate safeguard of the soundness of the real economy ("ultimate," in that they come into play if all other self-correcting mechanisms fail).

Shocks and disturbances of small-to-medium magnitude can be efficiently handled by the inbuilt feedback mechanisms of the financial markets. It is the "perfect storms" that have the potential to create havoc and destroy wealth on a massive scale. Given this state of affairs, it is not surprising that the regulatory bodies that are mandated to control the stability and proper functioning of the international financial system are basing more and more of their regulatory demands on the estimation of the probability of occurrence of extremely rare events. In statistical terms, these requirements are expressed in terms of what are called, in technical parlance, "extremely high percentiles." For instance, the regulators are requesting more and more frequently, and in wider and wider contexts, that a 99.9th, one-year percentile of some loss distribution be calculated for regulatory capital purposes. This is just the definition of Value-at-Risk (VaR), which we will discuss in detail in the following chapters. At this stage, we can take this expression to mean that financial institutions are required to estimate the magnitude of an adverse market event so severe that an even worse one should only be expected to occur once every thousand years.

Let us pause and "feel the magnitude" of this statement. A more familiar (although not strictly identical) question is the following: "How bad must a flood/snow fall/drought be for you to be confident that we have experienced a worse one only once since the battle of Hastings in 1066?" Again, let us pause and feel the magnitude of the statement. How would you try to estimate such a quantity? What data would you want to have? How many data records would you need? And where would you find them?

As we saw, it is not just the regulators who have a strong interest in keeping the financial cogs turning smoothly. Banks and other financial institutions to a large extent share the same concerns—if for no other reason than because surviving today is a pretty strong precondition for being profitable tomorrow. There is far more to the risk management of a financial institution than avoiding perfect storms, though. Modern (i.e., post-Markowitz) portfolio theory sees the trade-off between expected return and risk (variance of returns) as the cornerstone of modern finance. In this light, possibly the most common and important questions faced almost every day at different levels of a bank are therefore of the following type: What compensation should we, the bank, require for taking on board a certain amount of extra risk? Should we lend money to this fledgling company, which promises to pay a high interest but which may go bankrupt soon? Should we begin underwriting, distributing, and making a market in bonds or equities, thereby earning the associated fees and trading revenues but accepting the possibility of trading losses? Should we retain a pool of risky loans, or are we better off repackaging them, adding to them some form of insurance, and selling them on?

Of course, how a financial institution should choose among different risky projects has been the staple diet of corporate finance textbooks for decades. Down in the financial trenches, it is a pressing question for all the decision makers in a bank, from the most junior relationship manager to its CEO and finance director. The risk policy of the bank (what is these days called its "risk appetite") is typically set at a very senior level in rather broad and generic terms. But it is only after the (often rather vague) risk appetite policy has been articulated that the real questions begin: How should these lofty risk principles be applied to everyday decisions and, most importantly, to strategic choices?

The standard textbook answer to these questions used to be disarmingly simple: "Just discount the expected cash flows from the new prospective projects at the 'appropriate' risky rate. Compare how much, after this discounting, each new project is worth today. Choose the one with the greatest present value today. Next problem please."

Even glossing over the difficulty in assessing the "appropriate" rate of discount, this way of looking at the budgeting and capital allocation process appears to suffer from at least one important shortcoming: unless the bank already has an "optimal" mix of risk,[1] the approach appears to neglect the *interaction* between the new projects and the existing business activities. Diversification or concentration of risk (i.e., the undesirability of putting all of one's eggs in one basket, no matter how strong the basket looks) is not readily handled by the discounted-cash flow method.*

To overcome this shortcoming, a new approach, termed the "economic-capital project," has recently been suggested. Unfortunately, there is no consensus about the precise meaning and applicability of the term, as it is often used in different, and even

---

*A brief caveat in passing: it may not be optimal for the banks to diversify, but for investors to do so. More about this later.

contradictory, ways. In chapter 8 I will therefore try to explain what it promises (a lot), and what it can deliver (alas, I fear somewhat less). I will frame that discussion in the wider context of the use and misuse of traditional statistical tools for financial risk management. For the moment, what is of relevance in this introductory chapter is that the make-or-break condition for the economic-capital project to succeed, and for a lot of current quantitative risk management to make sense, is that it should be possible to estimate the probability of extremely remote events—or, in statistical jargon, that it should be possible to estimate extremely high percentiles.

"NOT EVEN WRONG": SENSE AND NONSENSE IN FINANCIAL RISK MANAGEMENT

One of the points that I make in this book is that the very high percentiles of loss distributions (i.e., roughly speaking, the probability of extremely unlikely losses) *cannot* be estimated in a reliable and robust way. I will argue that the difficulty is not simply a technical one, which could "simply" be overcome by collecting more data or by using more sophisticated statistical techniques, but is of a fundamental nature. Of course, more data and more powerful techniques *will* help, but only up to a point. Asking what the 99.975th percentile of a one-year loss distribution is is not a tough question, it is a close-to-meaningless one. Famously, Wolfgang Pauli, one of the founders of quantum mechanics, dispatched the theory of a student of his with the ultimate putdown: "Your theory is not correct. In fact, your theory is not even wrong. Your theory makes no predictions at all." This is not quite the case with some utterances from hardcore quantitative risk managers. These statements *do* contain predictions. Unfortunately, they are untestable.

This claim is in itself an important one, since so much effort appears to be devoted to the estimation of these exceedingly low probabilities. This, however, is not the main "message" of my book. Apart from the feasibility issue, I believe that there is a much deeper and more fundamental flaw in much of the current quantitative approach to risk management. There is a "sleight of hand" routinely performed in the risk-management domain that allows one to move from observed frequencies of a certain event to the probabilities of the same event occurring in the future. So, for instance, we observe the historical default *frequency* of AA-rated firms, and equate this quantity to the *probability* that a AA firm may default in the future. This association (frequency = probability) implies a view and an application of the concept of probability that, at the very least, should not be taken for granted. I believe that this "sleight of hand" is indicative of the way we look at probabilities in the whole of the risk-management arena. The philosophy that underpins the identification of frequencies with probabilities is defensible. In some scientific areas it is both sensible and appropriate. It is not, however, the only possible way of understanding probability. In the risk-management domain I believe that the view of probability-as-frequency often underpins a singularly unproductive way of thinking. At the risk of spoiling a point by overstressing it, I am tempted to make the following provocative claim. According to the prevailing view in risk management:

> We *estimate* the probabilities, and from these we *determine* the actions.

For most of the types of problems that financial risk management deals with, I am tempted to say that the opposite should apply:

> We *observe* the actions, and from these we *impute* the probabilities.

This statement may strike the reader as a puzzling one. What kind of probabilities am I talking about? Surely, if I want to advertise my betting odds on a coin-tossing event, *first* I should determine the probability of getting heads and *then* I should advertise my odds. The estimation of probability comes first, and action follows. What could be wrong with this approach?

In the coin-flipping case, probably nothing (although in the next chapter I will raise some reasonable doubts as to whether, even in this stylized case, the approach really always works as well as we may think). The real problem is that very few problems in risk management truly resemble the coin-flipping one. It may come as a surprise to the reader, but there are actually many types of probabilities. Yet the current thinking of risk managers appears to be anchored, without due reflection, to the oldest and most traditional view. It is a view of probability (called the "frequentist view") that applies when we enter a statistical "experiment" with random outcomes with absolutely no prior beliefs about the likelihood of its possible outcomes; when our subsequent beliefs (and actions) are fully and only determined by the outcome of the experiment; and when the experiments can be repeated over and over again under identical conditions. Unfortunately, I will show in the next chapter that none of these requirements really applies to most of the financial-risk-management situations that are encountered in real life.

Fortunately, there *are* views of probability that are better suited to the needs of risk management. They are collectively subsumed under the term "Bayesian probability." Bayesian probability is often seen as a measure of degree of belief, susceptible of being changed by new evidence.* The frequentist probability is not dismissed, but simply becomes a limiting, and unfortunately rather rare, case. If the conditions of applicability for the frequentist limiting case apply, a Bayesian is likely to be delighted—if for no other reason, because there are thousands of books that teach us very well how to compute probabilities when we flip identical coins, draw blue and red balls from indistinguishable urns, etc. But the abundance of books on this topic should not make us believe that the problems they (beautifully) solve are quite as numerous.

Unfortunately, the "Bayesian revolution" has almost completely bypassed the world of risk management. Sadly, quantitative risk managers, just when they claim to be embracing the

*See chapter 3 for a fuller description.

more sophisticated and cutting-edge statistical techniques, actually appear to be oblivious to the fundamental developments in the understanding of the nature of probability that have taken place in the last half century. This cannot be good, and it is often dangerous. This, in great part, is what this book is about, and why what it says matters.

WHAT DO WE DO WITH ALL THESE PROBABILITIES?

There is another aspect that current risk-management thinking does not seem to handle in a very satisfactory way: how to go from probabilistic assessments to decisions. Managing risk in general, and managing financial risk in particular, is clearly a case of decision making under uncertainty. Well-developed theories to deal with this problem do exist, but, rightly or wrongly, they are virtually ignored in professional financial risk management. Most of the effort in current risk management appears to be put into arriving at the probabilities of events (sometimes very remote ones), with the implicit assumption that, once these probabilities are in front of our eyes, the decision will present itself in all its self-evidence. So, these days it is deemed obvious that a quantitative risk manager should be well-versed in, say, extreme value theory or copula theory (two sophisticated mathematical tools to estimate the probabilities of rare or joint events, respectively). However, judging by the contents pages of risk-management books, by the fliers of risk-management conferences, or by the questions asked at interviews for risk-management jobs, no knowledge, however superficial, is required (or even deemed to be desirable) about, say, decision theory, game theory, or utility theory. A potpourri of recommendations, rules of thumb, and "self-evident truths" do exist, and sometimes these are cloaked under the rather grand term of "industry best practice." Yet, it only takes a little scrutiny to reveal that the justifications for these decisional rules of thumb are shaky at best, sometimes even contradictory. Alas,

I will argue that some of the lore around the economic-capital project is no exception.

What can we do instead? To answer this question, I will try to explain what the theoretically accepted tools currently at the disposal of the decision maker have to offer. I will also try to suggest why they have met with so little acceptance and to explain the nature of the well-posed criticisms that have been leveled against them. I would like to suggest that some of the reasons for the poor acceptance of these decision tools are intrinsic to these theories and do reflect some important weaknesses in their setup. However, some of the reasons are intimately linked to the "type of probability" relevant in risk management. Therefore, understanding one set of issues (what type of probability matters in risk management) will help with solving the other (how we should use these probabilities once we have estimated them). This link will also provide a tool, via subjective probabilities and how they are arrived at, for reaching acceptable risk-management decisions. In essence, I intend to show that subjective probabilities are ultimately *revealed* by real choices made when something that matters is at stake. In this view probabilities and choices (i.e., decisions) are not two distinct ingredients in the decisional process, but become two sides of the same coin. Decisional consistency, rather than decisional prescription, is what a theory of decisions in risk management should strive for: *given that* I appear comfortable with taking the risk (and rewards) linked to activity A, should I accept the risk–reward profile offered by activity B?

In this vein, I will offer some guidance in the last part of this book as to how decisions about risk management in low-probability cases can be reached. Clearly, I will not even pretend to have "solved" the problem of decision making under uncertainty. I will simply try to offer some practical suggestions, and to show how the line of action they recommend can be analyzed and understood in light of the theoretical tools that we do have at our disposal.

CHAPTER 2

THINKING ABOUT RISK

"You acted unwisely," I cried, "as you see
By the outcome." He solemnly eyed me:
"When choosing the course of my action," said he,
"I had not the outcome to guide me."

Ambrose Bierce

In this chapter I take a look at how human beings *actually* react to risk. I intend to show that we can be both surprisingly good and spectacularly bad at dealing with uncertain events. Very often, the same individuals can display a very keen and subtle intuition of risk, but then, faced with a different situation (or perhaps even with the same situation "framed" in different terms) can fail miserably at producing an acceptable risk assessment.

Risk blunders are not the prerogative of the man in the street. Experts and extremely intelligent people have fared just as badly, and at times even worse, when thinking about risk.[1] Fermat and Pascal, two of the towering minds of the seventeenth century, argued that the fair value of a bet should be just the expectation of its payoff. If this rule were reasonable, you should be happy to wager all your wealth (your house, your savings, everything) for a fifty–fifty chance of doubling it. Please pause for a second and ask yourself whether *you* would.

It was Bernoulli who first highlighted how unsatisfactory this answer was. More constructively, he also proposed a better solution. He did so with the story of Sempronius, a late-Renaissance merchant. A sketch of his argument is very instructive. In

Bernoulli's story, Sempronius stores in his warehouse at home precious goods worth 4,000 ducats.[2] He also owns other precious goods worth 10,000 ducats in a warehouse located in a distant land that can only be reached by sea. The seas are perilous and pirate infested. Experience has taught Sempronius that, on average, only one ship in two makes the journey home safely. The other is lost forever. Sempronius has an idea. His goods are gold, spices, silk, and precious stones, all very light and easy to transport. He can easily ask his merchant friends to load them in a corner of their large ships and they will not charge him for the service. Why doesn't he divide his foreign goods into four parcels (each worth $10,000/4 = 2,500$ ducats) and entrust them to four different ships (which will take different routes back home)? Note that, by doing so, Sempronius has not changed the expectation of his final wealth: since the probability of any ship reaching home safely is still $\frac{1}{2}$, if he put all his wares in one ship, he can expect to add $10,000 \times \frac{1}{2} = 5,000$ ducats to his wealth at home; if he divides them over four (independent) ships, the expected loss from each ship is $2,500 \times \frac{1}{2}$ ducats, giving an identical total expected loss of 5,000 ducats. Yet, something suggests to us that the expectation of his wealth is not the only thing that matters, and that he will be better off with four ships than one. Many eggs and a single basket spring to mind. Laplace and Fermat refused to be convinced by this argument, and kept on arguing that, in evaluating an uncertain prospect, one should only look at the expectation of the outcome. No advantage whatsoever would be reaped, they claimed, by entrusting the precious wares to four different ships. What do *you* think?

This is but one striking example of bizarre thinking about risk and of the fact that being very clever may, at least in this field, not always help. On the other hand, there are areas related to risk and probability where even the uninitiated fare reasonably well. Take Shakespeare, famous for many things but not, to my knowledge, for his mathematical insight. He appears to have had a clearer perception of the diversification problem than Fermat and Laplace, at least insofar as we can judge from the words he puts in the mouths of Antonio and Salarino:

> *Salarino.*   My wind, cooling my broth,
> Would blow me to an ague, when I thought
> What harm a wind too great might do at sea.
>
> ...
>
> And, in a word, but even now worth this,
> And now worth nothing?
>
> ...
>
> *Antonio.* Believe me, no: I thank my fortune for it,
> My ventures are not in one bottom trusted,
> Nor to one place; nor is my whole estate
> Upon the fortune of this present year:
> Therefore, my merchandise makes me not sad.
>
> The Merchant of Venice (1.1.22–48)

So, luckily, not everybody was as dogmatic as Fermat and Laplace: indeed, a few centuries after Sempronius, Antonio, and Salarino, Nobel prize winner Markowitz was to use Bernoulli's (and, apparently, Shakespeare's) insight to provide an astonishingly parsimonious and convincing description of investors' behavior in terms of expected return *and risk* (variance). His model is obviously not without flaws, as many modern critics are all too eager to point out, but, if judged by the ratio of how much it explains to how many input parameters it requires, it stills sets a standard of parsimony and explanatory power.

Bernoulli's argument is actually quite a bit subtler than what I have just sketched, but, for the present discussion I simply want to pause to comment on the choice of the name and of the profession of Bernoulli's fictitious character. First of all, he is neither a mathematician, nor a philosopher, nor an exceptionally wise man, but a good, solid, commonsensical merchant. To a reader of the time, his name also betrays his "common" extraction. Even if "Sempronius" may sound fancy to us, to Bernoulli's reading audience, well at ease with their Latin, the name was almost automatically associated with the names Titus and Caius. Titus, Caius, and Sempronius were the exact Latin equivalents of Tom, Dick, and Harry (and, indeed, in Italian the expression "Tizio, Caio e Sempronio" survives to this day to indicate the three men-in-the-street par excellence). So, Bernoulli does not want to introduce a character of exceptional wisdom and intelligence and ask how this extraordinarily gifted individual would crack a difficult problem of choice under uncertainty. He was asking himself what Tom, Dick, and Harry would do. The solid and commonsensically appealing answer to a risk-diversification problem offered by Sempronius is a good example of what I mentioned in the opening lines of this chapter: sometimes experts can be spectacularly bad at thinking about risk (Fermat and Pascal were); but at other times even laymen seem to be able to find unexpectedly good risk solutions. And, as this story suggests, over-intellectualizing a risk problem can be a very efficient route to producing risk nonsense. Witness, again, Fermat and Pascal.[3]

As we saw, Bernoulli failed to convince Fermat and Pascal. But we do not have to go back a few centuries to find bewildering statements about risk and stubborn refusals to use common sense. As late as 1938, the then-standard reference work on financial investments by Williams implicitly recommended that investors should place all their wealth in the investment with the maximum expected return.* This recommendation was not made in the get-rich-quick investment column of an evening paper. His book on investing was published by no less august an institution than Harvard University Press. Surely, that must have been the "best industry practice" of the time. Again, I would invite the reader to pause and think about the practical implications of such a recommendation. Would you really consider for a second investing all of your wealth (and, while you are at it, why not borrow some extra money on your credit card and leverage up a bit) in, say, the latest and hottest Internet or biotechnology stock, just because it seems to offer the most dazzling expected returns? Much as in the case of the recommendation of Pascal and Fermat,

*J. B. Williams (1938), *The Theory of Investment Value* (Cambridge, MA: Harvard University Press).

we should perhaps be thankful that the good Semproniuses of this world have routinely discarded "expert" risk advice.

The second half of the twentieth century was an important time for the development of a coherent way of thinking about risk: it was in this period that these commonsensical insights about risk aversion and diversification became embedded in a solid conceptual framework and became the cornerstone of modern thinking about finance. I will not look at these developments in detail, but I will discuss below some important aspects that are relevant for our discussion.

PERCEPTIONS OF RISK

Risk is absolutely central to modern finance. The concept of risk, in turn, is inextricably linked to how we understand probability. Despite the central role played by probability and probability updating in modern finance, these concepts have almost always taken the backseat. Investment theory, for instance, has certainly moved on from the days of John Burr Williams, but it still almost invariably assumes that investors "just know" the objective probabilities attached to the different possible future states of the world.* I think that this state of affairs is unsatisfactory. If we want to describe how human beings *actually* make their choices in the presence of uncertainty, we had better make sure that we truly understand how probabilities are *actually* used in decision making—rather than how stylized hyperrational agents endowed with perfect God-given statistical information *would* reach these decisions.

This line of inquiry has recently been taken up by behavioral finance and experimental psychology, with an impressive number of studies on the "cognitive biases" that, supposedly, make us make "wrong" choices.[4] The existence of these biases has been

---

*To give just one example, in Markowitz's seminal book about portfolio diversification, the possibility that probabilities may be imperfectly known only makes its appearance on p. 250 of a 384-page book.

amply discussed in the area of finance called asset pricing. This is the branch of finance that is devoted to the understanding of how the prices of different securities are arrived at: why is the price of Microsoft shares $160, rather than $320 or $16? Can this market value be linked to "fundamentals" about the prospects faced by this company and by the economy in general? This is a very interesting field of study. There is more to cognitive biases, though, than asset pricing. Risk management, the discipline concerned with assessing the probability of and, most importantly, *reacting to* uncertain events, should also be of major interest to behavioral finance and cognitive psychology. Unfortunately, these disciplines have been applied much less systematically to the management of financial risk. This is surprising, because I think that it is much easier to make a case for the influence of cognitive biases on risk-management decisions than it is to do so for asset pricing. Why should that be the case? In a nutshell, because in the case of asset pricing there exists in the market an inbuilt mechanism (the shrewd investor) capable of correcting the effects of these irrational biases and preventing them from spreading. If the same biases, however, distort our probabilistic assessment, and this assessment is *used for risk-management purposes*, it is much more difficult for an "arbitrageur" to exploit, and hence correct, our mistakes. If I have "irrationally" paid too much for those hot dot-com stocks, you, the cool-headed investor with a clear assessment of probabilities, will ultimately find a way to make money out of my stupidity, and thereby push the prices back toward fundamentals. So much for asset pricing. But when "irrational" probabilistic assessments are not used to "make a price," but to inform risk-management decisions (say, to allocate capital), there is little direct opportunity for a shrewd investor to take advantage of them and correct them away. These probabilistic "errors" will therefore result in inefficient allocation of resources to the management of risk (e.g., spending too much on very remote risks, and too little on more pressing ones), in onerous and ineffectual regulation, and in unnecessary hindrance to financial innovation—in short, in a waste of some time and lots of money.

The absence in risk management of a simple mechanism capable of correcting cognitive biases has an immediate implication. If it is possible to identify contexts in which human beings (as beings with a social and an evolutionary history) systematically prove poor at assessing risk, it would be helpful to structure our risk-management practices in ways that tend to minimize, not amplify, our cognitive limitations. This might seem almost too obvious to state. Unfortunately, current quantitative management of financial risk appears not just to disregard this rule, it actually often seems to work against the grain and to act as a "cognitive bias amplifier." More about this later.

Fortunately, this is not virgin territory, and empirical studies of how real, intelligent people actually use probabilities have been published in their thousands. So, what are the more-or-less well-established facts about how members of the species *homo sapiens* deal with uncertain events?

First of all, psychologists recognize two modes of probabilistic assessment, helpfully called System I and System II.[5] The former provides fast, approximate, but not very accurate responses. The latter is more deliberative, much slower, and correspondingly more accurate. Some neurophysiologists believe that the distinction is "real," i.e., that different parts of the brain are actually engaged in System I and System II cognitive operations.[6] Be that as it may, System II responses appear to be the application of the general reasoning abilities of human beings that could be used for a variety of complex problems—in particular, to problems of choice under uncertainty. In a way, there is nothing specifically probabilistic about System II reasoning. It is System I responses that are more interesting. It is tempting to play armchair evolutionary biologist and to speculate about the evolutionary advantage conferred upon an early member of our species by the ability to apply simple rules of (opposable) thumb to situations of uncertainty.[7] I can readily imagine important situations in which speed of reaction is at a premium over precision of probabilistic assessment. Our ancestor is in the jungle and a bush suddenly starts to rustle. It does not matter greatly if the probability of the rustling being due to a crouching leopard poised to spring is 42.8% or 61.7%: quickly running away is an appropriate response in either case.

The evolutionary advantage of developing such a rough-and-ready probabilistic assessment is clear. The subtlety of this rough assessment, however, deserves some discussion. Note in fact that a careful balance must be struck between what in statistics are called type I and type II errors*: the humanoid ape that moves away from rustling bushes too slowly (i.e., whose probability assessment of a threat is systematically too low) will not live long enough to spread many of his genes. However, the cousin ape who runs away like a nervous ninny at the first rustling of a leaf will not fare much better either: by the end of the day he will have spent most his time fleeing rather than feeding, mating, building shelter, etc. Therefore, the quick-and-dirty rules that our ancestors developed did indeed have to be quick, but, after all, not too "dirty": there is no safe way to err, no precautionary principle that should be invoked by default.

Moving from speculation to experimental fact, is there evidence for the existence of these System I probability assessments? Indeed, rules of thumb, or "heuristics" as they are referred to in the psychology literature, have been systematically found. The most common, and the easiest to understand, is familiarity. Having regular first-hand exposure to a risk source affects (increases) our perception of the probability of its occurrence. Salience has a similar effect: if we *personally* see a person drowning, our assessment of the risks of swimming in open waters will be different (again, greater) than if we simply read about it.[8] For salience to be effective, we do not have to physically witness the event in question ourselves: experiments have shown that just mentioning it, describing it in a detailed but "objective" and "clinical" manner, or describing it vividly and graphically will all increase our probability assessment *and how much we are prepared to pay to avoid this*

---

*Type I and type II errors have nothing to do with System I and System II responses. The terminology "type I error" and "type II error" comes from statistics and describes errors stemming from rejecting too rarely or accepting too frequently a wrong hypothesis.

risk. And they will do so exactly in this order. Johnson[*] quotes a beautifully revealing example: before boarding a flight, people are prepared to pay more when offered a flight insurance policy to cover against "terrorist insurance" than for a policy offering protection from damage arising from all causes. Surely terrorist action is a (rather small) subset of all the bad things that may happen when a very heavy metal box full of people, fuel, and luggage moves at high speed through the air. Yet the probabilistic actions of the boarding passengers do not bear out this very obvious truism.

Similarly, recent events will have a greater impact than distant ones: the purchase of earthquake insurance increases greatly after the occurrence of an earthquake, and declines steadily as the memory of the event fades. Similar behavior has been observed for floods and flood insurance.[†]

Going back to our System I probability assessment, note that these heuristics are not necessarily "wrong." They may be wrong in the idealized context of a probability model, but the main concern of our hunter-gatherer ancestor was not passing statistics tests, but escaping crouching leopards. So, if leopards have recently moved into a region (perhaps because of snow at higher altitudes), giving greater weight to recent sightings of leopards rather than to their long-term frequency of occurrence in an area may provide a better rule of thumb to stay alive. Buying flood insurance after a flood is only irrational if we assume the underlying flood-producing mechanism to be time homogeneous (i.e., not to change over time). It no longer looks so silly if climate change is making floods more frequent or more severe. The heuristic bypasses (rather, short-circuits) the System II analysis of the evidence about changes in climate and their impact, if any, on floods. Despite its inaccurate nature, it can be very effective, at times more effective than System II analysis.

---

[*]E. J. Johnson (1993), Framing, probability distortion and insurance decisions, *Journal of Risk and Uncertainty* 7(I):35.

[†]See, for example, P. Slovic (2000), *The Perception of Risk* (London: Earthscan).

Similarly, salience may not be so silly after all: seeing can be superior to hearing about, especially in an evolutionary period when trustworthy refereed journal articles were pretty thin on the ground. I might have told you about crouching leopards, but was I not, after all, the same reliable source who also told you about the deadly threats from unicorns, two-headed monsters, and basilisks?

The familiarity and salience heuristics are very familiar to any financial risk manager who wants to catch (and hold) the attention of a senior manager: given two possible scenarios of identical statistical probability of future occurrence, much more attention is always paid to the one that resembles (or, indeed, is a repeat of) a vividly remembered instance of market turmoil. To this day many banks still run "historical scenarios" that repeat the unforgettable 1998 events that connected over a period of a few months the Russian default on its domestic debt to the quasi-collapse of the Long-Term Capital hedge fund.

THE WISDOM OF CROWDS: OF PHARAOHS, CAKES, AND MOVIES

A great part of the vast behavioral finance literature is devoted to showing that human beings are not "Bayesian animals," i.e., that they do not live up to the standards of rationality embodied in the probability rules that tell us how to update our beliefs in the light of new evidence. The rough-and-ready System I heuristics, in other words, would appear to prevent us from reaching the best probabilistic conclusions we could from the available data. As a consequence, our decisions would be systematically suboptimal.

This bold statement deserves some finer analysis. Are we really *always* so bad? Are the System I heuristics *really* so crude? Are these rules of thumb uniformly bad, or are there some areas in which they actually do a pretty good job? And, if this is the case, what lessons can we draw from this?

A recent work by Griffiths and Tenenbaum sheds some interesting light on these questions.* The authors asked a large number of subjects to make some bold guesses. Suppose that you are one of their subjects. You would then be told, for instance, that a friend is reading to you a line from her favorite poem, and she tells you that it was line 5 of that poem. What would your guess be of the total length of the (unknown) poem? Or, if you met an eighteen-year-old man, what would your prediction be for his residual lifespan? Or, imagine that someone tells you that a movie has grossed $10 million to date, but you do not know how long it has been running for. What would be your estimate of the total box office take for that movie? Or, again, you walk into a kitchen and observe from the timer above the oven that a cake has been cooking for thirty-five minutes. What would you guess for the total baking time? Finally, suppose that someone told you that a Pharaoh who reigned in Egypt around 4000 B.C.E. had been ruling for eleven years. What would you predict about the duration of his reign?

All these questions have something in common. You probably know something about the question at hand before being told the "new evidence": unlike the Martian that you will meet in a few pages, you therefore have some prior beliefs about human lifespan, about how long it takes to bake a "normal" cake, about the gross takings of movies, the length of poems, etc. You are then given some evidence (how long *that* cake has been in the oven, the age of *the* man in question, the gross takings of *that* particular movie, etc.). Presumably, this will be an important component in arriving at your answer: if you were told that the age of the man whose residual lifespan you have to guess is seventy-five instead of eighteen, I presume that your answer would be very different. Similarly, your answer would have been different, I imagine, if you had been told that the line number of the poem read to you was 1,723 (for starters, Shakespeare's sonnets are definitely out). And so on.

*T. L. Griffiths and J. B. Tenenbaum (2005), Optimal predictions in everyday cognition, *Psychological Science* 17(9):767–73.

The other feature that all these examples have in common is that there is a unique, statistically "correct" (System II) way of arriving at the right answer, i.e., of combining known prior statistical information about life expectancy, length of Pharaohs' reigns, box-office takings of movies, etc., with the new information you have been given. In other words, we know what the "right" answer should be, but in order to arrive at it a lot of empirical knowledge and a rather complex (definitely System II) statistical process would be needed. To arrive at the right answer you would need to have at your fingertips the correct actuarial information about conditional life expectancy, about the length of Pharaohs' reigns, about cakes' baking times, etc. You would also have to know quite a bit about Bayesian analysis, Gaussian and Gamma functions and integrals thereof, conjugate priors, and lots of other marvelous statistical stuff.

Griffiths and Tenenbaum, however, were not interested in testing your knowledge of Bayesian statistics. They wanted to explore how good your heuristics (your System I mechanisms) are in arriving at a rough-and-ready estimate for all these questions. Here is how they instructed the subjects: "We're interested in your intuitions, so please don't make complicated calculations—just tell us what you think!"*

The unexpected result of their study was that the "guesses" were surprisingly good. The predictions about the box-office takings of movies (and about their runtimes), about lifespans, about the length of poems (and of marriages) were indistinguishable from their corresponding optimal Bayesian predictions. Similarly good were the predictions about the cakes' baking times. This is remarkable because, despite the "homely" nature of the example, I am told that the correct distribution of baking times for cakes is surprisingly complex.

As for the predictions about something as remote from everyday experience as the length of Pharaohs' reigns, even these were only slightly longer than the correct (Bayesian) answer. Interestingly enough, the "mistake" did not come from an inappropriate

*Ibid.

use of System I heuristics (the probabilistic, and interesting, part of the problem), but from inaccurate factual knowledge: people thought that the typical duration of a Pharaoh's reign was longer than in actually was. When this "factual" mistake was corrected for, the prediction turned out again to be surprisingly good.

In short, Griffiths and Tenenbaum conclude that the

> result of [the] experiment reveals a far closer correspondence between optimal statistical inference and everyday cognition than suggested by previous research. People's judgements were close to the optimal predictions produce by our Bayesian model across a wide range of settings.[*]

Not bad for a bunch of quick-and-dirty System I heuristics, presumably developed by our ancestors to deal with crouching leopards and falling coconuts!

WHERE THE PROBLEMS REALLY ARE

The results discussed above are both surprising and, to some extent, flattering. Perhaps we are not so bad at thinking about probability, after all. If the results of these experiments are anything to go by, we can perhaps cope with complex statistical models not only at a System II (reflective) level, but even at a System I (intuitive) level. If this is the case, despite the naysayers, we *should* rely heavily in setting up our risk-management systems on complex statistical models. And since this is the route embraced by current financial-risk-management thinking, the whole enterprise may seem like a pretty good idea after all.

The fact that statistical heuristics seem to work well for a set of problems should not, however, make us automatically conclude that they will work as well in all kinds of probabilistic settings. Are there situations in which System I heuristics are more likely to let us down? And are these situations of relevance in risk management?

[*]Ibid.

If we think about our evolutionary story, I have already argued that an ability to assess in a rough-and-ready way the risks of pretty frequent occurrences confers a clear evolutionary advantage. So, System I should allow us to deal (imperfectly, but adequately enough to survive) with probabilities in the range, say, 10–90%. But the more remote the risk, the more difficult it is for the evolutionary advantage of being able to assess this risk efficiently to establish itself. Even if I can assess the probability of one-in-a-million events more accurately than you, the incremental reproductive success of my children and grandchildren (who carry the smart statistical genes) over yours can be easily swamped by random statistical fluctuations. As the probability that must be estimated becomes smaller and smaller, the signal-to-noise ratio just becomes too small to make an evolutionary difference. Being good at telling when rustling bushes hide a crouching leopard gives your genes a much better chance of spreading than my ability to assess the risk of a volcanic eruption (even if the very rare volcanic eruptions are more dangerous than a leopard).

Indeed, this is just what modern psychology experiments show. As usual, actions, especially when they involve parting with money, are very telling. Let us look at the insurance premia people are willing to pay to protect themselves against different risks. The first "irrational" response occurs when the (perceived) probability of the risk is too low. Many experiments suggest that when this happens the probability is mentally set to zero, and the willingness to pay for protection insurance drops correspondingly.*
When the probability is perceived to be still low but greater than a certain threshold level, however, we fall into the opposite "irrationality": not only do we buy insurance, but we do so even at prices that are very disadvantageous actuarially (i.e., even if the expected value of the payout averaged over many insured parties is much lower than the premia collected).† In other terms, when the perceived probability of occurrence is very small, we appear

*See, for example, D. Coursey (1993), Insurance for low-probability hazards: a bimodal response to unlikely events, *Journal of Risk and Uncertainty* 7:95.
†See Sunstein, *Laws of Fear*, p. 75 ff.

to categorize events in two groups: "impossible" ones, for which we are not prepared to pay insurance; and "possible" ones, for which we are ready to pay (and *over*pay).

"Peace of mind" also plays an important role in how much we are happy to pay for insurance: "people are willing to pay relatively little for a small increment in safety, but they will pay far more when the additional increment is the last one," eliminating all residual risk.*

There is yet another bias of relevance for rare events. *Large* proportional differences in *small* probabilities have been shown to make very little difference in the response of most people. Cass Sunstein at the University of Chicago organized an interesting experiment with graduate students.† He asked them how much they would be prepared to pay to reduce the probability of cancer risk. To analyze the results easily, the students were divided into two groups: the first group was told that, to eliminate an existing probability of contracting cancer of 1 in 100,000, they could pay $0, $25, $50, $100, $200, $400, $800, or more. The second group was given the opportunity to pay the same possible "fees," but this time to eliminate a cancer risk *ten times smaller*. The average "insurance cost" offered by the two groups of students was $71 and $194: a ratio of less than three times for a risk that was ten times bigger. If you are unimpressed by this finding, let me translate the problem to the medium-probability range: would we find it reasonable to pay only three times more to eliminate a 40% risk of an unpleasant event than a 4% risk of the same event?

Even more interesting was the second part of the experiment: two other groups of students were created, and they were given the same insurance opportunities and the same probabilities. They were also given, however, a vivid, although factually not particularly informative, description of the cancer itself. Salience largely crowded out the "objective" probabilistic assessment, and more powerfully so than in medium-probability settings. The average premium now showed an even weaker link to the stated

*Ibid., p. 76.
†Ibid., p. 78.

probability: the students were now barely willing to pay twice as much to eliminate the *ten-times-higher* risk.

Another mechanism that becomes particularly effective at very low probabilities is the "outrage" effect. When certain remote outcomes are emotionally very charged or evocative, they elicit far stronger responses than more neutral, but equally unlikely, events. When outrage is at play, often the subjects even become probability insensitive, and react in the same way to stated risks of 1 in 100,000 or 1 in 1,000,000 (again a tenfold difference in risk). More tellingly, in a study quoted in Cass Sunstein's *Laws of Fear*, subjects were confronted with two probabilistically identical (and very remote) risks: one stemming from nuclear waste (high "outrage"), one from radon contamination (low "outrage").* Despite the fact that the risks had been described as equally unlikely, the subjects were much more prepared to act to avert the nuclear waste risk than the radon contamination risk. Indeed, the effect of outrage was roughly equivalent to a 400-fold difference in risk probability![†]

THE RELEVANCE FOR FINANCIAL RISK MANAGEMENT

The academic literature on the subject is immense and, clearly, I have only skimmed its surface. However, one can already discern a few recurring themes that are very relevant to the management of financial risk. Let me highlight a few:

1. Human beings appear to deal with probabilities in qualitatively distinct fashions: a deliberative System II mode, which allows for a more accurate, but slower, assessment of risk; and a System I mode, which provides quick responses, heavily influenced by identifiable heuristics.
2. In the medium-to-high probability range these rules of thumb are far from perfect, but they do not seem to perform too badly. When the most likely occurrence of one such

*Ibid., p. 80, and references therein.
[†]Ibid., p. 81.

medium-to-high probability event must be estimated, heuristics have actually been shown to be surprisingly effective. Some instances of apparent System I "irrationality" can be explained and partially justified.

3. Where the System I mode of operation really breaks down is when the probabilities at stake are very low.* When this is the case, the heuristics soon cease to provide useful guidance, and the behavioral responses become very difficult to explain in a "rational" framework.[†]

Why is this relevant to financial risk management? Because, as I have mentioned in the introductory chapter, both the industry "best risk-management practice" and the regulatory framework increasingly point to the estimation of the probability of extremely unlikely events as a desirable tool to control, manage, and understand risk. But very low probabilities of very disastrous occurrences constitute just the domain where human beings have been shown to be cognitively extremely poor! Emphasis on the estimation of extremely unlikely events therefore acts as an *amplifier* of the probabilistic cognitive difficulties of *homo sapiens*.

Admittedly, human beings no longer have to rely only on System I methods to deal with probabilistic events. Indeed, the whole libraries of books that have been written on statistics are a testament to the power and sophistication of our System II mode of operation. This may well be true, but having to rely on only one mechanism when two could help and reinforce each other does not strike me as a brilliant idea. The weight on the shoulders of System II analytical methods is actually even greater, because it is not just a matter of having to do *without* the System I heuristics:

---

*One of the most egregious and, for risk-management applications, most pernicious instances of breakdown of the System I mode of operation is the so-called unconscious "belief in the law of small numbers" (see A. Tversky and D. Kahneman (1971), Belief in the law of small numbers, *Psychology Bulletin* 76(2):105–10). This term describes our overconfidence in the stability of observed patterns (e.g., the stability of early trends) or, more generally, in extrapolating from relatively little statistical information.

[†]One can, of course, invoke "alternative modes of rationality," but this is a relabeling rather than an explanation.

we actually have to *fight against* our evolutionarily honed prob-abilistic rules of thumb, i.e., against voices whispered from deep inside our psyche.

Resting the management of financial risk on the assessment of extremely low-probability events therefore strikes me as an exercise in working against, rather than with, the grain. Still, an optimist could try to look on the bright side and say, "It can be done." Unfortunately, I will argue in the following chapters that the nature of the problem is such that the System II analytical methods cannot help us either. This is a bold statement. To under-stand how I can defend this claim, we must begin by looking in more detail at the very concept of probability and at how it is used in different contexts. This I do in the next chapter.

CHAPTER 3

THINKING ABOUT PROBABILITIES

Here's one useful rule of thumb: there are very few fields in which every single practitioner is an idiot. If your understanding of a field is such that all practitioners of it must be idiots, then probably you're not understanding it correctly.

Ted Rosencrantz in *Bayesians versus non-Bayesians*

DIFFERENT FACES OF PROBABILITY

What is the probability of obtaining heads when tossing a given coin? What is the probability of the next president of the United States being a Democrat? What is the probability that *The Iliad* and *The Odyssey* were written by the same person?

In posing these three questions, I have used the same word: "probability." Yet a moment's thought clearly shows that it has a very different meaning in the three contexts. The first has to do with an event (the tossing of the coin) that can, in principle, be repeated many times under virtually identical conditions. We can ideally think of repeating this experiment as many times as we wish with the same coin and of recording how many times we get heads. From this set of coin tosses we can establish the frequency of the outcome "heads," and we find it "natural" to associate the probability of an outcome with (some limit of) this frequency. For this reason, this type of approach to probability is often called "frequentist."

When we deal with the second question (the one about the next president of the United States), matters are not as straightforward. The most glaring difference is that in this case we certainly do not have the ability to repeat the "experiment" (i.e., the election of a U.S. president) many times under identical conditions and to record the frequency of the different outcomes. Perhaps we can look at what happened in the past and draw from this some information. However, the conditions under which past elections occurred were certainly not identical. If we want to venture a guess about the probability of reelection, the observed frequency with which, say, incumbent presidents have been reelected certainly gives us some information. Yet, you may believe that it is more important to look at whether the economy is doing well or poorly at election time than it is to look at incumbency. And as for my political-scientist friend, who has written a book about the U.S. presidency during the years of the Vietnam war, he believes that neither incumbency nor economic conditions are really important, but what really matters is whether the country is bogged down in a messy war in a foreign land. And so on.

As more evidence accumulates (more economic data are released, the results of more opinion polls are known, etc.), the probability of the next president being a Republican or a Democrat will tend to converge toward one or zero as election day approaches. The important point is that, even if we are faced with a cliffhanger (as the elections of 2000 and 2004 were), there *will* come a time when we all agree about the outcome. Before CNN has called the last state, we can in good faith disagree about the probability in question (and for this reason this type of probability is often called "subjective"); but, when the last dimple on a Florida election card has been called, we know the answer.

With the third probabilistic question, however (the one about Homer), speaking of probability is fraught with even greater problems. Certainly we cannot repeat the experiment over and over again. We have already encountered this difficulty in assessing the probability of whether the next president of the United States will be a Democrat (in the Homer case, by the way, it is even less clear what the "experiment" is). But in the third example there is an additional problem: no matter how much evidence future archaeologists, linguists, and historians may uncover, we can never reach the same level of consensus about the authorship of *The Iliad* and *The Odyssey* that, *after* election day, we will reach about the party affiliation of the next U.S. president. New evidence may push the "probability" of Homer being the author of both *The Iliad* and *The Odyssey* to virtual certainty, yet a reasonable person in good faith may still beg to differ. If we had made a bet about the next president of the United States we would, eventually, be able to settle it. There is no way that a bet about the authorship of *The Iliad* and *The Odyssey* can be settled in a way that a bookmaker would accept. Speaking about betting may seem frivolous, but, as long as "betting" is given a sufficiently broad meaning, this way of looking at probabilities is actually central to my future argument. Betting, in this widely understood meaning of the term, becomes a metaphor for taking action at a possible cost in a situation of uncertainty.

The third (Homer-related) type of probability raises some extremely interesting points: indeed, as my lawyer wife explains to me, these are just the probabilities of relevance in the legal context (as the expressions "on the balance of probabilities" and "beyond reasonable doubt," which apply, respectively, in the civil and criminal context, testify). However, in order to keep some focus to the discussion, I will not deal with Homer-like probabilities in the rest of the book. This is no big loss for our purposes because the only probabilities we have to deal with in the context of the management of financial risk are of the first (frequentist) and second (subjective) type.

SUBJECTIVE PROBABILITIES AGAIN

When we try to make predictions, a model of how the world works tells us what variables can affect the outcome of a certain phenomenon. Indirectly, this model tells us what the *relevant* past information is. It is important to stress, however, that the "model" that informs our search for relevant information may, but need not, be a formal model. The term encompasses the wide range of "mental structures" that help us in making sense of the data we already know before conducting an experiment. If I have no clue as to how a medical thermometer works, I may think that holding it upright or upside down may affect the reading of the mercury column. Or perhaps I should shield it from electric fields? If I have at least a rudimentary understanding of physics, however, I will be able to "guess" that the reading will be due to the thermal dilation of the mercury up a very narrow tube and that, therefore, electric and gravitational fields will have a negligible influence on the reading of the temperature of the patient. Even if we try, in most real-life situations we cannot help having a "model" in this sense, i.e., a way of organizing the information pertaining to the world we live in. Indeed, we shall see in a few pages what troubles a coin-flipping Martian will get itself into just for not having such a model. The reason for stressing this point is that statisticians who believe that coin-flipping (frequentist) probabilities are the only ones worth discussing tend to downplay (or deny) the importance of models in the sense just discussed. This is not my view. I believe that information other than the data at hand is almost always useful; and I intend to argue that in risk-management applications it is essential.

So, the first role of models is to tell us which past information is relevant. Models seen as mental structures, however, are not static; rather, they interact with new evidence in a very dynamic and subtle way. How evidence should be incorporated into our new beliefs is the bread and butter of Bayesian statistical analysis. Faced with new evidence about the "world out there," Bayesians say, rational beings will update their probabilistic assessment about future events in a well-defined and optimal manner: according to Bayes's rule. Markowitz did not beat about the bush when he tersely said "the rational investor is a

Bayesian."* In the eighteenth century Richard Price made an even more sweeping statement:

> [Bayes's solution] is necessary ... in order to assure foundation *for all our reasoning concerning past facts, and what is likely to be hereafter.*[†]

So, there are not seven, four, or even two ways to update our probabilistic beliefs given new evidence: if we are "rational," we all have to agree how the new piece of information should change our probabilistic assessment.[‡] What, then, is Bayesian statistics?

According to the Bayesian view of the world, we always start from some prior belief about the problem at hand.[1] We then acquire new evidence. If we are Bayesians, we neither accept in full this new piece of information, nor do we stick to our prior belief as if nothing had happened. Instead, we modify our initial views to a degree commensurate with the weight and reliability both of the evidence and of our prior belief.[§] It all sounds very commonsensical, and the statistically innocent reader may find it surprising that intellectual wars have been fought over something so apparently benign (it is the fierceness of these intellectual wars, by the way, that has prompted my choice of the opening quote for this chapter). What is all the fuss about?

To understand why the Bayesian approach to probability is very different from the frequentist one (and, I believe, much more relevant for financial risk management) we must understand a bit better how it actually works. I will try to explain this by looking at a couple of examples.

---

*H. Markowitz (1987), *Mean-Variance Analysis in Portfolio Choice and Capital Markets*, p. 57 (Oxford: Blackwell).

[†]R. Price (1758), *A Review of the Principal Questions and Difficulties in Morals* (London: T. Cadell; reprinted by Oxford University Press in 1948), my emphasis.

[‡]Why *must* we? Because, as we shall see, if we *act* on the basis of these probabilistic assessments, and we do not follow Bayes's rule in revising them, someone will take advantage of us with our consent.

[§]More precisely, "[the probability of an event given the new evidence] is proportional to the product of [our prior probability distribution] and [the probability of observing the evidence given the event]." I am afraid that this is the best I can do while sticking to my rule of not using any formulae.

Suppose that you are told that there is a room full of children—you cannot see them but you have reason to believe that they are aged between eight and twelve. From inside the room someone shouts out the height in centimeters of one child after the other. From these observations you want to determine the distribution of ages in the population. Your "model" in this case would be made up of two components: first, your reason to believe that the age of the children in the room is between eight and twelve; second, your experience of how tall children aged eight to twelve are. You also have some degree of confidence in these two distinct beliefs. The game begins, and the first number you hear is 160 centimeters. That is very tall for a child of about ten years of age. The second height is 170 centimeters, the third 164, and the fourth 181. Your reaction to these numbers progressively changes as you hear the various heights being called out. After hearing the first you classified the observation as an outcome probably referring to a (tall) twelve-year-old child. Given your model the observation strikes you as a bit strange (i.e., you are a bit less confident about your prior beliefs about the height of preteens and about the population of the room), but you continue recording data. The second number shouted from inside the room (170) is even more "strange." By the time you hear the fourth number you are no longer automatically classifying all these outcomes as one freakish reading after another. You are beginning to reassess your model. Perhaps you did not know as much as you thought about children of that age. Or perhaps the room is full of adults, not children. *That* would explain things nicely. As each new piece of evidence accumulates, it is classified as exceptional, run-of-the-mill, mildly surprising, just-what-was-expected, etc., on the basis of your prior model; but, *and this is the more interesting bit*, it also continuously changes, perhaps imperceptibly, your confidence in the model itself.

Moving from the height of children to a more realistic example from finance and risk management, suppose that you have a model based on financial data that tells you that the economy should now be in a mild recession.* If this is true, the number of companies that are defaulting should be relatively high. You wait for the next monthly release of default statistics from Standard & Poor's and, when it arrives, it actually shows a very low number of defaults. You mentally classify this occurrence as rather exceptional (given your prior belief about the state of the world we are in), but you also have a twinge of doubt about the reliability of your model. The next month brings another low reading: another exceptional result, or should you perhaps revise your model? The third month brings a very high number of defaults. You are now left either with a good model and two exceptional (and therefore unlikely) outcomes, or with a bad model and one unlikely result. What do you do? How do you choose between the alternatives? How strong was your confidence in your model? How reliable are the data?

In short, the interaction between models and data is not a one-way street. Data can only be interpreted in the light of *some* model. But, in turn, models are (or should be) also consistently revised in the light of the quality of the predictions we make with their help. Repeated failures should give rise to some healthy doubts about the validity of the mental structures with which we began organizing the data. Typically, our revision will not be from black to white. We will not convert overnight from apostles to implacable adversaries of the model. More reasonably, we will engage in a dynamic process of to-ing and fro-ing from the model to the data and back to the model.

We can now understand the opening description of Bayesian probability updating a bit better. *Before* seeing the outcome of

---

*The example was actually very topical not very long ago. In 2006 the U.S. yield curve became "inverted," with long-dated bonds yielding less than short-dated ones. Typically this is a sign that the economy is, or is about to enter, a recession. Other macroeconomic indicators, however, suggested that no recession was present or imminent. In this situation of uncertainty, commentators, pundits, and policy makers were anxiously awaiting each new release of data (the new "evidence") to update their beliefs about the state of the economy. For a statistician this was just real-life Bayesian probability updating happening day after day.

our next prediction, we have a certain prior belief in the validity of the model. We then receive new evidence and observe how
well it agrees with the prediction. If the outcome is in line with
what the model had predicted, we strengthen our belief that the
model was correct to start with. But if the model predicted something strongly at odds with our observation, our confidence in
the model should be at least a bit shaken—the more so, the more
unlikely the observation was *given our model*. We start with prior
beliefs about how the world works (the "model"); we observe the
outcome of the prediction (the "evidence"); we reach posterior
beliefs (a new model, and one that is better, if for no other reason
than we may have become more skeptical about it).

This interaction between evidence and prior beliefs is inextricably associated with subjective probabilities. In the coin-flipping
case (where frequentist probabilities appeared to be adequate),
we needed very few prior beliefs about coins: we just had to flip
one over and over again. When faced with the question about the
next president of the United States, however, without a set of prior
beliefs we would not even know where to start looking for evidence. Does the economy matter? Does incumbency? How about
being bogged down in a messy war abroad or the hair color of the
presidential candidate?

WHAT IS A PROBABILITY AFTER ALL? SENSE AND NONSENSE
WITH FREQUENTIST AND SUBJECTIVE PROBABILITIES

The probabilities we come up with when we answer a question
such as, "Who will be the next president of the Unites States?" are
called "subjective probabilities." Why do we call them probabilities at all, rather than "hunches," "guesses," or the like? Because,
with a bit of care, they can be shown to have exactly the same
logical properties we expect from "hardcore" frequentist probabilities. To get a glimpse of why this is the case, suppose that I
slightly rephrase the question about the American election in the
following terms: "You *must* enter a bet on the outcome of the next
presidential election, but you do not know which side of the bet

you will be forced to take (i.e., whether you will be the bookie or the punter). What odds would you advertise for the next president being a Democrat?"* The number you come up with then possesses some interesting properties. Suppose you gave a 60% chance to the next president being a Democrat. If you did so, you *must* give a 40% chance (and be ready, if forced, to enter a corresponding bet at these odds) to the next president being a Republican. Why *must* you? Because, if you did not, you could be forced to enter a set of bets *at your own chosen odds* where you would lose money for sure. And *this* you would not want.

So, unless you are willing to lose money with certainty, you have to come up with two (positive) numbers (say, 0.6 and 0.4) that add up to 1 for two mutually exclusive events, either of which must come true for certain. With a few extra bells and whistles, these are exactly the properties that define the sets of positive numbers that we are ready to call probabilities.

Having said that, there are a few important caveats. While *logically* the frequentist and the subjective probabilities can be shown to share the same fundamental formal properties, in practice they are used in a very different manner. More importantly, statements that we consider meaningful for one type of probability (frequentist) can be, to say the least, puzzling in the context of the other. To see why this is the case, let us consider the following examples.

Suppose that you are armed with infinite patience and a really sturdy coin. There is nothing stopping you from coming up with a perfectly meaningful statement such as, "The chance of this coin landing heads is 0.500 001." If you made such a statement, I may ask you lots of questions, such as how many coins you tossed to reach such a precise conclusion and how controlled your experimental conditions were. Based on your procedure I will be in a position to decide whether the result you obtain is statistically significant. If sufficient experimental care was taken in reaching your conclusion, the statement about the minute biasedness of the

---

*Forcing you to take the bet and then hiding under a veil of ignorance about which side of the bet you will take removes both your possible reluctance to bet and your risk aversion.

coin can make perfect sense. If we substitute "electron," "photon," or "muon" for "coin," statements of this type are indeed commonly made in physics, and they often turn out to have important implications—it *can* make a difference, that is, if the probability is 0.500 001 rather than 0.499 999 or 0.500 002.

Suppose that now, however, you were asked the question above about the next U.S. president and that you answered it by saying, "I believe that the probability of a Democrat being elected is 0.500 001" or "I believe that the probability of Ralph Nader being elected is 0.000 032." Do these statements not sound bizarre? If I asked you how you reached such a conclusion, how could you methodologically explain your procedure? *Logically*, there is nothing stopping you from making these probabilistic statements (and, by the way, to avoid being at the receiving end of a bet that is certain to make a loss, you must also stand by the equally weird-sounding statement that you believe that a Republican will be the next president with a probability of *exactly* 0.499 967). But I have never heard anybody actually expressing their views in these terms. And, unlike in the coin case, I would have no idea how these numbers could possibly have been arrived at.

More importantly, when it comes to president-of-the-United-States-type statements, I have never observed anybody *behaving* as if they took the super-precise probabilities above as literally true. In other words, if the probabilities are of the subjective type, nobody I have ever met would *behave* in any respect differently if they said that there is a fifty–fifty chance of a Democrat being the next president (and that Ralph Nader should take up fishing).

The bottom line is that frequentist probabilities, no matter how small or sharp, *can* influence our behavior if the phenomenon at hand warrants such precision. Subjective probabilities can be shown to be logically identical, but they look, feel, and smell different from frequentist probabilities—and are *used* differently. The distinguishing feature is not that in one case I am dealing with "coin-like" objects (electrons, photons, muons, etc.) and in the other I am talking about people (presidents of the United States). I can make a perfectly meaningful frequentist probabilistic statement about people, such as, "The probability of a newborn baby being female is 0.523 45" or "The probability of a randomly chosen individual in a well-specified population having red hair is 0.1221." What matters is the repeatability of the "experiment" or the observability of what we are interested in over and over again under effectively identical conditions. We can indeed observe the outcomes of many past U.S. presidential elections, but they did not take place under identical conditions. The following quote* describes the situation extremely well:

> The traditional frequentist methods ... are usable and useful in many particularly simple, idealized problems; but they represent the most proscribed special case of probability theory, because they presuppose conditions (independent repetition of a "random experiment" but no relevant prior information) that are hardly ever met in real problems. This approach is quite inadequate for the current needs of science.

(And, I would add, for the current needs of risk management.) This way of looking at probability in general, and at frequentist and subjective probabilities in particular, is very fruitful in that, rather than opposing the two types of probability, it sees one (the frequentist) as a special case of the all-encompassing general case. Perhaps surprisingly, the general case is the subjective probability. A simple example can explain why this is the case and why it is so important.

THE STORY OF THE MARTIAN AND THE BIASED COIN

A Martian has just landed on earth, a planet he has never visited before. In particular, he has never seen a coin, let alone flipped one. The Martian has landed next to you. Not knowing how to strike up polite conversation, you take a coin out of your pocket (I said *your* pocket, not the Martian's pocket, or the pocket of a party magician). This is any old regular coin, which you have just

---

*From the introduction to Jaynes, *Probability Theory: The Logic of Science.*

received from the shopkeeper at the corner store. You toss the coin four times. Both you and your Martian friend record the outcomes of the four coin tosses. All four tosses happen to yield heads.

What do *you* conclude about the fairness of the coin? What is *the Martian* likely to conclude? Let us start with you. Personally, I have never in my life encountered an obviously biased coin. I know that they are very common in statistics books, but when I have to choose whether to serve or receive at the beginning of a tennis match I accept any old coin that my opponent produces. If you (not the Martian) are at all like me, you also probably believe that most coins are very close to fair. Seeing four consecutive heads may strike the two of us as only very mildly odd. Since we would have been just as (mildly) surprised if we had observed four consecutive tails, the probability of us being this surprised with a fair coin is between 10% and 15%. Would you draw any strong conclusions about the biasedness of the coin from this outcome? Personally, I would not. I may have a small niggling doubt that might prompt me to toss the coin a few more times just to check. But, if I were forced to bet on the next outcome on the basis of the available evidence, I would be likely to require odds of fifty–fifty for heads or tails. What would *you* do?

Things look very different to our Martian friend. He has never seen a coin. He does not even know that coins are for buying goods. For all he knows, and judging from his four observations, they could just as well be devices that earthlings have invented to produce heads after a toss. He cannot be sure of this, of course, but in his mind the possibility that heads are *much* more likely than tails is very real. If forced to bet on the outcome of the fifth coin toss, he will not accept fifty–fifty odds. For him heads is *much* more likely than tails.*

*I am assuming here that the Martian is not endowed with Laplace's views linking probability with symmetry. As one referee of my book pointed out, the Martian "might have a Laplacian intuition that a half was a good call based on his appreciation of the simple symmetry of flat objects, such as Martian skimming stones." If one so wanted, one could refine the thought experiment by preventing the Martian from seeing the coin itself. The main conclusion does not change.

You and your Martian friend have observed the same experiment, yet you reach very different conclusions. How can that be? Because, Bayesian statisticians say, we almost never approach an experiment with random outcomes without some prior ideas about the setting and the likelihood of the possible outcomes. New evidence modifies (*should* modify) our prior beliefs and transforms them into our posterior beliefs. The stronger the prior belief, the more difficult it will be to change it. If we really and truly have *no* prior beliefs about the situation at hand, as was the case with the Martian when he observed the coin flips, then and only then will we be totally guided by the evidence. This is the situation that is dealt with with infinite care and precision in "traditional" statistics books. Yet it remains a rather special situation.

Going back to our example, a lifetime's experience with coins has created in you and me a very strong prior belief about the (lack of) biasedness of coins. The rather weak evidence from four consecutive tosses will only mildly shake our prior belief. Our *actions* (i.e., our next bet) are only mildly affected by what we have observed, if at all.

Matters look very different from the point of view of our Martian friend. He has never seen coins in his life, and therefore he is very open-minded about their workings (in statistical terms, his prior beliefs about coins are very diffuse). The same evidence therefore has much greater power in making him change his prior belief (rather, in his case, in allowing him to form an opinion at all). He, not you, should make slavish use of all the formulae he will find in the "traditional" statistics books, and that will allow him to estimate all sort of marvelous things, such as rejecting the null hypothesis that a given coin is fair at a certain confidence level, etc. Neither you nor the Martian are acting "irrationally" in drawing very different conclusions *and in acting very differently*, i.e., *in betting differently on the next outcome*.

Why have I chosen to put much of the last sentence in italics? Because I want to stress that actions (in this case, betting) are central to the argument. Betting, in this context, is clearly a metaphor for a wide range of actions, namely for all those actions where you weigh the positive and negative outcomes and decide what steps to take when something that matters is at stake. When you insure your house against fire you are effectively making a bet (the premium paid is the amount you wager, the compensation you receive in case of fire your payout). If, instead of leaving your money in your (safe) bank account, you invest it in equities, you are making a bet. When you look at the sky in the morning and decide to leave your umbrella at home, you are making a bet. When you decide to marry you are making a bet. After observing your actions, I can deduce something about your subjective probabilities. The more actions I can observe, the fuller my picture of the full range of subjective probabilities you assign to the events you face. Note how different this way of looking at things is from the traditional prescription first to calculate the (frequentist) probabilities and then to act accordingly.

Of course, the differences should not be exaggerated. As mentioned above, subjective probabilities do become very similar to frequentist probabilities if we can repeat an "experiment" over and over again under exactly the same conditions. Why would that be? Quite simply because if we can truly repeat the same random experiment over and over again under identical conditions, the cumulative weight of the evidence becomes overwhelming. If we have an open mind, sooner or later it will (or it *should*) outweigh any reasonable prior belief. If, while tossing coins with our Martian friend, I saw forty consecutive heads, even I (the staunch believer in fair coins) would begin to suspect that there is something fishy about this particular coin.

So, when it comes to risk-management applications, the relevant question is not what type of probability is the "correct one" in the abstract. Rather, it is whether the particular problem at hand makes one approach or the other more profitable. The surprising fact is that most real-life risk-management problems lie much closer to the subjective end of the spectrum than to the frequentist one. Being good at guessing whether the next president of the United States will be a Democrat is much more useful in risk management than guessing whether my coin will land heads at the next throw. And since we saw that repeatability is an essential factor in deciding what type of probability is more relevant, it is time to look at this aspect of the problem in detail.

PLAYING ONCE AND PLAYING MANY TIMES

Risk management is not just about probabilities, but about using them in making choices. One important aspect of our behavior toward risk is how we deal with the repetition of a random event. Therefore I now turn from the type of probability of relevance in risk management to the actions inspired by these probabilities.

Faced with identical odds, if our interaction with a random event is of a one-off nature we often behave very differently than if we face exactly the same situation over and over again. The business of selling insurance seems to offer an obvious analogy. It is easy to find a competitive quote for life or theft insurance (where the probabilities at play are almost exactly frequentist and we deal with many essentially indistinguishable atomic events). It is very difficult, and expensive, however, to find insurance against terrorist events, whose probability of occurrence is of a subjective nature and which are, thankfully, rare. Repetition, however, is not a simple restatement of the principle of diversification. Let us see why this is the case.

I intend to make my point by means of an example (with a few twists). With this example, first I intend to show that repetition is important because it can radically change the way we behave when faced with a risky prospect. Few surprises here. More interestingly, I will also show that introducing a relatively small degree of uncertainty into our probabilistic information can change our actions in a dramatic fashion. Unfortunately, the classic (frequentist) view of probability makes it much more difficult to take this uncertainty into account, i.e., to change our actions. This is another reason why using subjective probabilities makes a lot more sense when, as is the case in risk management, we want to reach our best possible decision under uncertainty. So, here is the example.

We have a coin which is biased sixty–forty in favor of heads. Would you bet twenty times your yearly salary on the outcome of a single throw? Before answering, do visualize the amount of money we are talking about. We are not playing a dinner-party game with a few dollars at stake—at least not a game played at the dinner parties I go to. If you lose, your total wealth will take a massive blow, you may have to sell your house, you may even end up bankrupt. On the other hand, if you win, you may be able to retire tomorrow, if that is what you desire, or to buy that Stradivarius or a Ferrari, depending on what gives you pleasure in life. The odds are stacked in your favor by three to two. Would *you* enter this bet? I have never met a single person who answered seriously in the affirmative.

Now we change the game. We use the same biased coin (still sixty–forty in favor of heads), and flip it a thousand times. Each time heads appears you win twenty times your annual salary. Each time tails appears you lose the same amount. You only settle the net gain or loss after all the 1,000 coin tosses have taken place (so that you cannot go bankrupt after a couple of unlucky tosses at the start). Would you enter this bet? To help you with the mathematics, I have carried out a back-of-the-envelope calculation. Given the rules of the game, I have worked out that the probability of you losing anything at all is approximately 1 in 10,000,000,000. Greater losses are even less likely. When faced with too many zeros our heads begin to spin, so let us gain a feel for this number. Suppose that you choose, totally at random, one human being on planet earth. Totally independently, and also at random, I also choose an individual. If we have failed to pick the same person, then you win at least twenty times your yearly salary. If we *have* picked the same person, you have still not lost anything yet. For you to lose your bet I still have to toss a (fair) coin. If I obtain tails then and only then will you have lost twenty times your salary or more. Would you play this game? I have never met anyone that would turn down this opportunity. Rabin and Thaler are even more sanguine: "A good lawyer could have you declared legally insane for turning down this gamble."[*]

So far, I have not said anything too surprising, or too original. It seems to be just the principle of diversification at work under a different guise (over time rather than synchronously). Strictly speaking it is not, but, whatever name we want to give it, we are all rather familiar with the situation, and we would have all presumably answered in the same way—Rabin and Thaler certainly would have.[2] There is a last twist in the story, though. We no longer know with certainty that the coin is biased sixty–forty in favor of heads. We have conducted a series of experiments that leads us to expect the bias still to be sixty–forty, but we now have an uncertainty of plus or minus 15% around this estimate.[†] Note that our central expectation of the biasedness of the coin has not changed: on balance we still believe that the coin is more likely to be biased in our favor, and by the same ratio of two to three. However, we have now introduced some reasonable degree of uncertainty around this belief. So, the coin could be biased 75% in favor of heads, but perhaps it is actually biased 55% in favor *of tails*. We toss this uncertainly biased coin 1,000 times. Given this information, would you still enter the twenty-times-your-yearly-salary bet under the conditions stipulated above for the certain-probability case? Again, to provide a bit of help with the numbers, I have carried out some calculations on a piece of paper: if the coin is biased, say, 75% in favor of heads, the odds of you winning are even more staggeringly tilted in your favor than before—so much so that I will not even bother to write down the zeros. However, if the coin were biased 55% in favor of tails (a number still compatible with the uncertainty stated above), your probability of being on the *losing* side of the bet after 1,000 tosses has increased to over 99.9%. Suppose that the bias of 60% was arrived at because you knew that, with equal probability, the coin could either be

---

[*]M. Rabin and R. Thaler (2001), Risk aversion, *Journal of Economic Perspectives* 15(1):219–32. I agree, but see the first endnote for this chapter for a dissenting view.

[†]In frequentist terms, this apparently innocuous statement is, of course, meaningless. More about this later.

75% biased in favor of heads or 55% biased in favor of tails. This means that you stand (approximately) a one-in-two chance of losing the bet. What would *you* do? The majority of the people I have asked turn down this bet, despite the fact that *the expectation* of the number of heads obtained by tossing the coin a thousand times (not once!) has not changed from the previous example.

As I mentioned in the footnote above, the first two settings of this story have spawned an enormous literature. It is the last twist in the story, however, that has the greatest relevance for risk management. This is because in most of the stylized examples presented in risk-management textbooks, the probabilities of events are almost invariably treated as God given. So are percentiles, volatilities, correlations, etc. I rarely hear a Value-at-Risk number (which is, after all, a percentile obtained from a finite, and often not-too-large, sample) quoted as, say, $20,000,000 ± $2,000,000. This bad practice is very common, but also very dangerous, because Value-at-Risk (or other similar statistical constructs) should ultimately be used in risk management to make decisions. But the last part of the story shows that, if the decision is of the accept–reject type, *by neglecting the uncertainty in our statistical estimates we can reach completely, not marginally, different conclusions.* This has been recognized for a long time in asset management. In this multitrillion-dollar industry the standard Markowitz allocation scheme, which uses the very same correlation and diversification framework that is at play in Value-at-Risk, has been universally abandoned exactly because it is so prone to radically changing the suggested course of action for small changes in the inputs. Unfortunately, the same fundamental insight seems to have been lost in the translation to the risk-management community.

This is no coincidence. Current quantitative risk management is joined at the hip with a frequentist view of probability (even if it does not always realize that this is the case). With frequentist probability, it does not even make sense to say the probability of a coin being fair is 40%. The coin is either fair or biased, and that is it.[3] A frequentist may say that, given the experiments we have conducted, we can be confident at a certain level that the coin is, say, biased. Once we have attained this level of confidence, the coin is just fair: it does not exist in a quantum-mechanical superposition state of fairness and biasedness. But once the Rubicon of the 95%, or the 99%, or the 99.9% confidence level has been crossed, and the coin has been accepted at this confidence level as fair, it becomes psychologically much more difficult and cumbersome to reintroduce the effect of any residual estimation uncertainty in our decision making. Subjective probabilities, on the other hand, never cease reminding us that none of our parameters are sharp numbers (accepted or rejected), but come cloaked in a full probability distribution. But if, as the example above shows, a relatively small uncertainty in the probabilities can change our behavior in a dramatic fashion, subjective probabilities are better suited to the task at hand. This matters acutely for the current school of financial risk management, according to which we are to use a (sharp) Value-at-Risk number to decide whether, at the margin, we should enter deal A or deal B. A dangerous way to make decisions if a very reasonable degree of uncertainty in the "true" Value-at-Risk number can easily reverse our course of action. But I am getting ahead of myself: more about this later.

WATCH MY ACTIONS, DO NOT LISTEN TO MY WORDS: PROBABILITIES AS ACTIONS

For some readers encountering the term "subjective probabilities" for the first time it may have a liberating, but also rather unsettling, connotation. When we use subjective probabilities we do not limit ourselves to saying things like, "You should only talk about probabilities if you can toss coins, extract blue and black balls from urns, roll dice, and the like." We do not say, "Only if you engage in such (identically repeatable) activities can you assign objective probabilities to the different (combinations of) events." Rather, subjective probability theory says, "You have your own beliefs about events. If these beliefs taken together obey certain consistency conditions, and if, when new evidence appears, you update these beliefs in a particular way, then we can treat your degrees of belief about the various (combinations of) events as probabilities." At the same time, it also sounds too hand-waving. Surely, objective probabilities must be more "scientific" and more "respectable"? Are all beliefs not equally valid, after all? And, if they are, have we not demeaned the concept of probability? Not at all.

Subjective probabilities can be made every bit as "hard," "respectable," and, *if and when appropriate*, sharp and precise as your "objective" probabilities. I can give a few hints as to why this is the case. Let us start from your beliefs. Does *anything* really go? As we saw when discussing the party affiliation of the next president of the United States, if you really advertise two-way odds of 70% for a democratic win and 60% for a republican president, it is not difficult to see how you will land yourself in trouble. So, to begin with, consistency among your different stated beliefs is necessary to avoid your losing a lot of money very quickly. But there is more. You may also end up in situations where your freely chosen actions will get you into trouble (cause you to incur losses) with near certainty if you fail to update your beliefs (learn from experience) in a logically consistent manner.* Again, it is through actions that the inconsistency of your updated probabilities is revealed. And it is for this reason that, in explaining what subjective probabilities are, we started from the contrived situation of you being *forced* to enter a bet: the forced bet simply constitutes a metaphor for having to take a risky course of action. Finally, not knowing what side of the bet you will have to take (i.e., whether you will be the punter or the bookie) "cleanses" your advertised odds of risk aversion.

There is a lot more to subjective probabilities than consistency and rational updating, though, and this is what makes them so relevant for practical applications (such as risk management). Suppose that you believe that the probability of earth being hit

*That is, if you fail to update your prior belief on the basis of new evidence using Bayes's rule.

by a huge meteorite in the next month is 30%. Suppose that you also believe that, over the same period of time, the probability of a major breakthrough in nuclear fusion technology is 50%. Finally, you also believe that these two events are mutually incompatible: for some reason, if the meteorite strikes, then the nuclear fusion breakthrough will not materialize (fair enough). But, somewhat more surprisingly, you believe that the reverse is also true. If asked, you would consistently have to state that, in your opinion, the probability that neither event will happen is 20% (since the probabilities of mutually exclusive events add, 20% = 100% − 50% − 30%).

Your probabilities, and the link between the occurrences, might strike me as bizarre, but there is no denying that there is an internal consistency in your set of beliefs: all the probabilities are positive, they add up to 1, the joint probability of mutually exclusive events is 0, the probabilities of mutually exclusive events add, etc. At a formal level these may therefore seem to be perfectly good subjective probabilities. The problem is that you will not be able to do much with them. The moment you are forced to take some action on the basis of your advertised odds, you will immediately find parties (me, to begin with) all too willing to take the other side of the bet, or, rather, of the many bets that can be constructed on the basis of your (perfectly consistent) set of beliefs. To begin with I will sell you meteorite insurance in as large a size as you are ready to accept from me even for a very small premium. But note that, according to you, the probability of a meteorite *not* hitting the earth and of a breakthrough in fusion technology *not* happening in the next month is 20%. If you really meant what you said, you should be very willing to enter a bet where you pay up to five dollars for any dollar I wager on the event "next month will see no meteorites and no breakthrough in fusion technology." If you do not, I can be justified in forming the suspicion that your outlandish (albeit consistent) probabilities were not truly held beliefs, but cheap talk to impress your friends at a dinner party. You must be truly willing to back your beliefs with actions and ready to bear the associated price (or reap the reward) for degrees of belief to qualify as subjective probabilities. "Betting," as elsewhere in this book, is therefore a metaphor for taking a course of action whose future outcome has a real effect on us (e.g., buying insurance, investing in a risky project, spending money to avoid a flood or the spread of an illness, etc.). Having skin in the game is what turns wishy-washy utterances into real subjective probabilities.

Let me provide a less contrived example of what I mean. In the early to mid 1990s in the United Kingdom and in other European countries a widespread fear developed that a variant form of CJD might spread to humans. CJD is a fatal illness—also known as "mad cow disease"—that is well-known to affect bovines. The variant form of the illness was thought to have contaminated human beings via the ingestion of beef from cattle affected by the disease. The incubation time of the condition is very long (ten years or more) and the consumption of possibly contaminated beef had been taking place for almost a decade. Therefore, when the first human cases appeared scientists did not know whether they were observing the tip of an iceberg or whether the relatively few observed cases, tragic as they were, constituted a rather limited and circumscribed occurrence. "Expert scientists" were soon willing to go on record with statements to the effect that "it could not be excluded" that a catastrophe was unfolding.* The nonscientific press was all too eager to jump on the bandwagon, and extravagant claims were soon presented, such as that hundreds of thousands, or perhaps even millions, of lives could be lost over the next decade. Specific probabilities were not stated, but the prominence of the reporting only made sense if the possibility of this catastrophic event was nonnegligible: the newspapers, at least judging by the inches of column space devoted to the topic, were not talking about a risk as remote as being hit by a meteorite.

As the months went by and the number of cases did not significantly increase, the number of reported instances did not conform to the statistical pattern that would have begun to appear if we had

---

*They were probably happy to do so as well: the Warholian fifteen minutes of fame do not come so often to men and women in white coats.

been observing a tip-of-the-iceberg event. To "fix" what would be an anomaly if the catastrophe story had been correct, the estimate of the incubation period of the disease (about whose human variant very little was, and is, known) was correspondingly lengthened: we do not see as many instances as the Armageddon scenario would imply, the ad hoc explanation went, because a greater proportion of cases than we thought will take longer to manifest themselves.

Looking at the data available at the time with a statistical eye, I was becoming increasingly convinced that the magnitude of the potential effect was being greatly exaggerated. At just the same time, a well-educated, but nonscientist, friend of mine (a university lecturer) was visiting London and we decided to meet for dinner. As the conversation moved from one topic to another, he expressed a strong belief, formed by reading the nonscientific press, that the spread of CJD would be a major catastrophe for the U.K. population in the next five to ten years. He was convinced, he claimed, that "hundreds of thousands of people" would succumb to the disease. On the face of it, it would seem that I was faced with the expression of a perfectly legitimate subjective-type probability. But, was this really the case? I challenged him to enter a bet, to be settled in ten years' time, that the number of occurrences would not be consistent with a major epidemic. My friend refused to take me up on my offer, despite my very attractive odds (attractive, that is, given his stated subjective probabilities). He claimed that "one does not bet on these things"; that he found my proposal distasteful; that, anyhow, he was not a betting man; and so on. I explained that I was not trying to gain material advantage from a possible human disaster, but I was simply probing the strength of his convictions on the matter. Ultimately, the bet was not entered, and the evening was rather spoiled by my proposal. Yet I still think that my friend's utterances were not real subjective probabilities—just "cheap talk." By failing, for whatever noble reasons, to put his money where his mouth was, his statements failed to stand up to the most crucial requirement, after consistency, for qualifying as subjective probabilities: the willingness to back them up with "actions."

Also, the degree of likelihood implied by the newspapers' coverage was not an example of a subjective probability but of cheap talk. The newspaper would not stand to lose anything if, in five to ten years' time, their lurid projections failed to materialize: they would have sold a lot of copies in the scaremongering days, and, five to ten years down the line, the public would have been distracted by another clear and present (and similarly disastrous, and similarly "unpriced") danger. When the first human cases of CJD occurred, most (but, interestingly, not all) newspapers correctly and cynically sensed that they would ultimately stand to lose very little if their projections were wildly exaggerated, but that they would do rather nicely at the time from a "big story." By my definition, these newspapers were entering not a bona fide bet, but a one-way bet. Nobody could effectively take them on and benefit from their incorrect assessment of probability. As a consequence, once again, their stated (rather, trumpeted) probabilities were not true subjective probabilities.[4]

What is the point of this example? The point is to stress that, despite the name, subjective probabilities do not mean that "anything goes." Consistency and rational (Bayesian) updating are essential features, but there is far more. Probability-as-degree-of-belief does not mean that we are dealing with a wishy-washy, "new-age," "postmodern" version of good old objective probabilities. Extravagant implicit or explicit probabilistic claims (even if formally internally consistent) do not qualify as subjective probabilities. The term "subjective" does not mean that any probabilistic claim should command the same attention. Only if the claims can be easily and readily challenged and if they are backed by risky actions ("bets") can we truly talk of subjective probabilities. If these conditions are met, these "strong" subjective probabilities are as far from cheap talk as one can possibly imagine. Indeed, in many important fields they often give rise to the most accurate predictions that can be made; sometimes to virtually unbeatable predictions—unbeatable not because the predictions are always right, but because to this day nobody has found a consistent way of doing any better.

This is also very relevant to risk management. In many instances, it is thought to be best practice to elicit "expert opinion" from specialists—this is particularly true for operational risk.[5] This is all well and good, as long as we remember that "experts" do not live in a vacuum. When we listen to their predictions or risk assessments, we should always keep in mind how and to what extent they are rewarded for correct predictions or punished for false alarms. If an expert is held fully responsible if things go badly on his watch but is not correspondingly rewarded if things turn out better than expected, it is not difficult to imagine in which direction his predictions will be biased. As we shall see, this is one of the very good reasons why, when it comes to analyzing risky prospects, banks have set up a "division of labor" between "risk bears" (also known as risk managers) and "risk bulls" (also known as traders).

So, predictions with no gain or pain on "settlement date" are vacuous utterances. It is, however, necessary but not sufficient to have skin in the game for predictions to be derived from bona fide subjective probabilities. If the rewards and the punishments for making predictions are not "symmetrically" aligned with the correctness of the prediction (as is the case when one suffers too little or too much from a wrong prediction compared with the gain from a correct prediction), then what we have are not true subjective probabilities but risk-skewed ones.* I cannot open this new (and rather large) can of worms here. In the second section of chapter 10 I will discuss what this means in some detail in the context of management of risk in a bank. For the time being we should simply note that, as we leave the safe land of frequentist probability (with its objective and impersonal coin-tossing-like odds) and enter the murkier territory of subjective probabilities, matters quickly become not only more nuanced, but also unsettlingly complex and "fuzzy." This may be unfortunate, but no more so

---

*This is why I always insist that you should advertise your odds without knowing whether you will end up being the bookmaker or the punter.

than realizing that, for certain problems, assuming that balls are frictionless and that masses are point-like will just not do. If what I have discussed is an unwelcome surprise for some readers and I am the bearer of unpleasant news, please do not blame me for the fact that reality is more complex than we sometimes wish it to be.

It is not all doom and gloom. In many cases of relevance, there is a very important aspect of the view of probability-as-action that breaks down the often-artificial barrier between frequentist and subjective probabilities. Suppose that we are in those very special conditions where the frequentist approach to probabilities makes perfect sense (repeatability under identical conditions, weak prior beliefs, etc.). If what matters to us is the outcome of our "bet," and if the conditions for frequentist probabilities to make sense do indeed apply, then we as bookmakers will immediately and readily make use of the frequentist probabilities—since our "money" is at stake, we would be crazy not to. Focusing on the outcome of the "bet" automatically makes us nondogmatic probabilists, and allows us eclectically to embrace whatever tool we have at our disposal to arrive at the best prediction we can (i.e., at the prediction that you will find most difficult to profit from).

Where does this leave us as far as risk management is concerned? Roughly speaking, we can say the following. Whenever watching my actions (my betting, my worrying, my buying or selling insurance) is the best way of gleaning the underlying probabilities, these are likely to be of the subjective type. (If you want a good prediction about the party affiliation of the next president of the United States, do not bother with long statistical tables about past presidents—just look up the odds offered at your nearest betting shop.*) In those (rare) situations, on the other hand, when probabilities come first and actions follow from these, we are likely to be dealing with frequentist probabilities. (If something really hangs on the result of the next coin toss, I would not bother with soliciting opinions about its biasedness—I would just make sure

*This is not because the tables are of no use. It is because the odds will have been arrived at by looking at these tables, and at much else besides.

to have tossed that very coin many, many times beforehand). But I have argued above that in the real financial world very few problems are akin to coin-tossing problems. If I am correct, this entails that it is rare that in our risk-management decisions we are faced with such sharp and objective probabilities that we can be guided by them in the same precise way a coin-tosser can. Of course, "fuzzy" probabilities *are* also informative and *can* influence our decisions, but they are likely to do so in a much more complex and nuanced manner. "Fuzzy" probabilities may also suggest choices that are radically different from those made with "sharp" probabilities: recall the example about tossing a coin with uncertain biasedness a thousand times. Perhaps, if we cannot rely on probabilities to tell us unambiguously how to choose, the most we can hope for is decisional consistency. But what do we mean by consistency? And, in any case, how are we to link probabilities, of whatever nature, to decisions? This is what the next chapter is about.

CHAPTER 4

MAKING CHOICES

Non domandarci la formula che mondi possa aprirti
Si' qualche storta sillaba e seccha come un ramo.
Codesto solo oggi possiam dirti:
Cio' che *non* siamo, cio' che *non* vogliamo*

Eugenio Montale, Ossi di Seppia (1923)

WHY IS IT SO DIFFICULT?

Risk management is about decision making under uncertainty. There are well-established disciplines, going under the collective name "decision theory," that tackle this topic. Both utility and prospect theory, for instance, claim to offer *the* unique correct solution to *all* problems of choice under uncertainty. I do not believe that either fulfills this promise fully, but I cannot ignore their claims. To argue the case as to why they fall short of their promise, I must first give an intuitive explanation of what influences our risky choices and then explain, as sympathetically as I can, what utility and prospect theory offer. Once the terms of the problem and the proposed solution are made clear I will argue that, if one is interested in risk-management applications, there are problems both with utility and with prospect theory. Not all

---

*Don't ask us for the formula capable of unlocking worlds for you
Like a crooked syllable and as dry as a branch
Only this we can tell you today:
That which we are *not*, that which we do *not* want.

of their teachings have to be thrown out of the window, though. I will show that when other insights from behavioral finance are taken into account we may still be able to achieve less ambitious but still very useful practical results.

In the quote that opens this chapter, Nobel laureate Montale warned us not to look for a magic formula capable of solving all of our problems. I doubt that Montale had financial decisions in mind when he wrote these beautiful lines. Yet in many areas, including finance, the temptation to reduce our decision-making process to a simple rule is often close to irresistible—the more so when our decision is of a binary type: yes or no; black or white; invest or do nothing.

Decisions under uncertainty are at the heart of finance. Indeed, there is a common theme underlying investment budgeting, asset allocation, asset pricing, and risk management: how to arrive at a "good" trade-off between the benefits and the costs of an initiative—where, of course, the risks attached to an enterprise are among the "costs" associated with it.

So, how does the decision maker[1] begin to analyze a risky project such as a proposed trading initiative? A good starting point is to have a clear picture of what can happen if the initiative is entered into, and what the probabilities associated with these outcomes are.* We can then plot all the associated monetary outcomes against the probabilities associated with them and obtain what is called a *profit-and-loss distribution*. This is far from being an easy task, but, to get things started let us sweep these difficulties under the rug for the time being. One such curve is displayed in figure 4.1. It gives a graphical representation of the probability we associate with any given gain or loss.

By convention, the area under the whole curve is always set equal to one (the probability is normalized). Therefore, a point such as point A in figure 4.1 indicates that by entering this trade we incur a probability of 20% of losing at least $20,000,000 (this is

---

*I have discussed in the previous chapter what type of probability, "objective" or "subjective," makes more sense for financial-risk-management problems. We therefore leave this discussion aside, at least for the moment.

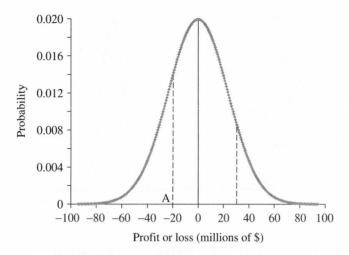

Figure 4.1. A profit-and-loss distribution. The area to the left of point A is 20% of the total area under the curve, indicating that there is a 20% chance of incurring a loss greater than $20,000,000.

because the area under the curve to the left of point −$20,000,000 on the x-axis is 20% of the total area). We also have a probability of 10% of making a gain of at least $30,500,000 (clearly, this is because the area under the curve to the right of point $30,500,000 on the x-axis is 10% of the total area). To the extent that all we are interested in is the profit or loss from a project, this *profit-and-loss distribution* curve contains all there is to know about the "trade" for us to reach a decision. If this all sounds too obvious even to mention, let us not forget that utility theoreticians do *not* regard this curve as a fundamental piece of information—they would rather talk about your total wealth before and after the investment. But we are getting ahead of ourselves.

If we are comparing two different investment opportunities ("trades"), we can draw the two associated profit-and-loss distribution curves on the same probability graph and compare where the probabilities peak, how wide the distributions are and, in general, make all sorts of interesting comparisons. Sometimes (but very rarely, as we shall see) these curves immediately suggest an

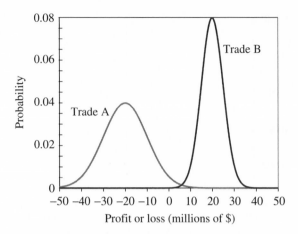

Figure 4.2. The profit-and-loss distributions for two trades (A and B). Which one would you prefer to enter?

obvious choice between two trades. Look at figure 4.2. Almost everybody would prefer the trade associated with the curve on the right (let us call it trade B): not only do I expect to make more money, but I will also have less uncertainty about the outcome. If you are at all like me, when real money is at stake you too prefer a certain dollar to an uncertain one (or perhaps even to an uncertain dollar and five cents).

Unfortunately, it is very rare for real trades to display profit-and-loss distributions like the ones in figure 4.2. This is simply because if this graph were available for all and sundry to see or to obtain, all and sundry would have already chosen trade B over trade A, or perhaps even "sold" trade A to build a leveraged position in trade B—wouldn't you? By so doing, however, the price for entering trade B would go up (because every man and his dog wants a piece of this particular action) and the profit would automatically decrease. By how much? Roughly speaking, up to the point when choosing between A and B is no longer such a no-brainer and the pros and cons of the two distributions become more finely balanced. For instance, perhaps one offers a bit more return, but with greater uncertainty. In short, you *might* find a

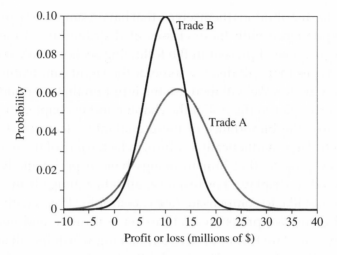

Figure 4.3. The profit-and-loss distributions for two other trades. Do you still find it just as obvious which one you would you prefer to enter?

$10 bill on the pavement, especially if the neighborhood where you find the note is thinly populated and houses the Institute for Metaphysical Speculation—but you will not find a sure-profit opportunity in the streets of modern financial markets, where there are not only lots of people walking but where these people also have a tendency to scour the ground with hawk-like attention for cents, dimes, and quarters (let alone $10 bills).

So, in practice you are much more likely to have to decide between two alternatives such as those in figure 4.3. Trade A looks more attractive on the upside (the probability of substantial gains is much greater than for trade B). With trade A we have a much greater overall uncertainty about the outcome, however; in partic-ular, the probability of ending up losing some money is consider-ably greater. Choosing between the two alternatives is no longer such a no-brainer.[2]

How can we begin to analyze these graphs in a systematic way? Are there some recurrent features in the associated trades that can help us classify these distributions and highlight common risk characteristics? Can we associate some numbers, distilled from the distributions themselves, that have a simple and intuitive correspondence with these classes of distributions? To answer these questions, I present in the following section a few stylized trade types that will display some of the significant features we are looking for. We will then use the intuition that we build from these examples in the rest of the chapter and in chapter 10. I cannot stress the importance of these qualitative features strongly enough. They synthetically capture, in fact, some of the reactions to risky projects that human beings have experimentally been observed to display.* For instance, all other things being equal we do not like to compensate rare catastrophic losses with many small gains; we prefer to avoid extreme positive and negative returns; etc. Any theory of decision making worth its salt should capture these features. This is why the intuition we are about to build is so important.

ROLLING DICE, BUYING LOTTERY TICKETS, AND SELLING INSURANCE

Suppose you set up a lottery that, for a change, is very risky for the organizer. You charge $100 for a ticket and promise to pay $1,000,000 to the winner. You have built a huge, and fair, roulette wheel with 12,000 grooves and the lottery (i.e., you) will pay out if the ball settles in *the* one green groove of your roulette wheel. The odds of the game are, of course, tilted in your favor—the odds would be fair if there were 10,000, not 12,000, grooves. But you stand to make a profit only on average. In reality you offer the prize of this lottery to one player at a time, one player per day. After the first day, and the first spin of the roulette wheel, you are very likely to be up $100. But there is a very small probability (1/120,000) that the ball may have settled on green on the very first spin of the wheel, and that you will find yourself $999,900

---

*See, for instance, H. Shefrin (2000), *Beyond Greed and Fear—Understanding Behavioral Finance and the Psychology of Investing* (Boston, MA: Harvard Business School Press).

in the red (the prize you have to pay out minus the price you received for the lottery ticket).

After one hundred days of playing this game the probability of you having had to pay out the jackpot has risen to just a bit below 1%. It is still very small but no longer totally negligible. Suppose you decide to do this for a living, and therefore plan to spin the wheel for 10,000 days (which roughly corresponds to 30 years of "work," give or take some holidays). At the end of your working life as a wheel spinner you have a 43% chance of being up exactly $1,000,000—this is the probability of the ball never landing on the green groove in 10,000 trials. Note that this is the maximum amount of money you can possibly hope to make: throughout your working life you collected $100 for 10,000 days and never paid out the jackpot. (This, by the way, is why the profit-and-loss distribution in figure 4.4 has zero probability mass for gains greater than $1,000,000.) There is also a 36% chance of you breaking even, because you had to pay out the jackpot once, and you will have still collected $100 × 10,000 = $1,000,000 in premia. And there are probabilities of 15%, 4%, and a bit below 1% of being out of pocket to the tune of one, two, or three million dollars, respectively. The whole profit-and-loss distribution is shown in figure 4.4.

What can we learn from this picture (and from the numbers behind it)? To begin with, we learn that you can expect (in a mathematical sense) to make money from this initiative: on average at the end of the 10,000 spins of the roulette wheel you should be up by $166,686. However, this piece of information by itself should not be enough to allow you to decide whether you want to do this for a living. Quite reasonably, you will want to look at the other outcomes and at the associated probabilities as well. Perhaps you do not fancy the possibility of being $1,000,000 in the red after a lifetime of wheel spinning. Perhaps the close-to-1% chance of losing $3,000,000 is just unacceptable to you. In any case, looking at this picture does help you make your decision.

What has spinning a roulette wheel got to do with "serious" financial decisions? Quite a lot, really. Many trades share the same

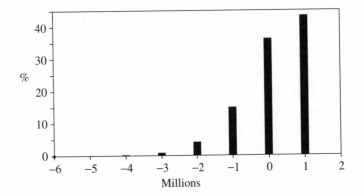

Figure 4.4. Your (discrete) profit-and-loss distribution after a life as a wheel spinner.

features of providing a small, dependable profit most of the time but of causing very large losses on rare occasions. A couple of examples will help.

Think of investing in the bond of an emerging-market country. There is some fear that the currency may be devalued but the government is trying to avoid this by enticing foreign funds into the local currency with high interest rates. By investing the foreign funds into the local short-term bonds, you are earning a nice interest rate on your investment with relatively high probability; but if the currency were devalued by, say, 40%, you would lose that fraction of your initial investment when you reconvert it into your own currency. Let us get a feel for the return and risk of this strategy with some realistic numbers. At the time of writing, you can get an almost riskless interest rate of between 3% and 5% by investing in the government bonds of most safe developed countries. In 2005 a bond guaranteed by the Iraqi government was offered on the international bond market yielding two to three times as much. If you invest $1,000 in this bond and hold on to it for a year, you stand to make $80–120 more than if you lent the same amount of money to Uncle Sam. If that sounds like a small amount, remember that your safe return is currently also pretty paltry, of the order of $30–40 per annum. If the Iraqi government were unable to honor its promise, however, you would stand to lose most of your initial investment, perhaps as much as, say, $800. By buying this bond you are effectively selling lottery tickets priced at $80, and with a jackpot (that you will have to pay out in the case of default) of about $800.

Let me give an example a bit closer to home. Suppose that you sell put options on a stock index, such as the Dow Jones. What this means is the following. The index today stands at 10,000. A friend of yours has invested $10,000 in this equity index. He is ready to take in his stride small fluctuations in the value of his investment but would be financially embarrassed (as the euphemism goes) if the index fell below, say, 8,000. You step in and promise to make good, dollar for dollar, any loss your friend will make beyond this level. So, if the index were to fall to, say, 7,600, you will pay your friend $400. If it fell to $7,000 you would pay him $1,000. And so on. Clearly you will not do this for free, but you will charge him a smallish premium for this insurance (smallish, that is, compared with your friend's investment). How this insurance premium (the cost of the lottery ticket, to keep our metaphors straight) is arrived at can be very complicated, and I spent a part of my professional life in pricing contracts of this nature (or more complex ones). Whatever the cost of the individual lottery ticket, however, it does not change the qualitative nature of the profit-and-loss distribution that comes from selling lots and lots of these put options: most of the time the index will not fall below the 8,000 level and you will just pocket the smallish premium. Occasionally a market crash will occur, or a protracted bear market will set in, the index will go through the safety level, and you will have to pay out a lot of money.* If we construct a profit-and-loss distribution for this type of trade, the curve may be a bit more or a bit less

---

*Real derivatives are not priced by assuming that you are a sitting duck and can only helplessly watch the index moving up and down. Derivatives are priced assuming that you will try to hedge movements in the index as best you can. (Actually, the Black–Scholes formula assumes that you can hedge *perfectly*.) This is not, however, the situation in the example. With some added bells and whistles, however, real "protection trades" do resemble the situation between you and your friend, and therefore the example *is* pertinent.

stretched, it may be centered somewhat more to the right or to the left, it may be a bit more or less skewed, but in essence it will still look like the curve we have drawn for the sold-lottery-ticket example.

A less exotic, but much more common, type of activity that has a sold-lottery-tickets profile is any form of lending. When you lend money, if everything goes swimmingly, you will at most get all your money back plus the interest. You will never get rich beyond your wildest dreams with this type of activity but, if you have done your credit analysis well, you are likely to reap small and consistent profits—you will keep on collecting the price of the lottery tickets. As one, or some, or many of the borrowers to whom you have lent the money find themselves unable to repay you, you have to "pay out the jackpot" (the money you lent) more and more frequently. When this happens, you will find yourself populating the left tail of the profit-and-loss distribution. Figure 4.5 was built supposing that you lent money to 1,000* companies each of which has a probability of defaulting of half a percent a year. As this figure shows, you can expect to make some money in excess of the riskless return from lending into this particular portfolio of bonds (although not much, about 50¢ for every $1,000 you invested). You can also work out that there is a 68% chance that you will at least break even. There is, however, a 13% probability that you may end up losing $8 or more for every $1,000 invested (lent out).

So much for selling lottery tickets. The other side of the selling-lottery-tickets coin is "buying insurance." In the context of our discussion, buying insurance need not have the literal meaning we normally associate with this expression. Indeed, that friend of yours who bought the put on the Dow Jones index from you did just that. Any trade where you expect to lose (a smallish amount of) money most of the time, but to reap a large reward on rare occasions is akin to buying insurance. Think again of the emerging-market example I presented when discussing sold-lottery-tickets

*We also assumed, in obtaining this figure, that the defaults were independent and that, in case of default, the recovery would be zero! We are not looking for realism here!

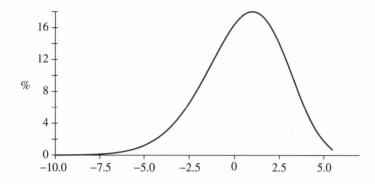

Figure 4.5. The profit-and-loss distribution (in millions of dollars) obtained from advancing $1,000,000 to 1,000 (independent) companies.

trades. Intuitively you can easily see that if you were able to set up the mirror-image transaction, a sold-lottery-ticket trade would turn into a bought-insurance one. Creating a mirror-image trans-action would, in this case, mean selling, rather than buying, an emerging-market bond. But buying stuff is easy (if you have the money). How can you benefit from selling something that you do not own? The following paragraph explains how this can be done, and clarifies exactly what the insurance premium and the payout are. If you are not interested in the mechanics of this trade you can skip the paragraph without loss of continuity.

Suppose that a trader has negative views about the economic outlook for this emerging country. How can he set up a trade that will make money if he is right? The government of the emerg-ing country has issued bonds that promise to pay 20% interest per annum. If the trader believes that the government will not default, he should buy the bond. But if he thinks that it will default, the natural trade to enter would be to sell it. How does one sell something one does not have? The trader can go to a friend who happens to have bought this bond, worth $100 today, and ask the friend to lend it to him. To allay the friend's fears about what is happening to his bond, the trader will also give his friend $100 in cash as security. Now the trader can sell the "borrowed" bond in the market. This (i.e., the proceeds from this sale) is where the money posted with the friend as security comes from. Recall that the trader's view is that the currency will soon depreciate. If he is right, he will be able to buy it back for much less, say for $90, in a week's time. He can then return the bond to his friend, get his $100 in cash back (the security is no longer needed because the bond has been returned) and pocket the difference. The $10 is the windfall profit that the trader stands to make. Where is the insurance premium? The friend has only "lent," not sold, the bond to the trader. Therefore he will still want to receive the high interest paid (20%) by the emerging-market bond. Similarly the trader has only posted the $100 with the friend for security reasons—he is still entitled to receive the (low, 3% say) interest that his dollars would have earned from a bank deposit. So, each day the trader has to pay his friend the difference in accrued interest between 20% and 3%. For a $1,000,000 investment this corresponds to a daily payment of $465. The money the trader can make if a 10% devaluation does occur is $100,000. (By the way, this is also telling us that the trader is betting that the 10% devaluation will happen in fewer than 215 days, because $465 × 215 = $100,000.) If we drew the profit-and-loss distribution from this trade, its qualitative features would be the mirror image of the sold-lottery-tickets profile: the tail on the profit side would now extend a long way to the right, reflecting the possibility that the currency may depreciate by more than 10%. It is now the maximum downside that is limited.

There are much simpler, but perhaps less obvious, examples of bought-insurance trades. The U.S. Treasury, for instance, issues bonds of different maturities at regular intervals. As soon as the new 10-year bond is issued, the almost identical 10-year bond that had been issued a few months before is no longer quite the "flavor of the month"—in the market's lingo it has become an "off-the-run" bond (while the newly minted bond is called "on-the-run"). Off-the-run bonds tend to yield a tiny bit more (i.e., to be a little bit cheaper for the same promised coupon) than on-the-run bonds. Is this not money for nothing? After all, they are both guaranteed by the U.S. Treasury and will both reliably pay their often-identical coupons every six months. Why should I buy the slightly more expensive on-the-run bond just because it is the "latest model"? Are hard-nosed traders not beyond being fashion conscious? Things are not quite that simple. It is true that *under normal market conditions* on-the-runs and off-the-runs are almost indistinguishable; but when exceptional turbulence hits the market the newly minted bonds have the important advantage of being a bit more easily traded (in the market's jargon, more liquid). So, the important point here is that on-the-run bonds behave a bit better just when the going gets really tough. In this sense they are a nice thing to have, just as it is nice to have fire or contents insurance for your house. They are a form of bought-insurance trade: the small yield you sacrifice every day when nothing bad happens is your insurance premium, the greater liquidity you enjoy when serious clouds gather over financial markets is the benefit you reap when you need it.

There is a fundamental snag with bought-insurance trades. When you buy real insurance, against fire, say, you do not really expect to make money "on average." You may shop around for the best quoted insurance premia, but you are very unlikely to estimate the probability of your house going up in smoke in, say, the next twenty years, multiply the yearly premia you pay by twenty, and decide whether to insure or not accordingly. If you are at all like me, you mainly want to eliminate, or mitigate as much as possible, the possibility of a really nasty event. Moving from real insurance to investment or business initiatives that have bought-insurance characteristics, we have seen that they share the common feature of paying out nicely when things are generally going badly. This is a very nice feature.[3] They also tend to be "safe"— you cannot lose more than the small premium you pay in—but on average not very profitable. The market expression for the small amount of money you throw away every day when nothing bad happens is "negative carry." You would enter a negative-carry trade not as a precautionary measure but to make money only if you thought that events were going to turn out worse, *and to do so more quickly*, than the market expects. When you engage in this type of trade you are, to use another endearing market expression, "an ambulance chaser." The emerging-market trader who had a negative outlook on the exotic currency, for instance, was implicitly betting that the currency would depreciate in less than 215 days (or he would have paid out more in negative carry than the windfall profit he would reap when the currency did devalue).

The main problem with this type of trade is that professional traders and money managers do not invest their own money, but are the agents of some ultimate investors (shareholders, hedge fund investors, and the like).[4] These investors often do not share the traders' detailed knowledge of market or investment dynamics. When you engage in bought-insurance trades, while nothing bad happens the only thing that these ultimate investors see is the effect of the negative carry: say, the interest rate differential between the emerging-country bond and the safe U.S. bond that bleeds away every day; or the much smaller but still negative difference in yield between the on-the-run and off-the-run Treasury bonds. Reassuring statements like, "Trust me, I'm a trader," find very little traction with investors who see that, for another quarter, their fund has underperformed those of their competitors (especially if these competitors have spiked their portfolios with some judiciously sold lottery tickets).

This is just what happened with the dot-com boom. Even if the existence of a bubble is very difficult to prove, every market professional with half a brain could see that the Internet shares in 2000 and in the early months of 2001 were ridiculously overvalued and that they were headed for a fall. However, they had also looked overvalued in 1999, and in 1998, and in 1997, and in 1996, when Greenspan first used the expression "irrational exuberance." A trader, or fund manager, who had begun "buying insurance" against a stock market crash in 1996 would have been posting losses against a boring index tracker for a good five years in a row. His view may well have been vindicated in the end but, with newspapers, TV channels, and amateur (and not-so-amateur) economists all waxing lyrical about the new economy and the this-time-is-different business cycle, which investor would have stomached one quarter after another of staggering underperformance? The negative carry, as we have seen with the examples of the emerging-market and off-the-run bonds, is equal to the difference in yield between the safe and the risky investment. With the dot-com sector outperforming the safe bank deposits sometimes by 20% per annum, would *you* have accepted to pay such steep insurance premia, especially when so many apparently knowledgeable "experts" were swearing that no clouds were gathering over the horizon? Sadly, many prudent, honest, and intelligent fund managers lost their jobs just by entering bought-insurance trades a bit too early, sometimes just a few months too early. The rug was pulled from under their feet by the negative carry. A similar fate befell investor extraordinaire George Soros, who had correctly "called" the Southeast Asia currency crisis of 1997, had broken the Bank of England in 1992, and had correctly predicted the Russia default in 1998. Yet, it was a negative carry trade on the NASDAQ that gave him his first important bloody nose. The NASDAQ did fall by 60%, but a few months too late. Because of his being "just off on timing," Soros conceded that: "We had our head handed to us."*

In short, if you sell lottery tickets, even if you have badly mispriced the insurance premium you charge for very rare events, from the outside you can still look very clever for a very long time before you are caught out. Conversely, even if you have calculated the value of the insurance you have bought more accurately than anyone else, from the same outside vantage point you can look very silly for just as long. The nirvana, of course, would be a *bought*-insurance trade or investment with a *positive* carry, i.e., a trade when you are protected when things go really badly and that also pays you a small premium every day, but this is only slightly less difficult to find than the unicorn.[5]

Sold lottery tickets and carefully and selectively bought insurance are the two most prevalent types of trades. This runs counter to the image of the trader popularized by Hollywood movies: a

*Quoted in P. Tetlock (2005), *Expert Political Judgement* (Princeton University Press).

cigar-chomping, thuggish-looking guy in red braces who stares at twelve screens at a time and always seems to shout (because shouting is his only means of expression): "The dollar is going to tank. Sell twenty zillion." I have now spent close to twenty years on or close to trading floors, but I have never met the guys in red braces. Sure enough, serious risk takers do exist on the trading floor, and they sometimes take very large, well-calculated gambles, but their decisions are ultimately much more similar to sold-lottery-tickets or, more rarely, bought-insurance positions* than to the rolling of dice the Hollywood image suggests.

With this proviso in mind, let us suppose that a trader did engage in a purely directional trading strategy, whereby he simply buys (or sells) assets with symmetric return distributions based on a straightforward view that they will gain (lose) in value. What would his profit-and-loss distribution look like? The trades or investment activities that would fall into this category are characterized by a symmetric and evenly balanced distribution of profits and losses, with good and bad events of similar magnitude having approximately equal probability. The ubiquitous normal distribution, of course, gives rise to such a split between good and bad outcomes, but it is by no means the only one that does. It *is* the only one obtained as a limit of the outcomes of a fair die. But you can imagine changing the numbers on two faces of the die: turn the 1 into a −3 and the 6 into a 10: your distribution of gains and losses will still be symmetric, but it will have much fatter tails (i.e., it will give much higher probability to extreme events) than the (close-to-normal) distribution obtained with the fair die.† Interestingly enough, you can think of the symmetric fat-tailed distribution generated by the funny die as originating from two separate simultaneous trades: one in which you sold lottery tickets (the −3 face, which will populate the far left tail)

---

*The best trades are actually a complex and skillful combination of simultaneously bought and sold insurance.

†Of course, even with a "funny die" (whose 1 face has been changed to −3 and whose 6 face has been changed to 10) the normal limit for the partial sums will still arise if we throw it forever. For *finite* sums, however, the resulting distribution may look very heavy-tailed.

and one in which you bought insurance (the 10 face, which will fatten the right tail).

It is surprisingly difficult to find trades that are truly of the dice-rolling type. You may think, for instance, that investing in the stock market provides one obvious example of such a symmetric distribution of outcomes[6]: are stocks not just as likely to go up as down, after all? It may be so for small-to-medium price moves, but market crashes do not have a counterpart in one-day "upward explosions." The S&P equity index, for instance, lost 30% of its value over four trading days in October 1987; it never gained anywhere close to that much in such a short period of time. Therefore, even when you invest in a mutual equity index fund you are to some small extent selling lottery tickets. Indeed, one of the ways to explain the so-called equity premium puzzle is by trying to estimate whether you are being paid fairly, too little, or too much for the lottery tickets you have sold.*

FROM DESCRIPTION TO CHOICE

I have introduced a way of synthetically describing many of the "trades" (or, for that matter, investment activities) that financial institutions engage in. What we would like to do, however, is not just describe, but choose: accept or reject, increase the size or reduce the exposure. How can we move from a description, such as the one given by the profit-and-loss distribution, to a decision-making rule? To fix ideas, let us start by looking at some simple cases.

Suppose that two trades have the same expected return and the same variance but one is of the selling-lottery-tickets type and the other is of the bought-insurance variety. Which one would you prefer? To help you make this choice, let us look at figure 4.6, which displays the profit-and-loss distributions from two hypothetical investments, imaginatively called A and B.

---

*It turns out that, if we look at the problem in this light, you would appear to have sold lottery tickets at a *very* high price.

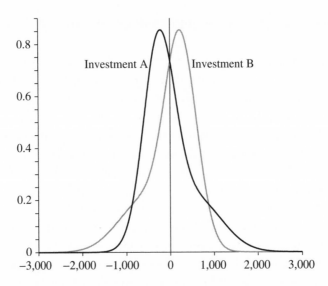

Figure 4.6. The profit-and-loss distributions from investments A and B (bought-insurance and sold-lottery-ticket types, respectively). The distributions from both the investments discussed have the same expectation and variance.

Investment A is of the bought-insurance type and investment B is of the sold-lottery-ticket type. The expected return from both investments is exactly the same, and so is their variance. With investment A we stand to make small losses with high probability: note how the probability of losses between 0 and approximately $1,000 is always higher for investment A than for investment B. Conversely, the probability of small gains (under $1,000) is always higher for the sold-lottery-ticket (B) investment. The ranking is reversed, however, when we look at really large gains or losses. Buying lottery tickets gives you a nonnegligible probability of gains of up to $2,000, with virtually zero probability of losses of the same magnitude. The opposite is true when you sell insurance. Remembering that there is no "right" or "wrong" answer, which trade would you rather enter? Would *your* answer change if I told you that the *x*-axis (which shows the magnitude of the profits and losses) is expressed not in thousands, but in *millions* of dollars, and that a loss of $2,000,000 would bankrupt you?

Empirically, it is generally found that, everything else being equal, investors tend to prefer profit-and-loss distribution profiles which are skewed to the right, i.e., bought-insurance trades. However, the preference for positive skewness (for a given variance and return) is not as "robust" as the preference for less variance (for a given return). Indeed, some authors* present a convincing case to explain why, under certain conditions, economic agents may prefer negative skewness.[†] For instance, suppose for a moment that the numbers on the x-axis represent units of your yearly salary. Would your choice between the two distributions have changed if I had told you that the investment that gives rise to the future profit-and-loss distribution in figure 4.6 has so far given you a loss of half your yearly salary? What if the investment had instead produced to date a gain of three times your yearly salary? The important point for our discussion is that different agents may have different responses to skewness, but they are in general far from indifferent to it. Recognizing its existence is therefore an important part of our decision making.

Now matters get more exciting. Look at the distributions in figure 4.7. The one with two peaks is perhaps less realistic, or at least less common, but it will help me to make a point. One of the two curves displayed is the ubiquitous normal distribution (ubiquitous in statistics texts, at least, if not in reality); the other an awkward-shaped distribution that looks so odd that it has no specific name attached to it. We will simply refer to it as the "bimodal distribution." Despite their very different appearances, they have two important features in common: they have the same mean and

---

*See, for example, N. N. Taleb (2004), Bleed or blow-up? Why do we prefer asymmetric profiles?, *Journal of Behavioural Finance* January 2004:75–79.

[†]As pointed out by Taleb in "Bleed or blow-up? Why do we prefer asymmetric profiles?" at least two different situations can give rise to a preference for negative skew. The first is when the profit-and-loss distribution, instead of being exogenously supplied, has to be inferred by the agent. In this case cognitive biases such as the law of small numbers (see again Tversky and Kahneman's "Belief in the law of small numbers," *Psychology Bulletin* 76(2):105–10) may make us underestimate the probability of rare negative events. The second is when the agent is sitting on what he perceives to be a loss. See the discussion on prospect theory in the rest of the chapter.

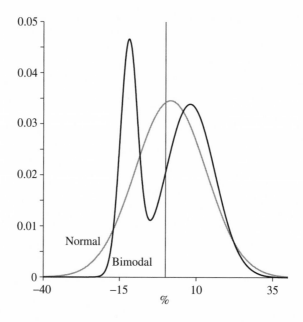

Figure 4.7. Two profit-and-loss distributions with the same mean and variance. Is it easy for you to decide which one you would prefer?

the same variance. Given this information, and after looking at the two distributions, which "trade" would you rather enter?

Let us try to analyze the two alternatives as we did before. The very large losses, of the order of 20–40%, are much more likely with the Normal than with the Bimodal trade: the chances of losing more than 25%, for instance, are about a thousand times greater with the Normal trade. Trade Binomial, however, gives a much higher chance of making a loss of between 10% and 20%. If we want to have a chance of making a return above, say, 30%, we should definitely go for investment Normal, which gives, however, a much greater probability of losses between 0% and 8%. This is all well and good but, unless you are endowed with exceptional insight and decisional resoluteness, after all this analysis you are probably still as puzzled and uncertain as you were when I first showed you these two distributions. And if you think that the Bimodal distribution is too far-fetched to be believable, I can assure you that you just have to sprinkle a trading book with a few digital options to obtain lunar landscapes considerably more complex than the Bimodal one.

In short, we have learned how to associate to trades or investment opportunities some important descriptive features. We probably agree that these features do have cognitive resonance, i.e., that they highlight aspects of our decision-making process that are likely to influence us. But it all looks very unstructured. It is all well and good saying that a given trade displays fatter tails than rolling dice, and it is skewed in the sold-insurance direction, but what can we do with this? Can we organize this admittedly appealing information into a clear decision rule? This is where the theory of decision making steps in. Its poster child (utility theory) and its more recent offspring (prospect theory) claim to have *the* unique answer as to how these disparate features can all be brought together into a coherent picture—*pace* Montale, how we can distill from them a magic formula that will "make us decide correctly." Until recently, the supposed "correctness" and superiority of utility theory made it *the* theoretically sound, and the only rational, way of reaching decisions, at least in academic circles. Its explicit application to practical decision making has never been enthusiastically embraced, however. If anything, down in the financial trenches it has often been dismissed as abstract, cerebral, and counterintuitive.* Are the practitioners who turn up their noses to utility theory unreconstructed philistines? Or do they display a shrewd intuition that not all was well in the kingdom of utility? Market practice, after all, may not always be perfect, but in my experience we shrug it off as silly at our peril. Be that as it may, one of the recurrent themes of this book is that risk management is not about measuring risk, or assessing probabilities, it is about

*Coating a bitter pill with sugar has always been a simple way to make it more palatable, though. And therefore many practitioners who would contemptuously dismiss the "ivory-tower" suggestions of utility theory find mean–variance optimization reasonable and intuitive—despite the fact that mean–variance recipes stem directly from a particular, and not terribly appealing, choice for the utility function, plus many more, and more unpalatable, assumptions.

making decisions in situations of uncertainty. A well-respected, intellectually sophisticated, and in many areas very successful theory that deals with exactly this problem does exist. Should we not at least take a good look at it? Perhaps this is where the answer to our decisional impasse lies. And if not, why not? These are the questions I try to answer in the rest of the chapter.

UTILITY AND PROSPECT THEORY

The Promise of Utility Theory

Modern utility theory bears little resemblance to the popular view (if there is one) of what utility theory is all about. If you have ever heard of it, you are likely to be familiar with statements such as, "John acted this way, because this course of action increased his utility" or "Between two courses of action, this one was chosen because it had a higher utility." "Utility," in this context appears to be a fancy word for "happiness," "satisfaction," etc. Actually, this is not quite how utility theory is currently understood by the majority of those who work in the field. Modern utility theory rejects the hedonistic interpretation of utility. Its first logical step is shared with the traditional (hedonistic) version of the theory. It begins by positing that your preference is always for more rather than less consumption (of any desirable good). Therefore, it can be graphically represented as an increasing function of consumption, as in figure 4.8. The second requirement is that this function should be concave, i.e., that the rate of increase in your satisfaction with consumption should decrease as you consume more and more. This feature is also shown in figure 4.8. Note that it is the *increase* in satisfaction that decreases, not the satisfaction itself. As Cochrane puts it,* the last bite is never quite as satisfactory as the first—but you would still rather have another piece of cake: indigestion is not on the cards. Why have we drawn our utility curve with these two features? Because, by themselves, these simple

---

*J. Cochrane (2001), *Asset Pricing* (Princeton University Press).

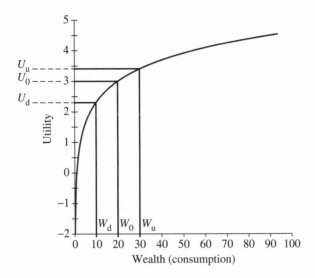

Figure 4.8. Explaining risk aversion with one picture: a plausible utility function. On the x-axis you read off the level of your wealth. The value on the y-axis that the curve associates to each value of wealth is your utility for that level of wealth. You start from an initial wealth (W_0) of 20. The utility associated with this initial level of wealth, U_0, is a bit below 3 (in whatever units). You are then faced with a fair gamble that could bring your wealth with equal probability to $10, W_d, or to $30, W_u. From the curve you read that your utility could therefore become 2.2, U_d, or 3.4, U_u. Your expected *wealth* has not changed (it is still 20) but, by entering the bet, your expected *utility* would *decrease* from approximately 3 to $2.8 = \frac{1}{2}(2.2 + 3.4)$. The expectation (2.8) is below your starting point (3) because the segment $|U_u - U_0|$ is shorter than the segment $|U_0 - U_d|$. This, in turn, is a consequence of the fact that our utility function is concave. If you are risk averse you will turn down the bet. That is why the utility curve of risk-averse investors is ever increasing, but concave.

features guarantee that what is described is the behavior of *risk-averse* agents. We will see why this is the case in a few paragraphs.

So, in the beginning (of utility theory at least) there was consumption—not wealth, gain, profit or loss, etc. Just consumption. It is consumption that individuals enjoy, and, since they like it so much, they try to maximize it, i.e., to arrange those conditions over which they have control in order to be able to consume as much as possible.

When there is no uncertainty about outcomes, the modern version of utility theory is rather boring. The utility theorist dons a white lab coat, *observes* your choices when faced with the different possible outcomes, and writes them down in a big notepad. The interesting bit comes with uncertainty. Suppose you are given different alternatives: say chocolate (that you like) and spinach (that you like even more). In our example getting spinach or chocolate is not a sure thing, though. Suppose that getting the desired goods is now uncertain, and a different degree of uncertainty attaches to the various outcomes. You prefer spinach to chocolate, so, presumably, you are willing to pay more to consume (certain) spinach than (certain) chocolate. But would you still pay more for a 60% chance of getting some spinach (and a 40% chance of getting nothing) than you would for a 95% chance of getting some chocolate (and a 5% chance of getting nothing)? Where is your breakeven? The beauty of utility theory is in the following statement: if your choices are consistent, your actions when faced with an uncertain choice can be described as if you maximized your expected utility. Let us see what this means. How do we use the utility-function tool, in other words, in order to make real decisions?

Let us start from a risky prospect. To each uncertain outcome we can associate two independent quantities: its probability of occurrence and "how much you like it"—or, more precisely, the utility you have been inferred to derive from consumption by *observing* your choices. For instance, you can think on the one hand of all the different monetary outcomes you could face if you invested in emerging markets, and of their associated probabilities. Or you can think of the outcomes and associated probabilities if you lent your money to technology firms; or of the less exciting outcomes and probabilities that would derive from depositing it at the local branch of your bank.

As a next step, you examine each course of action (emerging markets, technology firms, money in the bank) in turn, one at a time. For each outcome associated with this particular course of action you look at what would happen to your wealth (consumption, actually). Using the chosen utility function and the probabilities you knew from before, you associate to your terminal wealth in each state of the world a new quantity: the product of the associated utility *times* the probability of occurrence of that state. For each prospect, you add all these quantities (utility times the probability of attaining it) and call the result the "expected utility" for that project. You repeat the same procedure for all the different projects. How do you make your choice after all this? You simply choose the course of action (the project) that has the highest expected utility. When you have done so, you have *maximized your expected utility*. This, utility theory says, is how *homo economicus* makes his choices. "Old" utility theory used to say: this is how humans *should* make their choices—a prescriptive view of choice. "Modern" utility theory more humbly says: this is how humans *are (hopefully) observed* to make their choices.

It all sounds very contrived. Why should we make decisions following these rules? Why should this recipe be of any use for real-life risk management? To begin with, because one of the great accomplishments of utility theory is that it can account for risk aversion in a simple and natural way. Let us see how this happens. Take your current level of wealth as your starting point. From this reference point, consider the possibility of winning or losing, with equal probability, $1,000. Probably (unless your name is Laplace), you would not enter such a bet "for free," but would require some inducement to accept this evenly balanced disturbance around your current level of wealth. This aversion to risk can be rationalized by positing that you do not try to maximize wealth as such, but *a function of* wealth (i.e., roughly speaking, *a function of* the money you own). Much to the chagrin of modern utility theorists, let us think of this function as the "pleasure" you derive from (consuming) the corresponding wealth. This function should always be increasing (after all, you should prefer more money to less money), but, as your wealth grows larger, it should increase more and more slowly. Figure 4.8 then shows how your risk-averse behavior can be explained *as if* you maximized your expected utility: since the utility function *increases* at a *decreasing* rate, the expected utility for an even but risky bet is lower than the utility associated with the level of wealth you started from, and that is why you turn down the even bet.*

It is easy to see that this argument holds for any utility function that shares the same two features of being ever increasing and for being so at an ever-decreasing rate (i.e., for any increasing concave function). There exists an infinity of such functions, each perfectly capable of accounting, at a qualitative level, for risk-averse behavior. If we want to use this approach for risk management, what we need is one particular instance of this class of concave functions. Which one should we choose in practice? This is where the utility theorist in the white lab coat carrying the notepad comes back onto the scene. He will ask you how you would react to a simple, reasonable-sized bet: for instance, what compensation you would require to enter the $1,000 bet described above. From your answer, he will try to determine which one out of the infinite number of concave increasing functions best describes your aversion to risk. *By construction, this particular* utility function will perfectly describe your behavior for *that particular* bet, but we have not yet done anything interesting. We have simply restated your choice using a different language. The modern utility theorist goes a step further, though, and hopes that your behavior when faced with *other* bets will be consistent with the maximization of your expected utility *predicted by the particular utility function that has been associated with (calibrated to) you using the $1,000 bet.*[†] If this works, you now have a fully functional tool that can be used for *any* risky decision—in particular, for risk-management decisions.

Despite its elegance and conceptual simplicity, utility theory has attracted fierce criticism from a variety of quarters. Much of it stems from not appreciating what utility theory actually says,

---

*This argument should actually be the other way round: the utility function is concave because you have been observed to turn down even bets! Please do not go and repeat to modern utility theorists the sentence I just wrote.

[†] If not, he may conclude that he chose a utility function from the wrong functional family; or that you are inconsistent; or that the utility-functional approach is flawed.

or, for that matter, what a model, *any* model (of electrons, of condensed matter, of rational man, etc.), is supposed to achieve. Utility theory does *not* say that every man is perfectly rational. It does *not* say that man acts in every moment of his life by maximizing his expected utility. It does *not* say that all men have identical preferences, or identical investment goals.* It says that, if we model human beings *as if* they behaved in this way, we can explain in the aggregate many (not all) interesting phenomena. When it comes to asset pricing, for instance, it is sufficient for just one rational guy with extremely deep pockets to live by the rationality and utility maximization standards of utility theory for *all* prices in the market to be roughly the same as if every single investor were a similarly rational utility maximizer.[†] (And, by the way, close approximations to these hyperrational utility maximizers with deep pockets do exist, and are called hedge funds.)

The point I am making is that one should not judge a dish too hastily by reading the list of its ingredients: you would not give a lot of time to boudin noir, for instance, if you were told that it consisted of the congealed blood of pigs. More seriously, if you have been turned off by frictionless balls and point masses, I doubt you have got very far in your understanding of classical mechanics: certainly you have not reached the point when you can understand how these simplifications can be fixed. The following words (that I used as an opening quote to the previous chapter) were written by Ted Rosencrantz in the context of the Bayesian/frequentist debate, but apply equally well to the case of utility theory:

> There are very few fields in which every single practitioner is an idiot. If your understanding of a field is such that all practitioners of it must be idiots, then probably you're not understanding it correctly.

---

*This is the straw man that attracts the criticism of the most strident behavioral finance literature, or of all those authors who claim to have found a new grand unified theory of finance (and often of much else at the same time). The book *The (Mis)Behavior of Markets* by Benoit Mandelbrot is an example of this.

[†]See, for example, Shleifer, *Inefficient Markets*.

So much for what I consider the "naive" criticism of utility theory. A lot of valid (and far more "mature") criticism has been leveled at it. Part of the criticism has been directed at its apparently stilted assumptions. However, much more interesting objections have been raised to some of the *consequences* of utility theory. Since I have always found tasting the pudding more rewarding than reading the recipe, looking in some detail at these studies is worthwhile.

Let us start with Matthew Rabin, who has presented some very insightful examples that hold true for *any* utility function a rational person may have. Here are a few.* Suppose that we flip a fair coin. If it lands heads, you win $110; if it lands tails, you lose $100. Would you enter the bet? Pause for a second to think before continuing. (By the way, I probably would not.)

If "no" was your answer as well, you may be surprised to know that it follows with mathematical certainty that, *if you are a rational utility maximizer*, you will also turn down a fifty–fifty bet of losing $1,000 and winning $1,000,000, or $1,000,000,000, or, for that matter, *any amount of money*. If you stick by this choice, this is where you and I part company. Similarly, suppose that you and I have turned down an even bet of winning $11 or losing $10. Then, again, we should also turn down a fifty–fifty bet to lose $100 or gain any conceivable amount of money. Rabin presents many similar examples (see his table 11.1 in the book chapter quoted in the footnote). They all have the common feature of calibrating the utility function so as to give a realistic description of behavioral responses to small(ish) bets, but to imply an unrealistic attitude to large-scale risk.

The points made by Rabin should give pause for thought to any utility theorist. Do they imply however, that we should throw away utility theory *tout court*? If we look at Rabin's critique carefully we discover that it means that we cannot simultaneously explain risk aversion over very large and very small stakes

---

*The following examples are taken from "Diminishing marginal utility cannot explain risk aversion," by Matthew Rabin, which appears in D. Kahneman and A. Tversky (eds) (2000), *Choices, Values and Frames*, chapter 11 (Cambridge University Press).

with the same utility function. We cannot account for the behavior of people buying tickets for the National Lottery, choosing the best home insurance, and investing for their retirement portfolios using an identically calibrated utility function. Not a pleasant result, certainly. But let us not forget that very few theories enjoy such universal scale-invariance: even Newtonian mechanics breaks down if we look at objects that are too small (the domain where quantum mechanics kicks in) or that move too fast (where we need special or general relativity). This does not mean that in very many circumstances we cannot make profitable use of $F = ma$.

The crucial objection that Rabin raises is the feasibility of scale-dependent calibrations: once we have determined from one particularly simple risky problem which particular utility function applies to you, you may not be able to use this information if the further bets you are faced with are of a very different scale. For risk-management purposes this *is* a problem, but perhaps not an insurmountable one. We will have to make sure that, when we look at the "simple bets" that are supposed to act as beacons of our degree and type of risk aversion, we consider amounts of money at stake that are comparable with the applications for which we want to use our tool in anger. Some care might be needed, but it can be done.

Unfortunately for utility theory, there is more bad news. Another interesting line of criticism moves along the following lines. If people are rational, let alone utility maximizers, they should make their choices irrespective of how the alternatives are presented. If I ask you whether you would accept a fifty–fifty bet of losing $100 and you decline, you should also decline if I cunningly present the same bet as a fifty–fifty chance of winning the same amount. It sounds pretty obvious, but experiments have shown that it is enough to simply "shuffle the cards" a bit for inconsistent answers to the same choice problem to appear. Let us look at the two following alternatives.*

*The example is from Kahneman and Tversky, *Choices, Values and Frames*, and was originally published in 1984 in *American Psychologist* 39(4):341–50.

Alternative A. Would you accept a gamble that offers a 10% chance of winning $95 and a 90% chance of losing $5?

Alternative B. Would you pay $5 to participate in a lottery that offers a 10% chance of winning $100 and a 90% chance of winning nothing?

As usual, please pause to answer before reading on.

Most people accept alternative A but reject alternative B. The experimental bias in favor of the first alternative, by the way, is loud and clear, by no means a marginal effect. Was this your answer as well? (It was my answer, by the way, when I first saw the two questions.) A moment's thought, however, convinces us that the two "alternatives" in effect describe exactly the same situation: if you accept alternative B you certainly pay $5 to start to game, and then either win $100 with probability 10% (in which case your total gain is $95), or win nothing (in which case you are in the red to the tune of $5) with probability 90%. Yet, as I said before, when the same prospect was framed according to alternatives A and B and presented to college students, significantly different acceptance ratios were found according to how the bet was presented.

Why is this example relevant? Because it attempts to strike a blow at the very heart of rational choice (of which expected utility maximization is a special incarnation). If we can be fooled so easily by such a simple trick of smoke and mirrors, what faith can we place in utility maximization, which requires a much higher degree of internal logical consistency?

You may think that this is just another artificial laboratory experiment. In a way it is, but the issues it raises are very important. I will show in what follows that it contains in essence some important elements of a far more interesting, and more practically important, decision: the choice faced by many investors who have to decide between actively or passively managed funds. Since this is a trillion-dollar industry, we will be moving our focus from a graduate-school experiment in empirical finance to one of the leading industries on Wall Street. To appreciate the discussion properly, however, first we need to understand an alternative way of looking at how human beings made choices under uncertainty.

One constructive proposal as to how to "fix" utility theory is called prospect theory. In a nutshell, it makes two important statements that are at odds with canonical utility theory. What motivates our choices, it says, is not our total level of wealth (recall that in standard utility theory this ultimately means consumption), but gains or losses. What drives our actions, prospect theory says, is not how much we can ultimately consume, but whether a given course of action will bring about a gain or a loss. This is *not* the same as consumption because, as we will discover in a moment, gains and losses can easily depend on a sometimes-arbitrary reference point. The second important statement made by prospect theory is the following: we may well be risk averse when it comes to gains, but, to avoid losses, we will often accept very risky courses of action. So risky, indeed, that we can even become risk seekers. If this is the case, a concave utility function will still do for gains, but we will need to append to its left a portion with an *upward* curvature to account for losses. It may all sound rather abstract, but the following very important example will bring all of this vividly to life.

Let us look at what the discussion above implies for the choice between actively and passively managed funds. To set the scene, let me recall some of the basic facts about the investment choices faced by an individual who considers investing in the stock market. One easy option is to invest in what is called a tracker fund. A manager will take your money and buy some units of every stock in the index you intend to track (the S&P 500, say). There is no attempt to pick winners and avoid losers in this approach. The manager will just try to replicate the index as closely as possible by mimicking its composition. This investment strategy is termed passive, and the manger will earn a meager fee for his rather mundane and mechanical tasks.[7]

An active fund manager, on the other hand, will try to do something more exciting, i.e., construct your portfolio by picking winners and avoiding losers. A lot more work is involved, clearly:

reading balance sheets, talking to CEOs and CFOs, ferreting out hard-to-find information about companies, comparing companies in the same sector and across sectors, etc. All this work has merit and value even if, on the whole, markets are efficient.[8] And, given the level of effort and sophistication that active mangers have to put into their research, it is not surprising that they should ask for higher management fees than the passive index trackers: typically of the order of a few percentage points. The real question, there-fore, is not whether active managers can "beat the market," but whether they can do so after costs, and, if they can, by how much. Now, a multitude of empirical studies have shown that, *after all costs are factored in*, the extra advantage reaped by investing in an active fund is small, if it is present at all. Faced with this evidence and the alternative between investing in active or passive funds, how should the individual investor make his choice?

Here is one way to look at the problem. To fix ideas suppose that a passive fund manager charges half a percent per annum and an active one three percent. This is what the active fund manager might tell you:

> If you invest in the passive fund run by my dear friend and competitor Mr. B. O. Ring, you are *guaranteed* to underperform the market—indeed, I can even tell you by how much: by half a percentage point. Whatever the market does, you can be cer-tain to do the same, and then a bit worse (by Mr. B. O. Ring's management fee). If you want to have any hope at all of beating the market, you *must* invest in an active fund. You may start the race a bit below where the passive fund starts (by two and half percentage points), but at least you have *some* hope of winning. So, here is your choice: underperform the market by not much, but with certainty (with Mr. B. O. Ring's fund); or have a chance to beat the market with my active fund.

Many investors, after hearing this pitch, may reasonably go for the active fund. Who wants to be a certain loser, after all? But let us now hear the pitch from Mr. B. O. Ring:

Historically, equity funds have, in the long run, outperformed investments in Treasury Bills by a few percentage points. By exactly how much would take us down a long detour, but, in essence, if you invest in the stock market you can expect to make more money than if you invest in a money-market account. All empirical studies to date agree on this. Now, we do not know exactly how large this outperformance is, but it is certainly more than the meager half a percentage point that I charge for investing in my fund. So, if you invest with me, you have a well-documented chance of significantly outperforming an investment in Treasury Bills (at least in the long run). If you invest in the active fund run by my dear friend Mr. A. D. Venturous, however, you are already giving away in management fees some of your advantage over the Treasury Bills, and perhaps a substantial part of it. In addition, you are adding further uncertainty to your final investment outcome: you may end up doing a bit better than the market, but you can end up *much* worse, especially considering that you are starting the race two and a half percentage points behind me. And recall that, for all their sleek brochures, active managers have a really difficult task at hand: markets may not be perfectly efficient, but they are very close to being so.

The argument put forth by Mr. B. O. Ring sounds plausible as well: after all, who wants to risk giving up an almost-certain outperformance (over Treasury Bills)? Having heard the two sales pitches, which fund would you choose now? As usual, please pause for a second to make your choice.

It is important to point out that neither fund manager is "cheating" (i.e., providing you with false information) and that (with some caveats) neither choice is "wrong." Rather, two different mechanisms are at play: framing and loss aversion. We have already seen the first mechanism (framing) at play with the example about the $95/$100 gamble. This is exactly the strategy employed by Mr. A. D. Venturous and Mr. B. O. Ring: the first casts the problem by focusing your attention on the *loss* ("if you invest in a tracker fund, you are certain to *underperform* the market"—a true statement; "if you want to have a hope of not making a certain loss, you must invest in an active fund"—another true statement). The second manager frames the problem in terms of gains that you may end up losing because of your greed ("if you invest in a tracker fund you can expect to beat a riskless investment"—a true statement; "but if you go for an active fund you are at significant risk of losing this extra return"—again, another true statement).

There is more to the problem, though, than just the smoke and mirrors of framing: for the behavioral response to be different one must also require a different degree of risk aversion when we contemplate losses or gains. Prospect theory states (in concordance with utility theory) that we may well be risk averse when we are sitting on *gains*; but that we hate losses so much that we are happy to take extra risk (or even unfair gambles) to avoid them—and this is where utility and prospect theory part company. From the point of view of utility theory, if you give two different answers to the fund investment problem above depending on how it is phrased, you must be irrational because consumption is all that should drive your decisions and, for a given course of action, consumption is patently the same in the stories told by Mr. B. O. Ring and Mr. A. D. Venturous. We can see now why the switch made by prospect theory from wealth (taken as a proxy for consumption) to profits and losses as the relevant explanatory variables of our behavior is not as trivial as it may seem. It actually entails a radically different way of looking at how we make our choices. Classic utility theory puts consumption at its core. Prospect theory instead tells us that we care *intrinsically*, not instrumentally, about suffering losses or making profits, and that we behave differently to either.

Sometimes, telling whether we are sitting on a profit or nursing a loss is unambiguous. But in other circumstances, as in the example above, speaking of losses or profits depends on our starting point (certainly below the index—a loss that we crave to avoid— or above the riskless rate—a profit that we strive to preserve). If this is the case, what makes us tick is something other than, or in addition to, pure consumption.

How does prospect theory make these claims? First, by observing the behavior of individuals (hence the link with behavioral finance), as revealed by psychological experiments of the type described above. Second, by noticing regularities across individuals in the "irrationalities" (from the utility theory point of view) in their observed behaviors. Third, by arguing that the effects of these irrationalities can appear not just at the individual level, but also in the aggregate (say, in equilibrium prices). This can happen, for instance, if the actions of those deep-pocketed hyper-rational investors that could exploit the behavior of their irrational cousins, and thereby negate their effects in the aggregate, are hindered by institutional or other constraints.[9]

It all sounds very convincing. Should we then just switch from utility to prospect theory in our risk-management applications? We may need to ask a couple more probing questions to calibrate the more complex prospect function, but this does not seem to be beyond the ken of man. The ultimate goal—finding a coherent way to make choices under uncertainty—should be well worth the extra pain. Alas, not all is wine and roses in the garden of prospect theory either. There is at least one very important flaw in prospect theory seen as a normative discipline. Prospect theory does a very good job at accounting for how people mentally organize uncertain prospects in terms of often-arbitrary accounting frames; it describes well how we want to escape losses more than hold on to gains; it does a very good job, in short, of describing how human beings actually make their choices. Unless what is a gain and what is a loss is totally unambiguous, however, it can easily run into trouble as a prescriptive or predictive theory of behavior. Why should we worry? Is a loss not just a loss? Not necessarily. Suppose that your overall equity portfolio is up, but you have lost some money on its emerging-markets component. Do you have an overall gain, or a gain in one part of the portfolio (about which you should be risk averse) and a loss in another (about which you should be risk seeking)? And since when do you compute your gains and losses? The beginning of the fiscal year? January 1? The day you invested?[10] And should you look at your equity investments in isolation or together with your fixed-income positions? What about your pension fund?

This dependence on shifty reference points ("frames," in prospect-theory speak) is bad enough for many economists, but there is a more unsettling side to prospect theory. If you really made *all* your choices as prospect theory says, I could entice you to accept a series of freely entered transactions at the end of which you will find yourself where you started, minus some money that you *willingly* parted with. It is easy to see how this conjuring trick can be pulled off, for instance, just by playing fast and loose with what is a gain and what is a loss: *given the same transaction* I may be able to make you become risk averse (and pay above the actuarial odds to keep your perceived gain) or risk seeking (and pocket your reckless wager to escape the perceived loss). This is not a good place to be. It may be such an unacceptable place that many would ditch the whole enterprise.

This would be a pity, because in the context of the management of financial risk we can still make use of a lot of the insights offered by prospect theory. To begin with, strict accountancy rules dictate unambiguously what a financial institution can classify as a gain or a loss, and when the "investment clock" is reset. The ability to engage in a game of smoke and mirrors with frames is therefore enormously reduced. More generally, speaking in terms of gains and losses (rather than of total "wealth") employs a language with a very powerful resonance within a financial institution. Almost all the risk controls I can think of (limits, key risk indicators, Value-at-Risk, etc.) refer to *losses*, avoidance of *losses*, probability of *losses*. In exploring a new business opportunity we think of the *gains* we can make, of the *cost* of investment, of the *losses* we may incur.[11]

The point I am driving at is very simple: for all the theoretical inconsistencies of prospect theory, a profit-and-loss-based decision theory seems to me far more faithfully descriptive of actual behavior in financial institutions than a theory that rests on the concept of consumption (as utility theory does). Arbitrages may well lurk at the end of a long chain of transactions entered into on the basis of prospect theory. But perhaps at some point I will "smell a rat" and I will stop just short of the logical consistency that is required for you to trick me into giving up something for free. If my goal is to set up a set of risk tools that are aligned with the way activities are actually set up in a bank, for all its problems a decision theory that places profits and losses at its core is not a bad thing.

In chapter 10 I will therefore present some practical risk-management decisional aids that do not *explicitly* speak the language of utility or prospect theory, but that are eclectically inspired by both these disciplines. So, for instance, you will be invited in chapter 10 to determine something similar to your "certainty equivalent" (an important tool of decision theory) without knowing that that is what you are doing. If you think that this sounds a bit like Molière's *bourgeois gentilhomme*, who spoke in prose for his whole life without knowing that he was doing so, you would not be far off the mark. This "decision-theory-lite" approach has two important characteristics: it implicitly calibrates your risk aversion in situations of a realistic size (and so avoids possible Rabin-like problems); and, in order to retain some of the most useful insights of prospect theory, it is unashamedly cast in terms of profits and losses (not of consumption or terminal wealth).

Why not go the full hog and embrace, say, prospect theory in full? I do believe that prospect theory provides us with some very important and useful insights in to how human beings reach decisions under uncertainty (so does utility theory, by the way). I also believe that these insights are of relevance to financial risk management. However, both theories run into trouble when they are pushed the extra mile to obtain the logically consistent ultimate consequences of their useful-but-probably-incomplete insights. Witness, again, Rabin's examples. There is a lot to be gained in knowing when to stop and in avoiding throwing out the baby with the bath water. Newtonian action-at-a-distance may well be "wrong." However, I do not recommend discarding it lightly, especially if what you want to do is calculate the time it takes an apple to reach the ground from its branch and your alternative is using general relativity.

My approach is clearly neither revolutionary nor intellectually fully satisfactory. Despite this (or perhaps because of this) I believe that it can be useful.

PRACTICAL RULES FOR FINANCIAL DECISION MAKING

One of the appealing features of decision theory is that it throws us a lifeline when, faced with a picture like figure 4.7, we are drowning in a sea of decision making. Just put the profit-and-loss distribution in the input slot, turn the utility-maximization handle, and read your expected utility. Choose the project that maximizes this number. But, when it comes to choosing, humans do not like to put their fate in the hands of a counterintuitive and difficult-to-fathom black box. What happens when the handle is turned? What is the utility-maximization machine "making me choose"? We may put our lives in the hands of a surgeon or an aircraft pilot despite the fact that most of us know little about medicine or about flying a plane. But, when it comes to choosing, we feel robbed of our very humanity if an expert (or an expert machine) tells us what we *should prefer*. So, we like decisional aids, but we like those that are simple and intuitive and that allow us to peek under the bonnet even better. If what we see does not make perfect sense, no matter, at least we have done our "due diligence"—we are only human, after all. So, we like to say that risk means variance and that optimizing expected return against variance is how we make our choices among investments. The recipe makes intuitive sense, the equation "risk = uncertainty = variance" sounds plausible enough, and we embrace mean–variance frontiers. We have always been, we claim, mean–variance people. We like hurdle rates ("enter this initiative if its expected return exceeds a certain magic threshold"). We like return on capital as a decisional tool. Perhaps we adjust the capital for risk—but, by the way, what do we mean by risk? The variance? The 99.97th percentile? And what about capital? Regulatory or economic capital? Again, no matter. The prescription makes intuitive sense, and the details will take care of themselves—or, perhaps, some really clever quant will make sure that all the details are properly taken care of. Unlike the maximized expected utility, we think we understand (if not in detail at least in a broad-brush sort of way) where all these magic formulae come from. *We* are still choosing.

All these decisional tools (if we believe that they have been meaningfully estimated—this is sometimes a big *if*, as we shall see) are not wrong, of course. The expected return from a project, its variance, what happens if things really go pear-shaped, how much money the regulators would require us to set aside if we enter a given initiative, the return on the capital *we* would set aside to support the initiative, etc., are all useful pieces of information in reaching a decision. The problem is that, in isolation, no single piece of information, no risk metric, contains all the answers. More frustratingly, no simple *and intuitively transparent* distillation of these risk metrics into a single magic number seems to be able to do the choosing job for us. With Montale, we find ourselves unable to reach the magic formula capable of unlocking decisional worlds for us.

Where are we left with then? On the one hand, we have the apparently hopeless task of reaching decisions from a profit-and-loss distribution in its full complexity: a task with, literally, an infinite number of degrees of freedom. On the other hand, we seem to have crude one-dimensional rules based on an array of magic numbers, seemingly capable of helping us only with the simplest and most stylized problems. What should we do for the myriad of more difficult, subtle, and delicately balanced invest-ment decisions? What should we do, that is, in the real world?

Here is a blueprint for the way ahead. First, we must recog-nize our cognitive abilities and shortcomings in decision mak-ing. We should employ ways of reaching decisions that go with, not against, our cognitive grain. It is for this reason that I have devoted quite a few pages to discussing bought-insurance and sold-lottery-ticket trades: because many studies in empirical psy-chology suggest that these are important indicators that we make use of when we reach real decisions. We should then recognize that no single indicator of "risk," "goodness," or the like is bound to do the job fully. This would point to using many risk indicators simultaneously. Unfortunately, we must also acknowledge that there is a limit to how many of these we can profitably juggle. So we must retain intuition and cognitive resonance; avoid the temptation of the single magic formula; expand the number of decisional criteria, but not by too much. More (decisional tools) may not be better. We must, in short, use our silver bullets well and wisely. To do this I will offer in chapter 10 a few decisional aids, which do not absolve us from the duty of making a decision but help us in doing so. As I said, even if they do not admit to doing so explicitly, these decisional aids work by implicitly calibrating a limited-purpose utility function to a few important choices when we can see clearly what we are faced with. Without having to speak the language of ever-increasing, strictly concave utility functions, this approach will create in our minds three or four useful reference points. If we wanted to do so, we could try to relate these points to a utility function, but we will not need to. It is the points that matter, not the function behind them.

Before undertaking this plan, a few more steps are required. The first is perhaps the most important of all. We have not asked ourselves a pretty fundamental question: "Why does risk management bring value to a financial institution at all?" This is what the next chapter is about.

CHAPTER 5

WHAT IS RISK MANAGEMENT FOR?

THE VIEW FROM ACADEMIA

I heard you speak me a speech once, but it was never acted, or, if it was, not above once.

> *Hamlet* (2.2.433), probably referring to the view
> about risk management offered by academia.

After the discussion in chapter 1, it is pretty clear why regulators should care about the financial good health of a bank: just recall what we said about systemic risk, about the inherent "fragile robustness" of a bank, about the stake a state acquires in private banks via deposit insurance, etc. But what about the banks themselves? What do *they* care? Why would private firms, unfettered by regulatory constraints, engage in risk management at all? What is risk management for?

The questions may sound bizarre: isn't all risk "bad"? Is it not a motherhood-and-apple-pie statement that reducing risk is a good thing? Yes and no. The problem is that mainstream corporate financial theory does not give risk management *carried out by a firm* ringing and unqualified endorsement. According to the view from academia, in fact, reducing risk,[1] per se, has no intrinsic value and brings no benefits to the shareholders. How can that be? Have we suddenly forgotten about diversification, about not putting all of our eggs in one basket, or, if we have studied some finance, about efficient frontiers and all that jazz? All these concerns (which, ultimately, were Sempronius's and Shakespeare's) remain valid. According to corporate finance, however, the relevant question is not *whether* this diversification should be carried out but *who* should undertake it. Firm managers, the theory says, should not try to diversify because investors can more efficiently do so themselves. More precisely, a firm should not try to achieve a one-size-fits-all trade-off between risk and return by choosing a particular mix of business initiatives that will bring earnings volatility to a particular level *chosen by the firm*. Instead, let the individual investor decide to what extent he likes a high-octane, racy investment or a staid, predictable one, or something in between. He will be able to achieve his own desired degree of overall (portfolio) riskiness by investing to different degrees in safe, risky, racy, or perhaps even riskless investments. It is because of the ability of investors to know what individual firms are up to and to achieve diversification by themselves that mangers should simply concentrate on finding projects or investments ("trades") whose return exceeds their appropriate hurdle rate—or so, at least, standard investment and corporate finance theory preach: "Remember, a good project is a good project is a good project" correctly intone Brealey and Myers in one of the best-known university textbooks on corporate finance available in English.* They go on to argue that, faced with two possible investment opportunities, A and B, "investors would value A by discounting its forecasted cash flows at a rate reflecting the risk of A. They would value B by discounting at a rate reflecting the risk of B." There is no mention of diversification benefits anywhere. The two projects are valued "just as [if] they were mini-firms in which investors could invest directly." And, they continue, "[i]f investors can diversify on their own account, they will not pay any extra for firms that diversify. ... If the capital market establishes a [present] value PV(A)

*R. A. Brealey and S. C. Myers (1990), *Principles of Corporate Finance*, 5th edn, chapter 9 (Columbus, OH: McGraw-Hill).

for asset A and PV(B) for B, the market value of a firm that holds only these two assets is just the sum of PV(A) and PV(B)." There is no diversification term to be found anywhere. This is why, in their words, a good project is a good project is a good project, and present values add. As far as (introductory) corporate finance is concerned, this is the end of the story (and I am out of a job).

So, why do private firms spend (a lot of) money on risk management? Many answers have been offered in the academic literature. Some point to the asymmetric tax treatment of profits and losses (*after tax*, it is better to make $10 million for two years running than to make $100 million one year but post an $80 million loss the next); some to the reduction in the cost of financial distress; some to reducing conflict of interests between stockholders and bondholders; and still others to many other subtler, and for a practitioner perhaps even less convincing, reasons.

If these explanations are true (and they are), then where is the problem? The problem is not that these effects of risk management are not true, or are not beneficial. Rather, it is that, looking at the actual practice of risk management, listening to arguments aired at risk committees or board meetings, speaking to chief risk officers, etc., one does not get the feeling that these are the "true" reasons why risk management is carried out. Reducing the volatility of earnings (admittedly at the expense of giving up some expected return); limiting, at some cost, the impact of adverse economic conditions; giving investors few surprises around a chosen level of earnings volatility; and, yes, when all of this is taken care of, also avoiding bankruptcy—*these* are all reasons that find resonance with the praxis of risk management, but that find no place in the textbooks. And the risk managers, the executives and the board members will say, *this is just what the investors want*. Is corporate finance wrong? Are investors silly for agreeing to pay a lot of money to risk managers to do something that they could do themselves for free? Or are bank managers deluded (and wasteful), in imagining that investors want a ready-made diversification when they would actually rather carry it out themselves? The answer to all these questions is probably "no." To understand why investors may indeed want to delegate at least some of their risk management to the managers of a firm we have to look a bit more carefully at the conditions under which the theoretical results hold.

THE VIEW FROM THE TRENCHES

We have seen that the diversification carried out by a firm is not supposed to matter, not because diversification per se is irrelevant, but because each investor should be able to carry out the degree of diversification *he* prefers, and will not necessarily like the one-size-fits-all diversification chosen by the firm's manager. It is because of this ability that the manager should not worry about the different degrees of risk aversion of the (hopefully many) investors, but should just make sure that a good project is a good project is a good project.

For this "bespoke" diversification to be possible, however, external investors should know just as well as the inside managers what risk factors the firm (in our discussion, the bank) is exposed to. Would *you* feel confident guessing how much of last year's profitability of a complex bank such as, say, JPMorgan, Goldman Sachs, or Deutsche Bank came from their emerging-market exposure, how much from bonds (of which currency and maturity, by the way), and how much from transactions in foreign exchange? Are *you* confident that there are instruments in the capital markets at your disposal that would allow *you*, if you so wanted, to hedge the bank's exposure to the fees earned by their mergers and acquisitions division? And do *you* know that these institutions will still engage in the same risky activities this year? If your answer to any of these questions is "no," you may well choose to delegate at least some of the diversification task to the insiders of a firm. You may, in other words, give them a mandate to carry out some risk management.

These statements can be made more precise. In the real world the expected return and the volatility of a firm (the staple diet of modern portfolio management) are not God given, but must be estimated from noisy data, i.e., from the past performance of the firm itself. If the world never changed and if we had an infinite amount of data (and infinite patience), this would not constitute a big problem, at least for firms established in the infinitely distant past. As we have seen in the previous chapters, however, the relevance of information about the very distant past quickly decays: perhaps the management of the firm has changed; perhaps the competitive environment is no longer the same; perhaps the regulatory or institutional environment has been altered; and so on. So, in reality, the relevant information to estimate the trend and the volatility of a firm's results is far more limited than one would wish. If the results of a bank display high volatility, however, it can be very difficult for an outsider to detect a real positive trend from a few lucky strikes. Conversely, *from the inside*, if you are the CEO of a firm, you may easily tell that this year's poor results were due to a number of very unlucky events: say, a freakishly high number of unrelated defaults in your high-quality portfolio, which is unlikely to be repeated next year. But if you are an outsider, can you be as confident? Much as the CEO will sound knowledgeable, soothing, and reassuring at the next shareholders' meeting, the outside investors will harbor a nagging doubt that, in reality, the lending criteria may have become too lax, and the credit process sloppy.

If a firm is good and solid, its CEO has every interest in signaling to outsiders that it is not a lemon. But a large volatility in earnings can make it very difficult for investors to detect even a very good underlying positive trend. The senior management of a good firm in general, and of a good financial institution in particular, therefore have an interest in dampening the wildest fluctuations, so that the good underlying trend can be more readily revealed.

Matters, as usual, are not quite so simple: if return is a compensation for risk, by investing in risk management and dampening volatility senior management are also giving up some expected return. From the point of view of an external investor, however, the ability to spot with ease the good underlying trend may more than compensate for some loss in expected returns.

If this explanation is correct, one can easily account for investors' preference for "stable earnings," a preference that, as we have seen, is at best puzzling and at worst irrational, according to standard corporate finance theory (which assumes that the volatility and the trend of a firm are perfectly known to investors). Investors, in my explanation, like low volatility not because they have not read, or understood, the required reading for Finance 101, but because they like to be able to estimate the true trend of a firm's profits as accurately as possible, and fear that earnings noise will prevent them from doing so.

Let us do a back-of-the-envelope calculation to see if this explanation has at least the ring of truth. Suppose that we can describe the change in value of a firm as being made up of two components: a constant trend (drift) and a noise term (volatility). For this simple example I will make the assumption that the trend and noise terms are described by what is called a Brownian motion. The Brownian motion model has an illustrious pedigree, as its use in physics was pioneered by no lesser a figure than Albert Einstein in his *annus mirabilis* (1905) and, a few years earlier, by Bachelier.* It is not without flaws, but, for the purposes of our back-of-the-envelope calculation, the simple model of Reverend Brown will do perfectly well—especially considering that it has proven good enough for the work on derivatives of the Nobel prize winners Black, Merton, and Scholes.

So, let us consider a firm that is expected to grow by a very respectable 20% every year, plus a noise term (a volatility) of 25%. The Angel of Financial Investors (who exactly knows all the true statistical properties of stock prices and always tells the truth) has whispered these two values in your ear. Let us see whether the numbers make "sense" in light of the observed performance of

---

*L. Bachelier (1900), Théorie de la spéculation, *Annales Scientifiques de l'École Normale Superieure*, 3e Serie, Tome 17:21–86. For an excellent discussion see M. Davis and A. Etheridge (2006), *Louis Bachelier's* Theory of Speculation: *The Origins of Modern Finance* (Princeton University Press).

the firm. Suppose that the value of the firm today is $100. Given the information you have been given, we can *expect* that the value of the firm in one year's time will be centered around $120. But we know that the slings and arrows of outrageous fortune will add some noise to this value (i.e., add or take away some random return). By positing a 25% volatility we are effectively saying that, over a year horizon, the value of the form will be centered around $120 but with a finite dispersion. The dispersion is such that there is a 68% probability of finding the value of the firm between $95 and $145. Given the information provided to us by the Angel of Financial Investors, if, by the end of the year, we observe a price of, say, $99, we have no reason to believe that our angelic friend has been having some fun at our expense. We simply conclude that the firm in question has had a run-of-the-mill unfortunate year, and we hope that things will get better next year. If we fundamentally liked our investment before, we have no reason to reverse it now.

An acquaintance of ours is not on such friendly terms with the Angel of Financial Investors and has to estimate the values for the trend and the volatility of the firm from its past performance. He can only do so by looking at historical data. How many data points will he require to form a judgement about the true trend of the firm and about its volatility? As for the volatility, if our acquaintance makes use of ten years' worth of observations, and given the statistical features of the stock in question, his uncertainty (as measured by one standard deviation) about the volatility will be less than 6%. Even just five years' worth of observations will make his uncertainty just above 8%. Not splendid, admittedly, but at least something to work with.

When it comes to the trend, though, matters look much less encouraging. The problem is that the uncertainty in the trend does not decay as fast with the addition of extra data: collecting five years' worth of data will leave our friend with close to an 11% uncertainty (again measured as one standard deviation) in the estimate of the true trend—and even ten years of observations barely bring the error on his estimate below 8%. This means that after collecting data for five years he will estimate with a 68%

confidence that the true trend is approximately between 31% and 9%! Waiting five more years will only reduce his uncertainty (at the same level of confidence) to the range 28% to 12%. Since our investor friend has read the pages of this book about relevant information, he has every reason to feel discouraged: ten years ago the firm's main field of activity was forestry, and now it sells mobile phones! Perhaps, he thinks, he should just turn his attention to some other stock.

The CEO of the firm in question, however, knows that the Angel of Financial Investors has very few friends, and that most investors have to estimate trends and volatility themselves. What can he do? If he employed some skillful risk managers and managed to reduce the volatility of the firm from 25% to 10%, the investor in the story would be in a better position. The uncertainty in the riskiness (the volatility) of the firm would be reduced to just above 3% with just five years' worth of data. More importantly, at the same level of confidence that allowed our friend to estimate the trend as being between 28% and 12% when the volatility was 25%, he can now say that the trend should be between 23% and 17%. At long last, looking at investing in the firm begins to make more sense. In short, if the true parameters that describe the behavior of a firm are not known exactly *a priori* (i.e., if we live on planet earth), reducing the volatility of a firm's returns by engaging in risk management can make investing in the firm much more easy to understand, and therefore more appealing to investors.*

THE VIEW FROM THE PRESS

These back-of-the-envelope calculations can lend at least some degree of plausibility to my explanation of why firms engage in

---

*It must be stressed again that this greater appeal does not come from the reduction in the volatility per se: this almost certainly came at the expense of a reduction in returns as well. It came because investors were better able to estimate the true trend of the firm's return and thereby reduce their *overall* uncertainty of outcomes (uncertainty coming from the intrinsic volatility of the firm's returns plus uncertainty stemming from their ignorance). Investors ultimately care about uncertainty in consumption, wherever this comes from!

risk management at all (i.e., in order to allow the world to tell how good they really are). Does the explanation fit well with the way bank analysts and economic commentators look at the risk and return of financial institutions? Let me present in some detail just one of many examples I could offer, in the form of some quotes from the cover article that appeared in 2006 in *The Economist** on the bank Goldman Sachs: "By any measure, Goldman Sachs is a formidable company" the article begins. "The real reason why Goldman Sachs should matter to outsiders [is] because it stands at the center of a two-decade-long transformation of the financial markets and a new approach to risk." As examples go, we could hardly find a more pertinent one. The editor goes on discussing the derivatives exposure of the firm (more than $1 trillion) and the complexity of its business and asks three questions: "How exactly has Goldman Sachs ... achieved this? Can it be sustained? And what should happen if something goes wrong? Like most of its rivals, *Goldman is a difficult institution for outsiders to understand* [and] *precisely what Goldman is up to remains obscure.*"[†] (Recall, in passing, that you, the external investor, are supposed to be able to hedge the unwanted risk as you best please—how can you do so if even the basics of what the firm does are opaque? But let us move on.)

"[Goldman's] revenues are the most volatile among big investment banks and it has most days when it loses money. Overall, however, it makes the most money." Good, just as Investment Theory 101 says it should. A few paragraphs below, however, the article continues by saying that, "*Outsiders*—and perhaps even insiders—*find it difficult to judge whether Goldman's business is sustainably good or has thrived thanks to a dose of unsustainable good luck and skill.*" As a consequence, "the market doubts the run of huge profits can last. *Goldman shares are valued less richly than those of the competitors it obviously outwits.*" Almost verbatim the rationale for the existence of risk management I offered above.

---

*On top of the world, *The Economist*, April 29, 2006, p. 11
[†]The emphasis in this and the following quotes is mine.

Needless to say, showing that the financial press (and, presumably, the investors who read it) care about the volatility of earnings of a bank does not "prove" that their concerns are justified. I have simply offered an explanation of why these concerns may not be so silly after all. But I am not proposing to settle the issue of who should carry out diversification (the ultimate investors or the managers) with a couple of examples and a plausibility argument. The important point is that, *rightly or wrongly*, investors *do* care about (and penalize) earnings volatility. Accepting this reality and carrying out the financial risk management that can bring this volatility under control is therefore an imperative for any firm manager. In short, *this* is, in my opinion, what risk management is ultimately for.*

*If I was asked what the second most important reason for the existence of risk management was, I would suggest achieving a better alignment of the interests of bondholders and shareholders. The latter may well "own" the firm, but have to rely on the former to finance it efficiently. As I explain in chapter 9, volatility is much less attractive to bondholders (whose maximum upside is capped) than to shareholders. Signaling that the firm has an established, *long-term* commitment to keeping volatility under control therefore has a beneficial effect on the rate of return that current and future prospective bond buyers require.

CHAPTER 6

VAR & CO: HOW IT ALL STARTED

Why then can one desire too much of a good thing?

As You Like It (4.1.124), a reference, apparently, to the
enthusiasm with which VaR has been embraced.

HISTORICAL BACKGROUND

In the introductory chapter I pointed out that the roots of the
current debate about the use of quantitative techniques in risk
management can be traced all the way back to the eighteenth-
century Franco-Prussian debate about statistics and the state. I
then discussed the types of probability (subjective/Bayesian versus frequentist) relevant for risk management; the difficulties one
encounters in the search for a single indicator (a "magic formula")
to help us decide; and, finally, the raison d'être for risk management itself. Having started from the 30,000-feet view, I intend to
focus on a less sweeping vista of current quantitative risk management. To inject concreteness into the discussion, and to make a con-
nection between the theory discussed so far and the applications
dealt with in the second part of this book, I will present below a
broad-brush and selective description of some of the changes that
have occurred in the financial industry in the last few decades.

The idea that sophisticated statistical techniques could be
employed for the management of financial risk in the banking
industry began to gain widespread acceptability around the early
to mid 1990s. To understand why it happened when it did, and

why it happened at all, we must however look briefly at some aspects of the evolution of banking in the 1980s and 1990s.

For centuries, the staple diet of banks had always, of course, been lending money. As the joke goes, in the good old days (we are talking about the 1960s) the only piece of quantitative information a bank manager needed to know was the 3–6–3 rule: raise money at 3% (from the depositors), lend it at 6%, on the golf course by 3 P.M. This cozy state of affairs had been allowed to develop, and to be maintained, because it was thought that sheltering banks from the harsh winds of competition would make them safer institutions—in view of the inherent "fragility" of banks discussed in chapter 1, this is an outcome that, then as now, is deemed useful and desirable. What was less desirable was that the good old days were certainly good for bank managers and golf-course operators but not quite as good for depositors or borrowers—in short, for the economy as a whole minus the bankers and the golf-course operators. However, if one looked closely, there *was* in this arrangement an indirect benefit to the economy: society was, in effect, buying via the 3–6–3 arrangement a form of insurance against the systemic risk associated with bank failures. The real question therefore was, could the same degree of protection be acquired at a lower cost to society? Was the insurance fairly priced?

Over-cozy business arrangements are normally resolved by facilitating (or removing obstacles to) competition. One of the side effects of such a policy is that the most inefficient players will often end up going bust. As we have seen, though, a bank is not just any business, and the consequences of a bank failure have the potential to spread quickly and far more widely than the bank's depositors, employees, and shareholders. To square the circle, i.e., to increase competition while keeping the risk of failure down, a two-pronged approach was taken. On the one hand, the banking industry was deregulated in terms of the range of profitable activities it could engage in. On the other, it was re-regulated by taking a closer and more stringent look at the capital buffer banks would from now on be required to hold as a safeguard against going bankrupt. Competition was now fine, but going bust was still not on. As a result of product deregulation, banks were presented with the opportunity (and, if they wanted to survive, the need) to engage in activities they had not even contemplated in the good old 3–6–3 days.

As the banking industry was being opened to competition, another nasty (for the banks, that is) development was taking place. Traditional corporate borrowers, who had routinely come to banks to raise money for investment, began to discover that they could borrow money directly by selling bonds (i.e., standardized loans) to investors. This newfound liquidity, reach, and depth of capital markets was progressively allowing good-quality corporate borrowers to "disintermediate" banks—a fancy expression meaning that the middle man (the bank) was being cut out. Soon, a virtuous circle developed: as more and more corporate borrowers accessed the capital markets directly, these became larger, more liquid, more transparent—in short more inviting for more borrowers to access and for more investors to put money into. Again, however, the circle was (or seemed to be) virtuous for almost everybody, apart from the banks.

It was in this context that, from the 1980s onwards, banks began to engage more extensively in a specialized and complex new area: the trading of securities. More and more banks were finding themselves forced to complement their traditional, long-term, relationships-based lending activities by taking active part in the capital markets. Banks wanted and, at the same time, needed a piece of the new trading action and became involved in types of short-term, depersonalized transactions with which they had little familiarity in the 3–6–3 days: trading operations. Together, deregulation and disintermediation were changing the banking landscape. Because of disintermediation banks "had" to share a piece of the trading action; because of deregulation, for the first time in post-Depression history they were allowed to do so.

These trading operations evolved quickly from rather simple bond trading activities to trading in equities, in foreign currencies, in commodities, in securitized mortgages, etc. As soon as derivatives on all of the above began to appear, these were quickly added to the banks' trading activities too. Very soon, the opportunities for banks to combine derivatives with traditional borrowing and investment products became almost endless. So, by the mid 1990s a bank could routinely provide an unprecedented range of finance and investment products. It could offer to a borrower the alternative between borrowing at a fixed or a variable rate. It could offer guarantees that the borrowing rate over the life of the loan would not exceed a given level. It could offer a corporate client the ability to borrow *in the future* at a prespecified borrowing rate. It could provide cheaper-than-normal borrowing as long as the borrower was ready to take on board some form of market risk; it could arrange for the funds to be raised cheaply in the (typically high-yielding) currency for which there was investor demand, and for the repayment obligations to be translated into the currency of relevance to the borrower; and much more.

Financial innovations have the intrinsic feature of being self-reinforcing and, to some extent, "addictive" for their providers. As more banks compete for the same business, profit margins shrink. As a consequence, it becomes increasingly difficult for banks and other financial institutions to make (risk-adjusted) returns that exceed their cost of capital—in short, to be truly profitable. The attractive returns are to be found in the "next big thing," i.e., in the new "exotic" product or in the innovative transaction tailored to the needs of a particular client of the bank. Banks therefore see themselves forced to innovate, but, "[o]ver time, many of the most successful innovations become mainstream, enhancing market efficiency … and reducing the initial supernormal returns to the innovators, who must move on the next new thing; and so on."* The forces behind financial innovation therefore have been (and are) not only powerful, but, to a large extent, also self-feeding.

Because of these developments, by the mid 1990s trading activities in general, and complex financial transactions in particular, had become an increasingly important source of revenue for banks and other financial institutions. For many banks, trading revenues were no longer the thin icing on the far more substantial cake made

*Tucker, *Financial Stability Review* December 2005:76.

up of the traditional banking activities centered around lending and financing. They had become a major contributor to the bottom line. Therefore they required to be looked at carefully if the financial risk of a company was to be understood and managed effectively.

The development of trading activities and of derivative instruments were seen as very closely connected in the minds of the public at large, of the financial press, and of the regulators. Unsurprisingly, this was especially true when malfeasance, incompetence, or outright fraud brought some large financial losses to the headlines.

There was a new, and somewhat unsettling, feature related to understanding the risk associated with the new derivative transactions. If I have lent you $100 (perhaps in the form of a bond), it is easy to understand how much I stand to lose if you fail to pay me back. However, many derivatives (off-balance-sheet) instruments could be worth zero to you and me when we strike a deal. Yet the value of the contract will certainly not remain zero throughout the life of the contract. Its value will change over time and will depend on the future (and, therefore, as of today, unknown) behavior of the underlying financial quantity—interest rates, equity prices, etc.—to which the derivative contract is referenced (or "derived" from, whence the name). The risk associated with derivatives, depending as it does on the very imperfectly known future, is therefore much more difficult to assess and to communicate to external interested parties than the risk that comes with traditional (on-balance-sheet) lending transactions. What is the risk associated with a transaction that today is worth zero to both parties but could be worth millions in a few weeks' time?

As practitioners, regulators, and journalists were struggling to find a way to convey a sense of the money at risk when using these newfangled instruments, they began to refer to the notional amounts of the underlying swaps and options as indicators of the "volume" of the new market (and, by a logical sleight of hand, of the underlying risk). This was unfortunate, because these amounts, with many more zeros than a telephone number, convey a very distorted impression of the actual cash flows that change hands. This bad habit, however, was there to stay, and contributed to the impression that market risk in general, and derivatives-related market risk in particular, was becoming as important as traditional lending risk.

There was another entirely new feature associated with trading activities. Lending to borrowers often tended to be part of what is described as "relationship banking." The interest rate charged to a borrower reflected more than just the "cost of money." Embedded in it was the price for the implicit commitment that the bank would not walk away from the client at the first signs of financial difficulty. Sometimes this commitment would be formalized with a so-called credit line, but, more often than not, there would simply be the implicit understanding that, in a generalized economic downturn, a bank would try to provide financing ability to a fundamentally sound company that may be going through a rough patch. And, as a corollary, whenever money was extended to a company, the intention would be that the loan would remain on the balance sheet of the lending bank until its expiry. A loan may not have been for life, but it was certainly not just for Christmas.

Since loans were hold-to-maturity assets, their value could be reasonably accounted for in a rough-and-ready manner: for a reasonably good loan, if I had lent $100 I could expect $100 back, and its value was therefore recorded as $100. If there were some doubts as to the repayment ability, some reserves would be taken, and the value of the loan would be recorded as, say, $60. If the financial difficulties the borrower was in became so severe as to make repayment an impossibility, the loan would be written off and its value recorded as zero. These adjustments to the value of a loan would be made on a periodic basis. Unless dramatic bad news about a company suddenly surfaced, the review period would be of the order of weeks or months. Between these revaluation periods, the recorded value of the loans would not change.

Not so for trading transactions. Here, there is no relationship with a particular borrower that needs to be preserved. The counterparty is, in general, the impersonal "market." As a consequence, there is no natural length of time over which the transaction should be kept. Buying, say, a five-year government bond is, of course, a form of lending, similar in this sense to lending for five years to a local company. But the absence of an ongoing underlying business relationship makes the bond transaction fundamentally different: in the traded-bond case there is no trace of an implicit or explicit commitment to hold on to the bond until its maturity, let alone to buy a new bond (i.e., extend further credit) when the present one matures. Since there is no business relationship to preserve, the length of time a bank would hold on to a trading position could be much shorter. A few weeks, days, sometimes even hours or minutes, but certainly not years are the appropriate timescales for trading-book positions.*

This posed a new problem. If, when the dust has settled, I am reasonably confident that I will receive my $100 back at the maturity of a traditional loan, it is probably reasonable to record its value today as $100. But if I intend to dispose of my bond in the next hour, how should I value it? Will the market's assessment of the value of the bond in sixty minutes' time be the same as the current one? With megabytes of economic information pouring onto trading screens by the second, it almost certainly will not be. But, if this is the case, in the fast trading-book world I can stand to make a loss even if no borrower "defaulted." It is enough for the *perceived* probability of default to change as a result of the stream of information arriving by the second for the next "putative lender" to change the price he is now willing to pay for the bond I bought for $100 one hour ago. Information is instantly embedded in the prices. Unfortunately, losses can just as quickly become embedded in a trading book.

How large can these losses be? And how large should the prudential capital buffer be to safeguard an institution against the possibility of financial distress from losses from these short-lived

*The head of the foreign exchange trading operations for an international bank was famously asked how he made his trading decisions. "I employ," he said, "a mixture of short-term and long-term trading signals." "And how long are your long-term trading signals?" "Oh, it could even be a few minutes" was the half-serious, half-tongue-in-cheek answer.

trading positions? In an intuitive but imprecise way, the capital buffer should cover the possible losses arising from adverse movement in the underlying risk factors. But over which time period? To pursue the example of the traded bond, if I can sell it in the next sixty seconds, surely considering the possible adverse moves in interest rates between now and the bond maturity is irrelevant. A more relevant scale would be the magnitude of the price moves over the length of time needed to get out of the bond position if I wanted to. As mentioned above, this "holding period," i.e., this characteristic length of time over which a position can be liquidated, is, in normal market conditions, of the order of minutes or hours, sometimes even seconds. In difficult market conditions it can become considerably longer, but it is certainly not years. This apparently "technical" feature has important implications for the management and the quantification of financial risk.

As this new environment was evolving, some high-profile scandals began to alert the public and the regulators to the fact that trading-related losses could financially embarrass even large institutions (witness Barings Bank, Metallgeschaft, Sumitomo, Orange County, Bankers Trust). If the institution was not large, and poorly managed, mismanagement of items on the trading book could even sink a bank, as the case of Barings vividly illustrated. If one looked behind the newspaper headlines, it would have been apparent that, more often than not, it had not really been derivatives-related losses that had "sunk the bank." Old-fashioned fraud (perhaps disguised under the new name of operational risk) was still a very efficient way of losing a lot of money in a very short period of time. Sure enough, trading positions (perhaps in derivatives form) were often part of the chain of events that led to the most notorious losses, but more often than not as accessories to the crime rather than as the ultimate culprits. Given the ubiquity of derivatives in modern financial transactions, it should be no more surprising to find that a derivative was used as part of a headline-grabbing transaction than, stretching the point a little, a computer, a telephone, or a fax machine. Nonetheless, newspapers soon found that telling (and sometimes embellishing) lurid stories of how hundreds of millions could be lost by fast-living derivatives traders gambling away the bank's capital would cause little harm to their sales figures. If grabbing everybody's attention is what they were trying to do, they certainly succeeded.

The regulators took notice. Their reasonable concern was (or should have been) that when it comes to risk taking a bank is not just another commercial institution. If a widget maker goes bust, this is regrettable and unfortunate, but, in general, it does not create a danger for the economic system as a whole. The failure of a widget maker does not, to use one of the regulators' favorite expressions, pose "systemic risk." Banks are different, as the painful experience of the 1930s showed: the repercussions of bank failures can have devastating and lasting effects on the economic health of a nation or, in these globalized days, perhaps even of the world economy. The fact that banks are, by nature, leveraged institutions with a sizeable maturity mismatch between their short-term liabilities (the deposits and short-term funding) and their long-term assets (loans under various guises and other investments) does not improve the quality of sleep of banking regulators. Banks, in short, must not only be solid and solvent, they must also be *perceived* to be so.

To ensure that this would be the case, regulators imposed capital requirements on banks. Originally these requirements were crude and simple and mainly applied to the lending operations of a bank (the so-called "banking book"). The original rules stipulated that, for a "standard-quality" loan of $100, each bank had to set aside a capital buffer of at least $8. The reasoning was simple: for a loan portfolio of "typical" credit quality, even if 8% of the loans disappeared into thin air the bank still had to be, and had to be perceived to be, solvent and solid. The $8 of capital was there to provide a reasonable safety buffer between the lending losses and the depositors.

Clearly, the quality of a bank's loan portfolio played a role in the prudential level of capital reserves. This was taken into account via extremely crude but easy-to-understand rules that established a rough-and-ready equivalence between loans to different borrowers and the "typical" loan for which the 8% rule applied. The rules were so simple, and crude, that, by and large, they could easily be written in the top half of an A4 sheet of paper.* And as for the risk of a bank going bust because of trading losses, in the original framework this was clearly an afterthought—so much so that the trading-risk capital charges went under the banner of "add-ons." So, the set of rules used to determine a reasonable prudential capital buffer might have been adequate in the early 1980s. Unfortunately, by the 1990s the size and complexity of the trading operations undertaken by many banks was such that the bank regulators began to realize that the add-on approach was no longer adequate.

Regulators were not the only players to be worried by these market developments. Before the mid 1980s, and with a few exceptions, most banks that engaged in trading activities had rather simple and relatively easy to understand exposures to market risk factors. Very often their greatest market exposure would come from the money-market desk, linked to their funding and liquidity activities. Sometimes, internationally active banks would trade foreign currencies in large amounts. Equity trading could also be significant at some institutions. But, by and large, during the decade that ended with Tom Wolfe's *Bonfire of the Vanities*, trading-book risk was relatively simple to understand and, by and large, linear.† With the growth in the breadth and depth of the trading activities of financial institutions during the 1990s, however, risk managers soon found themselves faced with a very different environment. Banks were active in equities *and* interest rates *and* foreign currencies *and* commodities (and, often, in all of the above in derivatives form). It might have been easy enough for a risk manager to set prudential limits for, say, a money-market desk,

---

*To give an idea of how simple and crude these original rules were, lending to the government of an OECD country was deemed to be virtually riskless; lending to an OECD bank was deemed a bit more risky; but, below that, lending to Microsoft or to the corner store were reckoned to be equally risky.

†By "linear" I mean that, if I know the loss for a given move in a risk factor, I automatically know that, for a move half, twice, or four times as large in the same risk factor, the loss would also be half, twice, or four times as severe.

or an equity trading operation, or a swap trader in isolation, but how were these different limits to be made consistent with each other? How does one compare a limit for a parallel shift in rates with a limit for currency risk or a limit for equity positions? What about optionality risk? And was all risk just as bad? Could some trading-book exposure actually reduce and offset the market risk taken in other parts of the trading book? In short, how can one compare oranges and apples?

In this environment, a particular tool, Value-at-Risk (VaR), quickly gained popularity and widespread support. The idea behind this approach was intuitively appealing and deceptively simple. In itself, its perceived simplicity goes a long way toward explaining why it became so popular so quickly. There were deeper reasons, however, why the industry "needed" something like VaR. To understand these reasons we must look a bit more closely at this measure of risk.

ENTER VAR

Let us start from today's portfolio of trading positions held by a bank. Each of these positions will change in value in response to changes in one or more market risk factors (foreign exchange moves, moves in rates, changes in volatility, etc.). Let us assume that, implicitly or explicitly, we can assign a probability to any conceivable *joint* move in all the risk factors—the FX rates, the interest rates, the equity prices, etc. This is a formidable, and per- haps impossible, task, but let us remain at a conceptual level for the moment. The function that associates a probability to all these possible combinations of moves is called the *joint probability dis- tribution* for all these risk factors.* In statistics there is no richer or deeper information that we can ever hope to obtain about a given set of random quantities.

*A half-careful discussion should of course refer to probability *densities*, not to probability *tout court*. The mathematically acquainted reader should definitely mutate these *mutandis*. The mathematically innocent need not worry too much.

Let us leave this joint distribution aside for the moment. Let us instead concentrate on calculating what *hypothetical* profits and losses today's positions *would* generate if they were subjected to various arbitrary joint realizations of the changes in the market risk factors (the market prices, the rates, etc.). Let us not worry too much about how these joint changes in risk factors are chosen— about, for instance, how plausible they may be or about whether they have already occurred in the past. Let us just consider *all* the possible combinations of changes in risk factors and see what effect they would have on our real portfolio. So, for instance, we can record on a piece of paper how much money our *current* trading positions would make if, say, the Dow Jones index climbed by 5%, *and* interest rates fell by 0.5%, *and* the dollar weakened against the euro by 1%, etc. With a big enough piece of paper we can repeat this operation, at least conceptually, for all the possible combinations of changes in risk factors we can dream up. Once we have done this we will have a very long list of hypothetical gains and losses generated by our positions.*

What shall we do with this list? Some of the combinations I have come up with may be rather implausible; some very likely; some well-nigh impossible. How can I assess their relative importance? Perhaps some of the losses I recorded on my very long piece of paper were staggering, but the combinations of market moves giving rise to these losses have never been seen since financial records have been kept. Should I worry? And, if so, how much? Here is the answer.

Recall that the joint probability distribution of the risk factors contains all the statistical information about the joint occurrences of the market moves I have dreamt up. Intuitively, albeit rather hand-wavingly, I can therefore imagine doing the following. I can begin by looking at losses around a particular value, say, −$20,000,000. To be concrete, I am going to look at losses between

---

*These gains and losses, it is essential to stress, have nothing to do with the true profits and losses generated by the actual positions we held in the past—that is why I stressed the adjective "hypothetical" and used the conditional "would" at the beginning of the paragraph.

−$19,990,000 and −$20,010,000. I then go and check my very long piece of paper with all the recorded market moves and losses and I put a cross only next to the market moves associated with those losses that fall in the chosen range. (It may sound daunting, but this is the kind of stuff computers are really good at.) This is where the joint probability distribution of the risk factors we started from comes back to the fore. Using this function, for each combination of market moves giving rise to a loss in the chosen range I look up the associated probability. I write all these probabilities on another piece of paper, which I label something like "Probabilities for losses in the range −$19,990,000 to −$20,010,000." When I am done, I add them all up. What have I obtained?

By construction, this sum is just the probability of incurring a loss between −$19,990,000 and −$20,010,000 *from whatever market move*. Although this is not quite exact, when the mathematical i's have been dotted and the statistical t's crossed, this is how we can move from the *probability of joint moves in the risk factors* to the much more interesting *probability of a given profit or loss*. When I repeat this exercise for the whole spectrum of profits and losses, I have created the full profit-and-loss distribution. By this procedure we have collapsed the impossibly complex information contained in the joint probability about risk factors and in the infinitely long list of hypothetical market moves and associated profits and losses into a manageable-looking single curve.

We are almost finished. As a last step, given this distribution we can pick a point on the x-axis (a level of loss) such that, roughly speaking, only $(100 - X)\%$ of the losses are worse than this chosen level. This level of losses is called the Xth percentile VaR for the portfolio in question at the chosen time horizon. So, if X is 95% and the time horizon is one day, the chosen point on the profit-and-loss distribution is the 95th percentile, one-day VaR. That is what VaR is.

Why was this new tool so useful? What was all the fuss about VaR? To begin with, the units VaR uses are money. This is the one metric that should be easily understood, at least in a bank, by everybody, from the most junior back-office clerk to the board member: "With today's trading positions, VaR says, you are at risk of losing at least $10,000,000 in one trading day out of twenty." Arguably, the person who does not understand the meaning of this statement should not go anywhere near a bank.

The second important advantage of VaR was that the possible diversification effects arising from holding different positions was automatically taken into account. Take the example of just two trading positions: with the first we make money if short-term interest rates decline; with the second we make money if equity prices increase. We can rather easily work out the risk of either position in isolation. But what can we do with these stand-alone risk numbers? How likely are we to lose money on our equity position when we are losing money on the interest-rates contract? In other words, how are equity prices and short-term interest rates correlated? Clearly, when we have entered both trades the combined risk is certainly not the sum of the two—this would be a gross overstatement that implies that we always lose money in equities when short rates go up. In reality, one can construct a plausible argument to the effect that, if rates are unexpectedly cut, this should have a stimulative effect for the economy, and equity prices (which are forward looking) should therefore do rather well. This may sound plausible, but how can we get a more satisfactory picture of the joint risk of holding equities and being simultaneously exposed to interest rates?

VaR, again, appears to have the answer. It lies in the joint distribution of the changes in the two risk factors (equity prices and interest rates) in question. Recall that we said that a joint distribution contains all the statistical information we may possibly want about two random quantities. In particular, from the joint distribution we can understand the nature of the codependence between the two variables. We can answer questions such as, "Given that the short rate has moved up by, say, twenty basis points, what is the probability of equities rallying by more than 1%?" Even more interestingly, we can ask the question, "Given that the short rate has moved up by the same twenty basis points, what is the (conditional) distribution of changes for the equity price of interest?" So, as long as we *really* know the joint distribution, all the (possibly subtle and unexpected) codependences between financial variables are fully captured. The beautiful promise offered by VaR is that, *if* we can start from the correct joint distribution of the changes in all the market risk factors, the resulting distribution of the hypothetical portfolio losses will "know" in the most complete possible way about total and partial offsets among all our current trading positions. A properly functioning VaR knows about diversification. It knows about concentration of risk. It knows (statistically speaking) just about everything. In short, with VaR we seem to have found *the* way, if not to add, at least to compare apples and oranges.

FROM NUMBERS TO DECISIONS: TAKE TWO

In the example above we ultimately made a translation from the joint distribution for all the risk factors and the associated loss into a single number, the chosen percentile. But this one number was obtained thanks to a rather arbitrary choice (why the 95th rather than the 97th percentile?). The really fundamental quantity we started from was an infinitely richer function: the profit-and-loss distribution, i.e., the whole function that associates to any profit or loss its probability of occurrence. The richness of this information can, however, be somewhat bewildering. As I have shown in figure 4.6, for instance, if we compare two such distributions, one may have a greater variance but be more skewed toward the right (the profit side). Another may have a lower variance but display a greater probability of very large profits and losses. Which one should we choose? When it comes to making decisions, we would like to have a single number as an indicator of the "merit" or "quality" or "goodness" of the quantity under analysis, so that we can make our decision easily and unambiguously simply by ranking the outcomes in terms of our indicator. But how do we go from a full function to a single number?

Since we have already used the words "ranking" and "decision making," we seem to be begging for the concept of utility to be brought into play. Indeed, we saw that utility theory promises to associate a single number (the expected utility from a risky prospect) to a full distribution of possible outcomes. This single output number has a very desirable property: large number equals good, small number equals bad, bigger number equals better. Is this not exactly what we were looking for, i.e., a straightforward indicator to move from a helplessly complex quantity with an infinite number of degrees of freedom (a continuous function) to a simple number? As appealing as this approach may seem, we have discussed some of the problems of both a practical and a theoretical nature associated with the use of utility. Be that as it may, the concept of utility has been as much loved by academics as it has been reviled or, at best, ignored by practitioners. This may or may not be unfortunate. However, as discussed immediately below, if the regulators wanted to align their prudential framework with the risk-management practice actually used in the financial industry, this fact could not be ignored: bankers may well be philistines, unreconstructed Luddites, or ignoramuses, but if they do not want to hear the "U" word, there is little point in forcing them to use a decision-making tool they do not believe in.

And, by the way, is the skepticism toward this use of the utility concept really so unjustifiable? I have tried to explain that modern utility theory tends to avoid a prescriptive use of utility (it does not say, "You should choose this course of action *because* it yields a greater utility"). Instead it tends to have a descriptive dimension and, in a way, reverses the logical chain of thought. It says that, *since* you have been observed to choose A over B, *then* your utility for A must be greater than your utility for B. In other words, modern utility theory is "calibrated" by observing your elementary choices and then using this revealed ranking to describe more complex choice settings. But, if this is the case, you *first* have to choose between the distributions with different variances, skewnesses, and kurtoses and only *then*, on the basis of this choice, can you assign the various utilities.* These choices over distributions are taken to be your elementary preferences, and modern utility theory does not help you express them. It just observes you as you make them. So, even if we wholeheartedly embraced (modern) utility theory, we would still be back at square one.

This leaves us with our initial problem unsolved: once we have obtained this extremely rich function (the profit-and-loss distribution), what use can we make of it for decision making? The answer from the practitioners was pragmatic, simple, and straightforward, if somewhat inelegant. The first step is very simple: choose a level of loss such that the probability of a greater loss is rather small (say, 5% or 1%). How can this be done? Since the area under a probability distribution is the probability itself, and since if something happens with certainty we say that it will occur with a probability of 1, we want to choose a point along the x-axis (where we display profits and losses) such that the area to its right is rather close to 1. As we saw, the name given to such a point in statistics is a percentile. A "rather high" percentile may therefore identify loss such that, say, 95% or 99% of the losses would not be as severe (or, conversely, such that only 5% or 1%, respectively, of the losses would be more severe). But this is just the definition of VaR that I gave above.

Once we have chosen this "rather high" percentile, what can we do with it? Recall that we want to collapse a complex, multivalued function (the probability of losses) into a measure, or proxy, or indicator of risk that is as simple and as low dimensional as possible. Why not, then, associate the "risk" of a set of trading positions with the VaR at this "rather high" percentile and for this short holding period. Why a short holding period? Because VaR was originally devised to deal with positions on the trading

---

*Modern utility theory is expressed in terms of preferences over lotteries, where the term "lotteries" means "probability distributions" over a set of outcomes—exactly the situation we are faced with here. See, for example, D. Kreps (1988), *Notes on the Theory of Choice* (Boulder, CO: Westview Press), or S. Hargreaves Heap and Y. Varoufakis (2004), *Game Theory—A Critical Text*, 2nd edn (London: Routledge).

book that could be liquidated in a matter of, at most, a few days—positions, in other words, that the bank does not *have to* hold on to if it does not want to. Why a percentile between the 90th and the 99th? Because, given a reasonable holding period of one day, this would relate to losses made (exceeded) approximately twice a month or twice a year. This makes sense, as these are the magnitudes of probabilities human beings easily "relate to." Our actions can be modified by events that tend to happen roughly with this or with a greater frequency. In the morning I hear on the radio that there is a 20% chance of rain. This information can affect my behavior: it might make me take an umbrella, for instance. I make a trade-off between the inconvenience of carrying the umbrella and the one-in-five possibility of getting soaked in the rain and I easily reach a decision. But how many of us have chosen between cars, planes, and trains as our means of transportation for our next holiday on the basis of the respective mortality rates associated with those forms of transport? In this case it is our lives that are at stake (arguably something more important than not getting soaked in the rain). Yet, given the small likelihood of the event in question, I become far more influenced by other considerations, such as the cost, the length, or the comfort of the journey.

So, faced with the problem of managing the risk of complex and diversified trading-book portfolios, practitioners found VaR to be a useful tool, and sensibly chose a short holding period and a percentile somewhere between the 90th and the 99th. But where did this choice leave the regulators? In updating the outmoded regulatory framework referred to above, they found themselves faced with diverse and to some extent conflicting requirements. To begin with, they soon realized that the financial industry had made great strides in the management and quantification of financial risk, at least in the trading-book area. Therefore, to quote one of regulators' mantras, they embraced the laudable principle of "aligning the regulatory framework with the industry best risk-management practice." As VaR seemed to be the embodiment of this best risk-management practice, they embedded VaR at the very core of their new regulatory setup. They did so by requiring that prudential (regulatory) capital against trading-book positions should be linked to the total VaR generated by the same positions.

As they were moving toward this progressive and exciting goal, it soon became clear that the chief risk officers (CROs) of private banks and the national banking regulators might well have different prudential goals. The CRO must ensure that the results presented by his bank are commensurate with the shareholders' expectations not only about returns, but also about the volatility of returns. Of course, the CRO and the board will want to prevent the bank from going bust, but they will also want to address a whole range of more nuanced concerns. We have seen all of this in chapter 5 and we will discuss it again in chapter 9, so there is no need to labor the point.

All of this makes a lot of sense, but it poses a problem. As we saw, left to their own devices, private banks (whose risk-management philosophy the regulators were keen to embrace) had calibrated their VaR measure to levels of losses that would be exceeded somewhere between once a month and once a year. This time frame is not only congruent with the level of risk that is easily understood by "normal human beings," but is also well-suited to controlling and managing risk over time frames linked to the annual or semiannual reporting cycle. Surely, however, the regulators cannot equate the regulatory (prudential) capital to the level of losses likely to be incurred every few weeks or months. Crudely stated, regulators cannot allow a bank to go bust once a month, once a year, or, for that matter, even once every ten years. How can this gap be bridged?

The regulators were facing another dilemma. As they were drafting their voluminous rule book, the international regulatory bodies were roughly aware of the then-current level of regulatory capital set aside by the banking industry worldwide. What they presumably did *not* want to achieve was to draft a set of rules that would *reduce* the prudential capital already in the banking system as a whole. Depending on the level and "quality" of trading risk on their books, some institutions could find the new set of rules more burdensome and some others less so. But, whatever the fancy statistical models may say, the regulators would not accept a reduction in the overall capital buffer. There was no guarantee, however, that the "reasonable" holding period of a few days and the intuitively plausible "rather high" percentile between the 90th and the 99th would give a result anywhere close to the existing level of capital. After all, this combination of holding period and percentile had been devised and put to work by practitioners for their own risk-management purposes. It was not supposed to cater for the needs and requirements of regulators. It would have been surprising if it did. And, indeed, it did not.

To get out of this impasse, the regulators had to find a pragmatic solution. They could have followed at least two different routes. They could have asked for a much higher percentile (the 99.9th or the 99.95th, or whatever) and/or for a much longer holding period. This would certainly have increased the prudential capital. Or they could have lived with a relatively low percentile (the 99th) and a rather short holding period (ten days) but then applied a "fudge factor" to the resulting capital number to bring it in line with their prudential concerns (and with the amount of capital already present, in the aggregate, in the banking system). In the 1990s, when the regulators were grappling with the task of controlling market risk, they chose the second, apparently less elegant, solution. For reasons I will explain in chapter 10, I believe that it was the right choice.

Unfortunately, as regulatory attention moved from market to credit risk (and to liquidity and operational risk), and as the confidence in risk-management models began to grow, the emphasis progressively shifted from the ad hoc multiplier toward the first, apparently more elegant, solution. As a result, what I regard as science-fiction percentiles began to be discussed, proposed, imposed on, and sometimes even voluntarily embraced by banks. Worryingly, a sort of "percentile inflation" began to happen: no sooner had the 99th percentile been accepted than the 99.9th percentile became more and more commonly discussed; as the 99.9th percentile (which, through repeated use and mention, soon came to be considered a plausible level of statistical confidence) became embedded in some of the regulation, some banks began to talk about the 99.97th percentile. To the uninitiated eye, this evolution may seem to be "small change" once you have already accepted the 99th percentile. Not so. A 99th percentile with a ten-day holding period refers to events that occur on average once every four years. A 99.97th percentile with a one-year holding period refers to events that on average should only have occurred about once since Homer wrote *The Iliad*. I intend to show in the following chapters that the estimation of these percentiles is not difficult— it is meaningless. I am not alone in holding this belief, as the anonymized story below shows.

Three years ago, a very senior quantitative analyst at a large international bank that had (even by that time) devoted many tens of millions of dollars to this project asked me whether we could meet for a technical discussion as I was travelling through New York. The senior analyst was becoming progressively convinced (as the results of such high-percentile calculations were finally becoming available after years of data gathering, coding, and testing) that the output was extremely sensitive to small changes in the assumptions, to almost-arbitrary choices in the use and selection of data, etc. After several years of work, the heartfelt question he presented me with over a Starbucks coffee had little to do with econometrics or statistics. The words I remember best were: "How do I tell them?"

This is not a good state of affairs. It is wasteful and it is dangerous for the financial industry. There is also the wider danger that an unreflective acceptance of these statistical demands can quickly spill over from the financial area to the wider management of risks in society. I believe that a dangerous disconnect is forming between specialists (statisticians, mathematicians, econometricians, etc.) on the one hand, who are undoubtedly discovering more and more powerful statistical techniques, and policy makers, senior managers, and politicians on the other, who are ill-equipped to understand when, and how, and to what extent these sophisticated techniques should be used and relied upon.

Unfortunately, the mathematicians love and know a lot about mathematics but understand the financial and social topics their techniques are applied to less deeply. The senior managers, the politicians, and the policy makers know the "social" issues well, but are likely to understand the mathematics used to tackle them even less than the statisticians know the underlying problems. It does not help that quantitative analysts, for once granted large budgets to pursue the research projects they adore, are an unlikely source of dissent in this process. The senior managers and politicians who have allotted these large budgets are understandably impatient regarding subtleties and qualifications and simply want the "magic answers" they have been promised.

To understand how things have gone so wrong, we must look more carefully at how data interact with statistical models to produce answers. And we must understand very clearly that radically different types of probabilistic question can be asked in the risk-management arena. Each type of question can be meaningful, but only in the right context and under the right conditions. It is for this reason that in chapters 2 and 3 I tried to clear the probabilistic deck before beginning to deal with the financial problems in this chapter. I will now try to bring the two strands together.

CHAPTER 7

LOOKING BENEATH THE SURFACE: HIDDEN PROBLEMS

Mammon. You are incredulous.
Surly.   Faith, I have a humour
          I would not willingly be gull'd.

Ben Jonson, *The Alchemist* (2.1),
much the way I feel about all models.

SMART BUT NOT WISE

Despite the fact that the tone of this book has been kept as discursive and breezy as possible, in order to appreciate some of the weaknesses of a naive statistical approach to risk management it is necessary to take at least a peak under the bonnet. As we have seen, the basic idea behind VaR is very simple and appealing. "Just" assign a probability, it says, to each possible monetary outcome from your portfolio and examine some important features (often some rather high percentile) of the resulting distribution curve. This seems to make a lot of sense: since looking at a high percentile means looking at events that occur rarely, by so doing risk managers will be taking into due account those rare adverse events they are paid to worry about. If one looks at VaR in this light, it is difficult to see what could be wrong with it. What could be more desirable than having a tool that allows us to compare on an equal footing the financial risk arising from disparate risk factors and that does so by taking into account the complex codependence among them? An index that, to boot, expresses financial risk in the most natural metric of all, i.e., money?

For many applications VaR is indeed a very valuable tool. It does suffer from some technical problems,[1] but these are relatively easy to fix. Unfortunately, the appeal of this tool is so obvious and intuitive that we are naturally brought to use it in situations where it may no longer make much sense. By doing so one quickly moves by deceptively small steps from problems that are relatively well-posed to applications that are only superficially similar and for which the VaR question (let alone the answer) can be close to meaningless. This little-step-by-little-step transformation towards meaninglessness is not the prerogative of VaR. As Miller and Page* point out:

> Often, tools get mistaken for theories with unfortunate consequences; elaborate computer programs ... or mathematical derivations are occasionally assumed to make a real scientific statement, regardless of their scientific underpinnings. Indeed, entire literatures have undergone successive refinements and degradations, during each generation of which the original theoretical notions ... are crowded out by an increasing focus on tool adeptness. This often results in science that is "smart but not wise."

I strongly believe that these statements, made in a very different context, apply almost verbatim to VaR. We must therefore turn our attention not so much to the nitty-gritty technical details of VaR implementations, but to the very way we look at the quantitative management of financial risk.

In order to understand the nature of the conceptual problems we face I will first present a weather-related example that every reader should be familiar with. The remaining sections of the chapter then go into greater technical detail. They may have a more limited appeal for the generalist reader, who may therefore want to rejoin the discussion in chapter 8.

---

*J. H. Miller and S. E. Page (2007), *Complex Adaptive Systems* (Princeton University Press).

DEALING WITH THE RELEVANT PAST

The starting point of any analysis based on the application of statistical techniques to prediction is that the future should "look like" the past.* This statement need not be interpreted in a naive sense: it does not mean that the future should be *identical* to the past—indeed, the future may look like the past in very complex and subtle ways. However, if we do not have any confidence that past events have some relevance to what will occur in the future there is no point in trying to predict future events by using statistical analysis.

This obvious and seemingly innocuous statement can be given a bit more bite by requiring that the future should look like the *relevant* past. This statement may also sound rather uncontroversial. However, it has implications that are not totally obvious and that are at the heart of much of the discussion developed in the following chapters. I will therefore try to illustrate what I mean by "relevant past" using an example (predicting the weather) that readers should find familiar and intuitive.

Let us suppose that we have been asked to make a prediction about the temperature change from one day to the next. To make the setting more realistic, let us add that we have been asked this question by an energy company. The reason the company needs to know about temperature changes is that it wants to make sure that the increase in electricity demand will not be such as to put an unbearable stress on its distribution network. However, it has not told us (yet) what motivates its inquiry and it has not even phrased the question in very precise terms. The company has simple asked us about "changes in temperature from one day to the next." How would we go about answering this question?

---

*Of course, statistics has applications much wider than prediction: it can be used, for instance, to give us a succinct description of the salient quantitative features of a given state of affairs (say, the incidence of a given illness in a population, or the frequency of murders in the Victorian period, etc.). The applications of statistics that we are going to be concerned with in this book, however, relate to the use of statistics in order to make predictions about what will happen in the future. Hence the requirement that the future should "look like" the past.

To make things simple, let us say that we happen to be in a statistically blessed (and rare) position in that we have daily temperature readings collected by thousands of weather stations around the world. These temperature records go back many decades, and for some weather stations perhaps a century or more. If we are told nothing about the geographical focus of the question and about the reason it has been asked, we may use all of the available data (some collected from the weather station in Anchorage, some from the weather station in Timbuktu). We may use these data to calculate, say, the average of the daily temperature changes, their standard deviation, their probability distribution, and all sorts of marvelous descriptive statistics.

We can do a bit better: we may want, for instance, to follow a slightly fancier methodology, by weighting the data according to the density of weather stations: if we have four in the area around Boston and one covering half of Siberia, a simple average would tend to give an answer "where the light is" (i.e., under the proverbial lamppost) rather than where it truly lies. However, ultimately, there is not much more that we can do, unless we ask the energy company what geographical location the prediction is supposed to relate to. We do so and we are told that the area is Brewster, on Cape Cod, Massachusetts.

With this piece of information the relevance of our raw data immediately changes. We can safely disregard the Anchorage and Timbuktu readings and concentrate our attention on New England data. Note, however, that even if we had plentiful past weather reports collected exactly on Cape Cod we may not want to keep only the Cape Cod data. Perhaps we have better-quality data for Boston. Perhaps data collected for Long Island are also relevant since, despite being some 200 miles further south, Long Island shares some important geographical features with Cape Cod. More about this later.

The next reasonable question we may want to pose to the energy company is what time of year the prediction is supposed to relate to. We are told that the company's interest is in the temperature change between today and tomorrow. Today is July 1. This new piece of information, beside injecting a certain urgency into our investigation, also has the potential to make our prediction much more accurate: it is clear that we should scan our data looking for temperature changes that occurred in similar geographical locations and at "similar" times of the year. Unfortunately, the very information that improves the specificity of the data also dramatically reduces their quantity: temperature changes in December (and April, and October) all of a sudden have a much smaller bearing on our prediction than changes in June, July, and August. Roughly speaking, at a stroke we have cut our database by a factor of roughly four.

We are experienced meteorologists, however, and we have worked for years in weather prediction. In the course of our studies, we have devised an ingenious weather-simulation computer program, based on a much-praised theoretical model. Using the output of this model we know that on warm, dull, cloudy summer days the temperature variation is much more muted than on clear, bright summer days. So, we look out of the window, realize that it is a warm, dull, cloudy day and begin to sieve our data to look for temperature changes that occurred in the past around similarly warm, dull, cloudy days.

Once again, this is both good and bad news. On the one hand, ascertaining what initial weather conditions the prediction relates to has increased our potential predictive ability by allowing us to focus on more and more relevant data. But on the other hand, it has also reduced the amount of pertinent data, or, at least, has given different importance to the already geographically and seasonally restricted data set we are left with. In the light of our model, temperature changes that occurred in New England during clear, bright summer days belong to a somewhat different class and have therefore become less relevant.

A last twist in the story: the energy company now tells us that it is only interested in *exceptional* temperature changes because it wants to make sure that the distribution network will be able to cope with the extra load from air conditioners (remember the story about kettles being boiled on p. 12). This gives a new complexion to the problem. If *exceptional* temperature changes are what the energy company is interested in, we should probably look at those past (warm, dull, and cloudy) summer days when the weather changed dramatically. *These* are the relevant data. This is a relatively small subset of the already substantially culled New England summer data records pertaining to warm, dull, cloudy days. We started from tens of thousands of records (the totally unfiltered temperature readings collected all over the world) and, by a process of successive refinement, we are left with a few dozen highly "relevant" data points.

The example could be further embellished, but one important feature of the process should already have become apparent. By focusing our attention on more and more specific subsets of our data set we have achieved two opposing results. On the one hand, we have data that are more and more relevant, with the potential to produce correspondingly more relevant predictions. On the other hand, the amount of data we can rest our analysis upon has become more and more limited. There is a trade-off between the increase in accuracy coming from learning more precisely what the relevant conditions are and the loss of estimation power arising from the progressive loss of pertinent data.

There is more to the process sketched above than a simple progressive reduction of our data set. At one point in the story, for instance, we invoked the fact that we were "expert meteorologists." We made use of this skill to inject an exogenous informational content into our data. We did so when we said that temperature changes over warm, dull, cloudy days were "special" and belonged to a class of their own. Note that this piece of information did not come from "inside" our data and relied on the validity of an external model. If our model had been faulty, not only would we have thrown away useful data, thereby reducing the estimation power of our statistical tests, we would also have given the wrong weights to the residual data. The degree of confidence in our model (our "prior belief") therefore clearly plays a crucial role in the process. But this raises the question of where this confidence came from. Presumably, from *other* data, *other* information, *other* models, not from the same data we are analyzing now. We cannot pull ourselves up by our own bootstraps.

Another important observation is that "using pertinent information" does not simply mean throwing away all the past information that does not conform to a given pattern. The process is far more nuanced: is the information "contained" in the temperature change on a warm, dull, cloudy day *on Long Island* more or less relevant than the informational content of the temperature change on a bright, sunny day *on Cape Cod*? And how many miles of geographical proximity in our historical records should we trade off against closeness in time of the year? The important point is again that the answer to these questions is not "in the data" but relies on an external model of how the phenomenon at hand (in this case the weather) works.*

FROM THE WEATHER TO FINANCE

What is the relevance of this rather long weather excursus for the statistical modeling of financial time series? The parallel is actually very strong. Let us see why this is the case.

Financial risk managers attempt to predict the likelihood of changes in those financial quantities (the risk factors) that affect the value of the positions held by a financial institution. They may do so for strategic reasons (to assess whether a certain strategy offers a good trade-off between its expected return and the uncertainty in this return, for instance). More commonly, though, they will try to make predictions for prudential purposes: they want to make sure that a given strategy, however good it may look *ex ante*, will not bring about unacceptable losses if events do not unfold according to plan A (or B).

When they employ statistical tools to make their predictions, risk managers also enforce the assumption that the future will look

---

*Note that this "external model" may well have been, in turn, validated by statistical means. This is, however, a distinct application of statistics, and in the case of the weather prediction it is a sort of meta-statistical analysis.

like the relevant past. This could be done explicitly, by selectively using sections of past historical data according to their relevance to today's conditions. More commonly, risk managers will do so implicitly, by limiting the data set used for their statistical analysis to the relatively recent past (which, just by virtue of it being recent, is therefore assumed to be automatically representative of current conditions). The first approach is often used in credit-risk modeling* and the second in market-risk analysis, but the boundaries are fluid. In either case, looking at the relevant past makes the data more useful for prediction purposes, but reduces the amount of available data.

This mundane observation has an important consequence: if we want to ask "fancy" statistical questions (such as what happens far out in the tails of a probability distribution), the second possibility, i.e., just looking at recent data, is only an option if the frequency of data collection is very high. The interaction between the timescales of information-gathering and the prediction horizon may well be subtle, but, broadly speaking, the upshot is rather intuitive: if the data points are collected with a yearly frequency, by the time we have gathered enough data to allow a robust statistical estimation of the 99th percentile *of yearly changes* the first observations may no longer be relevant to the current state of the world. Whether it is or not depends on the problem at hand, not on our needs.

If we do not (or cannot) simply rely on gathering a lot of frequent and recent data, we must trawl our data set in search of relevant "patches" of past. This approach is not without its problems either, however. As in the weather example, in financial applications the selection of what constitutes the relevant past is not objective, relying as it does on our confidence in the validity of an external model—a model, that is, that tells us what portions of the past are, indeed, relevant.

I cannot stress enough the importance of the fact that what constitutes the relevant past is not "contained in the data" but comes

---

*For instance, when risk managers estimate current default rates using data that pertain to a "similar" phase of the business cycle.

from what I have called an "external model." To clarify this point, let me make a concrete financial example. Interest rates, especially short-term ones, are clearly affected by monetary authorities (in the United States, by the Federal Reserve). The actions of the Fed are in turn affected by the state of the economy: during inflationary periods, central bankers tend to increase rates to dampen demand, borrowing, and investment; during recessions, they tend to cut rates to achieve the opposite effects. In the third quarter of 2001 the U.S. economy entered a mild recession. Suppose that in the third quarter of 2001 you were required to predict what changes the Fed would make to short-term interest rates. To guide your prediction you may reasonably want to look at changes in rates that happened in the past at the beginning of a recession. So far, so logical. The 2001 recession, however, was atypical: it was the first postwar recession that had appeared without a rise in inflation and without the Fed having already hiked rates to bring it under control. All the previous postwar recessions in the United States had, in a way, been engineered by the Fed by "taking away the punch bowl just when the party got going." But throughout 2001 the Fed had been aggressively *cutting* rates. Are past data about rate changes associated with the "usual" (i.e., inflation-associated) recessions pertinent to the 2001 situation? Or are past data associated with low-inflation environments more useful for prediction purposes? Only an "external" model of the economy can provide the answer to this question. The data do not neutrally and objectively contain the information necessary to make this call. Choosing one model over another will give a radically different weight to the available information, and change our prediction every bit as radically. So, there is more to the sampling of the relevant past than a simple reduction in the number of available data points. There is also an assumption, implicit or explicit, about what constitutes relevance.

Another point of similarity between the weather story and financial reality is that, in their prudential rather than strategic mode, risk managers have to concern themselves with rather exceptional events. In technical parlance, they have to estimate high percentiles (the so-called tails) of the loss distribution. How can they do so? This is what I look at in the rest of this chapter.

HOW STATISTICIANS LOOK AT RARE EVENTS

Basically, there are three ways of building a probability distribution for some financial random variable (such as, for instance, the profits and losses made by a bank's portfolio) from past data and of analyzing financial events that occur "rarely." I examine them in turn.

Nonparametric (Historical-Simulation) Approaches

The safest method—safest because it relies on the smallest number of assumptions—is to embrace what is referred to as the historical-simulation method.[2] The idea is disarmingly simple. Let us consider a single market position that depends on a single risk factor. To fix ideas, we can think of a (long) position in the S&P equity index: we make money if the S&P index goes up and we lose money if it falls. Nothing could be simpler. We have at our disposal a long history of daily historical changes in this equity index. We want to estimate the likely magnitude of a very large loss for this position. In statistical terms, we want to estimate a high percentile of the daily loss distribution. How should we go about doing this?

As a first step we apply these past changes to our current position, i.e., we calculate the hypothetical profits and losses that would have been incurred if those past daily equity index changes occurred today (given our current position). We then rank the resulting profits and losses from the worst (most negative) to the best (most positive). Suppose that we had 1,000 observations of changes in the S&P index and, therefore, 1,000 ranked hypothetical profits and losses. Let us take the tenth worst hypothetical outcome, and let us assume that it was, say, −$20,000,000. We have 990 better (more favorable) outcomes and 9 worse outcomes. By definition, we have just built the 99th percentile.* What does this number tell us about the magnitude of the profit or loss that our position will make over the next move in the index? If the past is a good guide to the future, i.e., if the 1,000 recorded price changes are indeed representative of what I can expect tomorrow, the answer is simple: it is intuitively plausible to say (and can be justified under reasonable assumptions) that there is only a 1% chance (10/1,000) that the next move in the S&P index will bring about a loss greater than or equal to $20,000,000. This is just the VaR number we were looking for.

There are two important observations about this approach. The first is that we made very, very few assumptions about the distribution of the losses: we simply constructed it "brute force" from the available data and read the desired percentile off a long list of numbers. For better or for worse, in the whole procedure there seemed to be no "free parameters" to fit.† The second observation is that, with the available 1,000 data points, we could, at the very best, attempt to answer questions about the 99.9th percentile (i.e., the once-in-a-thousand-days event): to do so, we would just look at the worst outcome. But, given our data series, there is nothing worse than the 1,000th worst outcome, and, therefore, a question about the 99.99th percentile (i.e., the once-in-ten-thousand-days event) is, *with the purely nonparametric, historical-simulation approach*, meaningless. As usual, there exists a bagful of statistical tricks to get around this problem, but to deploy them we have to introduce a lot of assumptions that, up to this point, we had not been forced to make.

In short: the historical-simulation method is "dumb" but safe. It is, statistically speaking, the least powerful of methods, but it keeps us honest about what we can, and cannot, speak about.

*To be more precise, we have just constructed from our sample an estimate of the true 99th percentile of the population.

†As already mentioned, the parameter-free nature of the procedure is actually deceptive. The length of the data window is an extremely important parameter that determines, in an all-or-nothing, binary manner, which data we consider fully relevant or totally irrelevant.

The Empirical Fitting Approach

With the second approach we take a slightly more sophisticated route to constructing a distribution of profits and losses: we assume that this function is a member of one of the many families of distribution functions one finds in statistics books (the Gaussian, the Student's *t*, the Weibull, the Levy, the Pareto, you name it). Each member of these families will be identified by fixing a small number of parameters. For instance, in the case of the Gaussian distribution, there are only two parameters: its mean and its variance. Once these two parameters are fixed the specific member of the Gaussian family is uniquely pinned down.

How do we choose one particular family of distribution functions? Typically, this is done on the basis of an empirical fit to the available market data. There are standard statistical tests that can help us in deciding whether it is at all likely that the data we have collected might plausibly have been drawn from, say, a Gaussian, a Student's *t*, or a Levy distribution.

Again, there are two important things to note. The first is that, in this modus operandi, the main reason for choosing a given family of distributions is not theoretical, but purely empirical: our justification for choosing a Gaussian, a Student's *t*, or a Levy distribution is that, after choosing the best parameters for that family, the fit "looks good" (where the expression "looks good" may well be given a sufficiently sophisticated statistical meaning).

The second observation is more subtle. Once the particular distribution function has been chosen and its parameters estimated on the basis of the empirical evidence, we can, in principle, make statements about arbitrarily high percentiles—more simply stated, we can look as far out in the tails as we want. In this respect this approach appears to be much more powerful than the historical-simulation, nonparametric method described above. However, we are not quite getting something for nothing. Suppose that the most extreme observed point in our data

set corresponds to, say, the 95th percentile of the fitted distribution. *After the fitting*, we may well feel emboldened to make statements about a hypothetical point that would correspond to the
99th, the 99.9th, or perhaps even the 99.99th percentile. We must
bear in mind, however, that we have not seen, in our data set,
any point corresponding to such an extreme event. Even if the
available points lie very nicely on the estimated curve, we have
no guarantee that extra points, which we have not collected yet,
would eventually settle just as nicely on the outer tails of our
distribution.

If, as in the historical-simulation example, we had collected
1,000 points, roughly speaking these will give us information
about the shape of the unknown "true" distribution out to the
99.9th percentile. But, you may say, perhaps we were lucky, and
in the first 1,000 events we happen to have recorded a truly exceptional one, a perfect-storm kind of event. Would this not help?
Unfortunately it would not, because, just using the data at our
disposal, we cannot tell that this is, say, a one-in-a-million event.
Its presence simply makes us misestimate the parameters (typically, the variance, but probably in this case also the kurtosis)
of a distribution that "should not" contain such a point in 1,000
draws.

What is happening here can be understood very easily if we
think of the contrived but simple case where we have collected
only two observations. Since we can estimate the mean and variance of the population from these two observations, these two
estimates are just enough to fit (uniquely) a Gaussian distribution. And, by construction, the data (i.e., the two data points) "fit"
the chosen distribution perfectly. Once this "fit" has been carried
out we can then make bold claims about events that may happen
only once in 10,000,000 draws. The fact remains, though, that we
have collected only two observations and that, therefore, when we
make statements about events that occur much more rarely than
once every other draw we are fundamentally in a state of sin.
Again, what if one of our two observed data points were a truly
exceptional one (a "six-sigma event," to use a management-speak

expression)? Unfortunately, we would have no way of knowing that this was the case by collecting just two observations—its exceptionality would only become apparent after collecting thousands or tens of thousands of data points and noticing that none of these "later" events even came close to the first (or second). As things stand, i.e., with two observations of which one is "freakish," we are simply led to misestimating the mean and variance of our Gaussian distribution. (Our problems would begin to appear, however, as soon as we collect our third data point.)

The Fundamental Fitting Approach

The third approach to creating a profit-and-loss distribution is different again. Recall that the first (the historical-simulation method) was (almost) nonparametric, and, as it was described, appeared to be a statistical embodiment of the Newtonian dictum *hypotheses non fingo*. The second approach was, in spirit, essentially empirical. We had no a priori reason to prefer one distribution over another, but we examined with an open mind several candidates, exploring whether, after varying their parameters in the best possible way, the observed points happened to sit more nicely (in a statistical sense) on one curve or on the other. The important thing to remember is that we had no fundamental reason to prefer one distribution over another, apart from the quality of fit.

The third approach is more ambitious. It starts from a model of how reality *should* behave. Given this model, it derives what the distribution of losses (or of whatever other quantity the model makes statements about) *should* look like. This is the approach often used in the "hard" physical sciences: a model is created to account for some observable phenomenon and its consequences are extrapolated to situations never encountered before. This approach has been spectacularly successful in quantum mechanics. After quantum theory was formulated, amazing and surprising statistical predictions were made about the outcomes of probabilistic experiments involving very small particles. These predictions then turned out to be spectacularly accurate.*

Roughly speaking, the hallmark of a successful theory in physics is how far it can predict phenomena it has not been designed to account for (or "fitted to," in science-speak). The prediction need not be deterministic. As in the case of quantum mechanics, the theory can simply predict the type of uncertainty that a phenomenon "allows." More generally, if we have an *external* model (recall the temperature-prediction example here) that tells us how certain, possibly stochastic, phenomena behave, we can often say something very precise about the nature of their distribution. The emphasis is on the word "external": for this fundamental approach to make sense we cannot solely rely on the data we are now examining to gain confidence in the model. Once again, we cannot pull ourselves up by our own bootstraps.

Some examples may clarify the thought process behind the fundamental approach. For instance, if we *truly* know that the occurrence of some rare event is totally independent of whether the last event has happened five minutes or five years ago, and that two events can never happen at exactly the same time, we can derive that the number of events in any time interval of length t follows a particular distribution (called the Poisson distribution). Or, if we *truly* know that a particle suspended on the surface of a liquid solution is buffeted by minute random shocks of a certain nature, then we know that the probability of finding the particle a distance d from where it was when we first looked at it follows a two-dimensional Gaussian distribution. Or, to give a more financial example, if we *truly* know that price returns are exactly independent, then we can show that, irrespective of the distribution of

---

*For readers familiar with physics, I am not just referring here to the well-know slit interference experiments (to which, one could claim, the theory had been "calibrated" in the first place), but, for instance, to the probabilistic predictions of Bell's theorem and to their relevance in the context of the completeness and locality of quantum mechanics.

the individual price moves, the magnitude of large drawdowns*
follows just as exactly an exponential distribution.

The repeated emphasis on the adverb "truly" was not without a purpose. Very often we can assume that certain phenomena can be approximated by a certain model: perhaps returns are
"almost" independent; perhaps, as a first approximation, it is useful to regard a stock price as a suspended particle buffeted by random informational shocks; perhaps we are not too far off the mark
if we assume that the probability of occurrence of rare financial
events (say, a major equity market crash) can be assumed to be
independent of how recently one such rare event occurred. The
art of modeling boils down to finding the simplest description of
a complex phenomenon that still captures those features we are
interested in. This practice is by no means limited to the social
sciences: physics is full of frictionless balls, uniformly smeared
electrons, perfectly rigid bodies, etc. Nor should such an approximate treatment of reality be necessarily considered "inferior."
Few things are more rewarding for a scientist than finding an
outrageously simple model that does an outrageously good job
at describing a complex phenomenon. When we use a model in
this manner, however, it is never clear "how far we can push it":
the particle-in-a-suspension picture of a stock price may give us a
useful indication of the shape of the return distribution around its
center, but can we really trust it far out in the tails? (By the way, the
empirical answer is "no.") The assumption of independence in the
returns is good enough to produce a distribution of consecutive
losses† well described, *around its center*, by an exponential distribution. But are the extreme tails of the distribution described as
correctly? (Again, empirical observation tells us that this distribution no longer does a good job at accounting for the probability of

---

*Given a financial time series, a drawdown is the fall in price between a local
maximum and the next local minimum. Roughly speaking, the distribution of
drawdowns conveys information about the magnitudes of uninterrupted price
falls and their probabilities.

†With the term "consecutive losses" I am referring here to drawdowns
defined in the previous footnote.

exceptionally large consecutive losses.) The extrapolation to *arbi-trary* tails of the distribution (the murky areas required to make statements about the 99.9th percentile and beyond) requires the model to be *exactly* true. If we believe that the laws of quantum mechanics hold exactly (not as an approximation), the (probabilistic) predictions about the results of the double-slit experiment are not only true if we look "at the center of the distribution": they are "exactly" true even if we let billions of photons go through the two slits and predict the subtlest statistical effect.

One may say that such "exact" theories are perhaps only met in the hard physical sciences (if at all), and, for that matter, only in the purest and most fundamental subdisciplines of physics. The hope of us truly knowing the constitutive equations of motion of phenomena as "messy" and complex as those found in the social and economic sciences seems to be far too remote. Perhaps we are bound, or doomed, to using models as convenient approximations (useful crutches) that can only take us some of the way in our analysis. If this is the case, models have certainly helped us in our analysis of "common" instances of the phenomenon at hand, but we cannot extrapolate from a relatively small number of observations to the behavior under exceptional circumstances of whatever we are looking at. Once again, it seems that, with imperfect models, 1,000 observations only give us information about events that do not occur much more rarely than once in a thousand observations.

There may be some hope, though. It goes under the name of the most-often-quoted theorem in statistics, namely the Central Limit Theorem. It is so important, and its relevance for the management of the risk associated with rare financial events is so great, that I devote a whole section (immediately below) to a nontechnical discussion of what it "really" says. Before doing that, however, there is a beautiful magic trick often invoked to solve all these problems. The trick is called Monte Carlo simulation and more sins have probably been committed in its name than Dante managed to cram into his *Inferno*. The discussion in the next subsection is marginally more technical, simply because it presupposes that you have at least a rough idea of what a Monte Carlo simulation does. Explaining this technique from scratch would entail too long a detour for this book and the following subsection can therefore be skipped if you are not interested in numerical techniques *or if it has never crossed your mind to solve the data problems discussed above using Monte Carlo simulations.*

Beautiful Monte Carlo

The first and most important thing to understand about Monte Carlo is that it is a numerical technique, not a model. It can be used to get answers (typically, numbers) out of a variety of models—and, indeed, the more complex and the "richer" the model, the more likely it is that the Monte Carlo technique will be used to get some answers out if it. Whoever uses the expression "Monte Carlo model," however, is in a state of confusion. And if you ever read in the glossy brochure of a software vendor that he will solve all your problems thanks to a "sophisticated Monte Carlo *model*," make sure to bin the promotional literature straight away.

Without going into detail, what one can say is that Monte Carlo is a very efficient technique for sampling high-dimensional probability densities (the higher the number of dimensions, the more comparatively efficient the technique becomes). When we are dealing with more than three or four variables, Monte Carlo sampling is almost invariably more efficient than any other numerical technique known to man. The reason why this has become so useful for problems that involve several variables is that it does not suffer from the so-called "curse of dimensionality," but, as mentioned before, explaining what this means does not really belong in this book.

Why has Monte Carlo been invoked as a panacea for solving the problems discussed above of determining the tails of a distribution when we have insufficient or scarce data? Because it can produce as many draws as we wish from a given, prespecified distribution. From real life, we may only have, say, 1,000 data points, but, if we are patient enough, we can generate 10,000, 100,000, or zillions of "synthetic" data points using a Monte Carlo simulation. Surely this wealth of data will contain all the information we need to estimate the extreme properties of our distribution?

It depends. If we have strong a priori reasons to believe that the distribution we are interested in is of a particular type and that we exactly know what its parameters are, then Monte Carlo simulations can indeed be a very powerful tool to sample the tails of this distribution. But what do I mean by "a priori reasons"? I mean that, for the Monte Carlo technique to work its magic and really give me something that was not in the data already, I must have fundamental, a priori (i.e., "pre-data") reasons to believe that the distribution to be sampled is of a particular type (say, a Gaussian, or a Student's t, or whatever). In addition, I must also believe that I know to the required degree of accuracy the parameters of this chosen distribution. If indeed I am blessed with such "fundamental" knowledge, the Monte Carlo technique will give me probabilistic information, given time, patience, and computing power, about events as far out in the tails as I may wish. In this respect, however, I am in the same situation as with the fundamental approach, where the information about the true distribution was coming from "outside the data" (for instance, from my knowledge of the true market microstructure dynamics and of its governing equations, or form my knowledge of the weather on Cape Cod).

In more common situations, however, such a priori information is not available or is of dubious validity (especially in the tails). What we do have is a finite number of actual data points, painstakingly collected in the real world. On the basis of these data points I can choose an acceptable distribution and its most likely parameters given the data (i.e., I can follow the prescriptions of the empirical approach discussed above). This approach may well do a good job at describing the body of the distribution (where the points I have collected are plentiful); but, when it comes to the rare events that the timorous risk manager is concerned about, the precision in determining the shape of the tails is ultimately dictated, again, by the quantity and quality of my real data. *Once I have decided* from the real data that the best guess for the true underlying distribution is, say, a Gaussian with a mean of 0.875 and a standard deviation of 2.345, the Monte Carlo technique will allow me to sample the 99.9th, the 99.99th and, if I so desired, the 99.99998th percentile of *this* distribution* by creating zillions of synthetic data points. But the Monte Carlo technique will do very little to increase my confidence (over and above what the analysis with the *real* data had suggested) that a Gaussian was indeed the right distribution to use and that its parameters were truly 0.875 and 2.345. The resolving power to choose, *as far as the tails are concerned*, a Gaussian over a Student's *t* or a chi-squared distribution ultimately comes from the real data, not from the synthetic (Monte Carlo generated) points. If you have always been convinced of this, I have wasted your time. However, statements like the following give me some cause for concern:

> Moody's views a simulation approach … as a best practice approach. Other approaches extend VaR calculations parametrically to "tail" levels between 99.85% and 99.97%. These bring with them the same issues as for VaR—particularly the problems arising from the normal distribution assumption.

Moody's Investor Services, Risk Management Assessment (April 2005)

This statement can be interpreted in many ways—some perfectly correct, others slightly worrying. Let us not quibble about the fact that VaR does not necessarily mean VaR-calculated-using-the-normal-distribution-assumption. Let us also leave aside, at least for the moment, the issue of whether a 99.97th percentile can be meaningfully estimated at all. Let us suppose that we have to try and do our best and come up with an estimate of these percentiles. Moody's report mentions "other approaches" that try to extend the estimate to these far out tails. It expresses understandable concerns about these parametric methods, but appears (at

---

*This example is clearly contrived: if the true distribution were indeed Gaussian, I would not need Monte Carlo to sample it.

least to me) to regard simulations as a possible way out of the impasse. If the underlying parametric model is not sound and trustworthy, a Monte Carlo simulation will only allow the very precise calculation of an incorrect percentile. There is no modeling content in Monte Carlo or other simulation techniques. But perhaps, that is not what Moody's meant at all.

In short, if you have been captivated in the past by statements like, "In order to estimate percentiles higher than those directly possible from the data, we are going to use the Monte Carlo method," I hope you will look closely under *that* bonnet and see whether the hopeful risk manager is promising something for nothing. If not, please continue reading without any worries.

THE CENTRAL LIMIT THEOREM: ARE ALL CATS REALLY BLACK IN THE NIGHT?

As promised, there is still one reason to be hopeful that a fundamental approach may be possible and that, therefore, via Monte Carlo or by other methods, we may be able to explore what happens out in the far tails of a distribution. This hope rests on a beautiful theorem in statistics, known as the Central Limit Theorem, that roughly (and the devil is in this "roughly") states the following. Draw many times a random variable with a numerical outcome. To fix ideas, the random variable could be the height of a person randomly chosen in a given population; the time a radioactive particle takes to decay; the move in the price of a financial index; etc. We are going to stipulate two important features of these draws: that they should all be from the same probability distribution; and that they should be independent. Other than this, this identical distribution can be anything at all;* certainly, it need not be the normal distribution.

---

*The statement is too sweeping. There are other, more technical, conditions for the theorem to hold. The most important, at least for the standard version of the Central limit Theorem, is that the underlying distribution should have a well-defined second moment.

What do these two requirements mean? The independence requirement stipulates that the outcome of one draw should be unaffected by the outcomes of the previous draws and that, in turn, it should not affect the outcomes of the draws to follow. To stick with one of the examples above, the independence of draws means, for instance, that if I have randomly sampled the height of an individual, I will not then go on and sample the height of his seven sisters (who all happen to play for the local basketball team). The sisters may indeed end up being drawn, but with no greater likelihood than any other person in the population.

As for the requirement that all the draws should be from the same distribution, this means that I will not begin to draw from a population of basketball players and then switch to a population of professional jockeys (although drawing from the same mixed population of basketball players and professional jockeys is fine).

Now let us construct a new random variable, i.e., the sum of a fixed number of outcomes of my original draws. In other words, let us just add up several of the numerical values I have collected and consider their sum as a random variable in its own right. For the sake of concreteness, let us consider the case when the height of people was indeed the random variable I was sampling and I collected 1,000 records of heights from a homogeneous population. I can add up ten consecutive heights, record the value of this sum, call, imaginatively, the new variable "sum of ten heights," and label the first sum as the first occurrence of this new variable. From the original 1,000 data points I can clearly construct 100 realizations of the variable "sum of ten heights."

Now, here is an interesting question. Recall that we said that the distribution of the *individual* heights could have been anything at all. What will the distribution of their sum (i.e., of the variable "sum of ten heights") be? It would seem that, if we did not know the distribution of the original variables, there will be little hope of being able to say something about the distribution of their sum. Not so. As more and more terms are added to the sum (of independent terms), the distribution of the sum will tend to the normal distribution, irrespective of the (identical) distribution of the

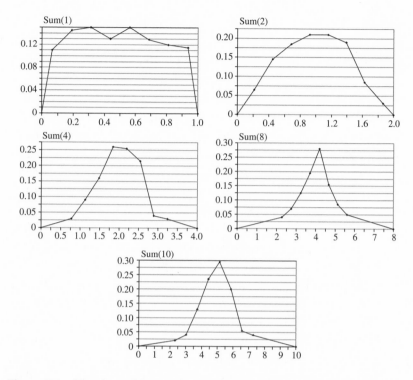

Figure 7.1. The Central Limit Theorem at work. The empirical distribution obtained with 200 realizations of the sum of 1, 2, 4, 8, and 10 uniform random variables. The theoretical distribution for a uniformly distributed random variable (a sum of one term) should be a rectangle. Notice how just eight terms produce a distribution that begins to "resemble" a Gaussian. Even four terms begin to produce a semblance of a bell curve, *especially around the center*. As far as the considerable numerical noise allows us to tell, note how the tails remain more problematic.

original variables. Figure 7.1 shows pictorially how the Central Limit Theorem works its magic. Note how the original distribution can be very different from the normal one, yet the distribution for the sum of the random variables "begins to look" Gaussian relatively soon.

The theorem is beautiful, and, to some extent, surprising. So beautiful is it, and so convenient, that it has been woefully overused. Why is it so convenient, and so relevant for the quantitative management of financial risk? Take financial returns—to fix our ideas, the change in price of a given stock. The individual (tick-size) returns may well be drawn from a very complex distribution, with skewness, excess kurtosis, and all sorts of statistical nasties. As we look at the returns over longer and longer periods, however, we are effectively adding more and more realizations of the same random variable, the "atomic" price move. If the aggregation time has not been so long that the characteristics of the generating mechanism that produces the "atomic" price moves has changed, we can hope that the returns have all been drawn from the same distribution. If we can also make the additional semi-heroic assumption of independence, the Central Limit Theorem then states that, as we add more and more elementary price shocks, the resulting sum (the cumulative price change) will look more and more like a normal variable. So, if what we are interested in are, say, weekly price moves and these are regarded as the sum of very many (probably thousands) of tick-size moves, the Central Limit Theorem tells us that the variable we are interested in (i.e., the variable "sum of thousands of mini price moves") will be almost exactly Gaussian. But, if this is the case, we know that just two numbers, the mean and the standard deviation, tell us everything there is to know about the *full* distribution of the sum. And if we know the full distribution, it seems that we can say all kinds of interesting things about the statistical properties of the cumulative price change. In particular, if we can justify from a fundamental point of view the choice of a given distribution (the Gaussian in this case), then we can make statements and predictions about the 99th, the 99.9th, the 99.999th, or any other percentile. If I have good reasons to believe that the individual returns are independent, the Central Limit Theorem therefore seems to offer just the fundamental justification for choosing the normal distribution that we are looking for, i.e., the tool we need to bridge our ignorance about the fundamental features of the market dynamics. The very complex microstructural features of real-life trading might produce a horribly complex distribution for the individual atomic price moves.

However, whoever has watched financial information trickle (and sometimes pour), one tick-size move after another, onto a computer screen knows that in an hour dozens of such minute price increments will be recorded. Therefore, as long as we are interested in the cumulative effect of "many" such moves, surely the daily (or, even better, weekly, or monthly) price moves, made up of the sum of very many such small moves, will have "almost-normal" distributions. Or will they?

Unfortunately, things do not work out quite so nicely. A first hint of the problem comes from a very simple recipe to generate random numbers (approximately) drawn from a normal distribution. The trick works as follows. Every computer (and even the ubiquitous Excel spreadsheet) provides a function, usually called something like RAND, that returns a random number drawn with equal probability between 0 and 1. Randomly drawing a number uniformly distributed between 0 and 1 can be visualized by imagining a ruler of length (in some units) exactly 1. Close your eyes and pick a point at random along this ruler. Record on a piece of paper the position of the point you have chosen—it will, of course, be a number between 0 and 1. As long as your eyes were properly shut and you really picked the point on the ruler at random, what you just did was to draw a sample from a uniform [0 1] distribution. Without using physical rulers, this is just what the function RAND does. Now, invoke this function twelve times, add together the uniformly distributed random numbers so obtained, and subtract the number 6. The result is a random variable that could, to a very decent approximation, have been drawn from a normal distribution of mean 0 and variance 1. Once again, the magic has been worked by the Central Limit Theorem. The original distribution (the uniform distribution between 0 and 1) does not look like a normal distribution at all, but when I add together enough terms, it does begin to look like one. The original (uniform) variables are all positive, so their sum must be positive as well. In order to get a mean of zero, I simply have to subtract $6 = 12 \times 0.5$ (0.5, of course, is the expectation of a [0 1]-uniformly distributed random variable). Why did we use twelve draws from a uniform distribution to start with? Because that is the number required to have a variance of 1 for the sum. It is so simple that it sounds too good to be true.

And, indeed, it is. We get a first hint of where the problem lies by looking at the tails of these almost-normal distributions. We know that a truly normal variable can assume, albeit with very different probabilities, all values from minus infinity to plus infinity. Yet, because of the way in which it was built our approximate normal variable will never produce an outcome larger than 6 or smaller than −6. By construction it just cannot. Suppose we have been exceedingly "lucky" and we have drawn twelve times from the underlying uniform distributions the highest possible number, i.e., 1. After adding these twelve freakish outcomes and subtracting 6, the highest number is $12 − 6 = 6$. The probability of obtaining a draw higher than 6 from a true normal distribution is indeed exceedingly small—and that is why the simple do-it-yourself recipe to construct a normal variable works remarkably well. But it is not zero. The Central Limit Theorem does an excellent job close to the center of the distribution. But, if we want to invoke it to gain information about what happens far out in the tails, that is just where it lets us down.

The problem, unfortunately, is fundamental and appears, to different extents, no matter what the distribution of the "atomic" draws is—the more different this distribution is from the normal, the more severe the problem will be. It is not that the Central Limit Theorem is wrong, it is that it is not very useful for the tails of a distribution. When it says that the distribution of the sum converges to the normal one, it says that the difference between the two distributions can be made smaller and smaller as more terms are added to the sum. Unfortunately, where the discrepancies tend to remain is just in the tails. Of course, for any *fixed* level of out-in-the-tailness (i.e., for any *fixed* percentile), I can always find a number of terms in the sum that is so large that the discrepancies between the approximate and the limit distribution become smaller than a given tolerance level. But, how large is large? The Central Limit Theorem does not answer this question, which depends on how different the original individual distribution is form the normal. If it was very close to normal to start with, very few terms may be enough even for a high percentile. (Indeed, if the original distribution happened to be normal, you need just one term in the sum for the distribution to already be correct all the way out to the highest percentiles.)

The statement above that for any given percentile level we can just add more terms can, of course, also be turned on its head, and can be expressed in a way that makes it sound much less encouraging. We can also say that, for any fixed number of terms in the sum, no matter how many, I can always find a percentile high enough that the approximation becomes unreliable.

But why can we not just add more and more terms to the sum? If we can, there is of course nothing wrong with this approach. But there are two problems, one obvious and one more subtle. The obvious problem is that, as we add more terms to the sum we reduce the number of new data points: in the example above, by adding up the height of ten individuals, at one stroke we "shrunk" our data set from 1,000 to 100. Well, it seems that we will just have to be patient and count for longer. Perhaps. Recall, though, that all the draws must be carried out from the *same* distribution (whatever it might be) for the Central Limit Theorem to hold (as we saw, switching from a population of basketball players to one of professional jockeys will not do). If I am not dealing with a presumably time-invariant physical phenomenon but with a social or economic phenomenon, the greater the time interval required to collect all the necessary atomic observations, the greater the danger that the world has, in the meantime, changed. And consequently, of course, so has the probability distribution of the phenomenon we are analyzing. When regulators blithely ask us to calculate the once-in-a-thousand-years worst credit event, it is not just a matter of collecting more data. It is a matter of where to find the relevant data. There may well be a chapter 11 in Geoffrey Chaucer's books, but there was certainly no Chapter 11 in Geoffrey Chaucer's times.

We started out with the hope of finding a way of looking significantly farther out in the tails than the number of observations at our disposal seems to allow. Everywhere we looked we found problems. We saw that a historical-simulation approach could not help us. We observed that empirical fitting of analytical distributions could not be relied upon in the very tails we wanted to explore. We discovered that a fundamental approach could not be trusted to be valid for exceptional events, when different generative mechanisms could be at play. We pinned our hopes on the Central Limit Theorem. If it had held for the applications we were interested in, we could have rescued the fundamental-approach enterprise simply by saying that the aggregate effect of many small individual shocks could behave in a (statistically) normal manner. Unfortunately, faith in our last hope was shaken by the observation that this beautiful theorem can let us down just where we needed it, i.e., in the tails. Indeed, I will show in a couple of pages' time, with some back-of-the-envelope calculations, if and when we have to worry. In the meantime, the important lesson that we have learned is that there is a subtle and unexpected interplay among how far out in the tail I want to look (the percentile), the number of observations I need to collect, the frequency with which data are collected, and the time invariance of the underlying phenomenon. We have not yet found a way of getting something for nothing.

DEALING WITH "ERRORS OF NATURE, SPORTS AND MONSTERS"

Errors of Nature, Sports and Monsters correct our understanding in regard to ordinary things, and reveal general forms.

Francis Bacon, *Novum Organum**

Whichever way we turn, we are faced, if not with an identical problem, at least with one that is very similar: it is as if nature

*Quoted in D. Sornette (2003), *Why Stock Markets Crash* (Princeton University Press).

allows us to examine rare events only at the price of collecting an amount of data commensurate with the rarity of the event itself.

At the margins, we can to some extent improve this state of affairs. Indeed, an entire branch of statistics (extreme value theory) is devoted to estimating what happens to a distribution in the far-out tails (i.e., to assessing the probability of exceedingly rare events). Its results are elegant and fascinating and some of its successes are certainly impressive.* Yet the small print requires careful reading for its results to hold. This caginess does not come from an application of the precautionary principle (of the we-don't-know-what-happens-out-there-so-we-shouldn't-do-anything-too-fancy type). There is hard evidence that, at least in finance, the world *is* fundamentally different in the tails: new regimes, new modes of interactions, different codependencies come into play.[3] Extrapolations, however clever, to exceptional regimes of well-understood behavior that prevails under the normal mode of operation are bound to land us in trouble just when we need them.

So we are left with the conclusion that whichever clever statistical trick we might turn to, the picture is not changed substantially. Unless we have a structural model that tells us how things *should* behave and that has been exogenously validated using data other than (and presumably more plentiful than) those we are examining, there is no escaping the consequences of a simple rule of thumb: if we collect 1,000 data points, we cannot say much about what happens much less frequently than once in a thousand observations.

Is this just a case of being patient, then, biting the bullet and collecting more observations? If we can do this, it will clearly help, but the other important constraint that we have discussed so far appears: the additional data set must be *relevant*. Sometimes we can try to get around this problem by collecting data more frequently: every hour instead of every day, or perhaps every minute.

*For a concise introduction to extreme value theory see, for example, A. McNeil, R. Frey, and P. Embrechts (2005), *Quantitative Risk Management* (Princeton University Press).

This costly and painful exercise, however, will only work in very special circumstances. If I am interested in, say, the distribution of intensities of hurricanes, I cannot "collect data more frequently": I will just have to wait for the next hurricane to arrive. This constraint applies, in general, to phenomena whose occurrence is intrinsically rare, or is, in any event, governed by a frequency beyond our control. The frequency of default of highly rated companies is obviously one example of great financial relevance. A "trick" around this waiting constraint might be to cast our net more widely and collect data from a larger population: perhaps not just hurricanes from the Gulf of Mexico, but also typhoons from the South Asia Seas and twisters from the Midwest; or, when it comes to companies defaulting, we might add highly rated European companies to a U.S.-based data set. But, once again, we must question whether the extra data are "relevant": does information about extremely violent hurricanes mainly gleaned from American ones allow us to make reliable predictions about the likelihood of a very strong hurricane in Hong Kong? Are large, highly rated companies "allowed" to go bust in Europe as readily as they are in the United States? Only an "external" model about hurricanes (or about what drives corporate defaults) will be able to answer these questions. And how did we validate *that* model? To an extent, if events occur at a given fixed rate that is beyond our control (like defaults of highly rated firms), and if they are generated by mechanisms that evolve with time, nature effectively draws a veil over the finer statistical properties of this phenomenon. Effectively, talking about a very high percentile of a phenomenon that cannot be sampled with arbitrarily high frequency and that is not time-stationary is tantamount to asking a metaphysical question, not an empirical one.

If we are in a hurry and cannot wait twenty years for an appropriate number of hurricanes to occur so that we can improve our data set, another alternative would be to go back into our archives to fill our data set backwards. But the usual nagging question has not gone away: are these data still relevant? Climate might be relatively stable over a considerable length of time, but the rarer (or finer) the effect we are interested in, the more small variations in the generating mechanism (the weather in this case) will affect our results. When it comes to hurricanes, of course, there is much ongoing debate at the moment as to whether an increase in sea temperature (as would be associated with global warming) has an effect on their intensity. The suggestion that this might be the case comes from (external) computer models of how hurricanes form. If these models are correct, even if we did have data about hurricanes collected by Captain Ahab while hunting for Moby Dick, it is not obvious that they would be all that relevant to today's conditions.

The picture gets darker. The more one thinks about it, the more absolutely-time-invariant phenomena appear to be the exception rather than the rule: from the perspective of an actuary working for an insurance company and assessing its liabilities in twenty or thirty years' time, longevity is clearly highly nonstationary. But many other characteristics of a population that one may assume to be virtually unchanging turn out to depend on the observation horizon once they are looked at with sufficient precision: the relative frequencies of male and female live births, for instance, has changed (and is changing) as prenatal screening techniques have become more widespread. Nor is the change in the male–female ratio the same in different countries where prenatal screening techniques are similarly widespread—so widening our data set by looking at synchronous data collected in different countries may not necessarily be useful.

Moving to longer timescales, the frequency of occurrence of earthquakes and their intensities are probably rather stable over human life spans—but they are certainly not so on geological scales.

Moving up another notch, the frequency of arrival of meteorites on the earth or the moon has probably not changed much over even longer timescales. However, the pitted surface of the moon indicates that things were a tad more "excited" during different astronomical ages of our solar system. Finally, theoretical physicists have to assume (and hope) that the nature of physical laws has remained unchanged since the first seconds after the Big Bang—but it is not self-evident that even this should be the case.

In short, faced with the task of making statistical predictions we cannot escape two fundamental limitations: first, for each phenomenon there is often a given intrinsic frequency of occurrence that cannot be altered, and which can only be circumvented by casting a wider and wider net (and thereby catching possibly "irrelevant" fish); second, there is always a maximum characteristic timescale over which the phenomenon can safely be considered to be self-similar and for which relevant data can therefore be collected. For any given level of required statistical "precision" these two factors together impose an upper limit on the quantity of relevant data that we can collect. This in turn roughly determines how far out in the tails we can safely look, because, as we saw, there is an inextricable link between the number of observations and the percentiles we can meaningfully access.

The similarity with the limitations of the Central Limit Theorem are striking: in that case we found that, for a *fixed* number of identically distributed and independent draws, there was always a percentile high enough that the normal approximation became too crude. Here we find that the number of useful observations is determined by the intrinsic frequency of data occurrence during the timescale over which the phenomenon can be considered to "remain the same." This creates an upper bound on the amount of relevant data we can even theoretically gather and, therefore, on how far out in the tails we can look.

MOVING TOGETHER (AND FAILING TO DO SO): CORRELATION AND CODEPENDENCE

So far we have looked at the difficulties in looking far out in the tails of the distribution of a single variable: the level of the S&P index, the temperature changes on Cape Cod, and so on. In the context of financial risk management the first distribution of this type that springs to mind is the profit-and-loss distribution. In some cases building a profit-and-loss distribution can be relatively easy. Indeed, if our "portfolio" is in effect a single long position (say, a long position in the S&P index), matters are conceptually very simple. In this case speaking of the distribution of profits and losses or of the distribution of the S&P index is almost the same thing—the two are linked by a simple proportionality constant.

But such a simplistic example is far too stylized to tell us much about the risk in the real portfolios of financial institutions, which will, in general, be influenced by tens of thousands of different risk factors. Recall that in chapter 6 we discussed the idea of creating a profit-and-loss distribution that "knew" about all the interactions between the various risk factors and the positions in our portfolio that were possibly highly nonlinear. In order to build this distribution we had to know (implicitly or explicitly) their *joint* distribution, i.e., we had to be able to assign a probability to every possible *combination* of realizations for the risk factors. Unsurprisingly, since we have tens of thousands of random variables that can affect market prices, the task is daunting to say the least. So daunting, in fact, that we may be tempted to take a completely different approach. Why not neglect all the thousands of underlying factors and their codependencies and simply regard the resulting profits and losses as the single random variable whose distribution we are going to study? The idea is appealing, but, unfortunately, it clashes head on with the constraints of self-similarity of the underlying generating mechanism. The problem is that, if we go down this route and consider the profits and losses made by a financial institution as the only relevant variable we are interested in, we are going to be faced with two sources of time dependence: one (which is unavoidable) is due to the fact that the distribution of the underlying risk factors (say, equity prices) may have changed over time; the other, which is almost "accidental" in nature, is due to the fact that the profit-and-loss profile of a given financial institution also depends on its trading style and on the regulatory constraints imposed upon it. The setting up of a new trading operation or simply the changing of the guard at the head of a trading desk can make different time segments of the profit-and-loss data qualitatively different. Suppose that, until yesterday, the head trader of Red Blood Capital used to run a double-or-nothing strategy. Whenever his positions showed a loss, he would double his positions waiting for the market to turn and to (more than) recoup his losses. When he finally ended up making money, he would cut down his position to zero. It is unlikely that such a trader would be around for long (the strategy he employs has, in probability theory, the endearing name "gambler's ruin"). Indeed, it so happens that just yesterday he agreed with senior management that he should spend more quality time with his family. But while he was in charge of trading, the monthly profit-and-loss distribution generated by his strategy was very skewed toward the left: the big (and bigger and bigger) losses are all there, but there are not very many large gains. Before employing the current head of trading, Red Blood Capital (at the time when it called itself Meek and Prudent Investments) had a different trading style: the then-head was a "momentum" trader, who kept on his positions as long as they were profitable, and would immediately cut them as soon as they showed a loss. Again, it is not difficult to guess the profit-and-loss distribution in the Meek and Prudent days: strongly skewed to the right, with lots of small wins and very few large losses. That was the distant and recent past. Today, after the refocusing of the life priorities of the Red Blood Capital head trader, the investment company has changed its name to Well Balanced Fund and now employs a trader who takes positions by tossing his favorite lucky coin. The profit-and-loss distribution generated by his trading model will look something like the famous bell curve.* Even if the risk-management function of Well Balanced Fund (aka Red Blood Capital, aka Meek and Prudent Investments) had kept a very long record of all the profits and losses made during the Red Blood Capital and Meek and Prudent Investments years, *and even if during these years the features of the market had not changed one bit*, the resulting historical profit-and-loss distribution would have

---

*At least as long as the underlying risk factors have a normal-like distribution—again, we are not going for realism here.

little or no predictive power about the future profits and losses of the Well Balanced Fund.

The point of this story is that there is something more "fundamental" and more stable in the behavior of prices than in the vagaries of trading styles. In reality, when we carry out the statistical analysis of a combination of financial positions, we strive to attribute the associated return and risk to two, completely different, sources: the rapidly varying (day by day) *sensitivities* to market risk factors (that come from the positions we have chosen and the trading styles); and the market risk factors themselves. Given today's positions, and for a given change in the market risk factors, the link between these changes and the profits and losses may be complex but it is fully deterministic. We do not need (and do not want) to pollute our statistical analysis, which is difficult enough as it is, with the fickle source of avoidable noise coming from the changing whims of the traders. The underlying fundamental variables are the changes in the risk factors. *These* are the quantities which may display the kind of regularity that we associate with natural phenomena. *These* are the quantities we want to treat statistically. Unfortunately, we are therefore faced with the problem of estimating the codependence among many thousands of risk factors.

Why is the task so difficult? Does any Excel-like spreadsheet not provide a handy function, called something like "CORREL", that returns the correlation between any two variables? Is correlation not all I need? I may well have thousands of variables, which will require the evaluation of millions of correlation coefficients, but are computers not cheap these days?

Matters, unfortunately, are not so simple. All the problems that we discovered while looking carefully at the case when only one risk factor affected the profit-and-loss distribution are still there, but many more have appeared. Let us do a back-of-the-envelope calculation. Suppose I have four variables, which I will call A, B, C, and D. How many correlations among them do I have? There are the correlations between [A and B], [A and C], and [A and D]; there are also the correlations between [B and C] and [B and D];

and, finally, there will be the correlation between [C and D]. (We do not have to count the correlations between, say, [B and A] or [C and B] because these will be the same as the correlations between [A and B] and [B and C].) Altogether we have six different correlations. A moment's reflection shows that for four variables I have $\frac{1}{2}(4^2 - 4)$ correlations. (I am subtracting 4 because the correlations of A with A, B with B, etc., are, trivially, 1; and I am dividing by 2 because of the symmetry between [A and B] and [B and A].) What does the number of independent correlation coefficients look like when I have 5,000 variables (as I said, this is a typical, and actually rather modest, value for the number of market risk factors to which a typical large financial institution is exposed)? A quick calculation shows that, for 5,000 risk factors, I have to estimate approximately 12,500,000 correlation coefficients using the available market data. How much "relevant data" do I typically have? If, as the regulators require for market risk applications, I collect (to remain "relevant") two years' worth of daily changes (and I have the full time series without any gaps for all the required 5,000 risk factors), this will still give me only 2,500,000 observations. It does not take a great knowledge of statistics to understand that estimating 12,500,000 unknowns (the independent entries of the correlation matrix) with 2,500,000 observations is, shall we say, a statistical challenge. I would need approximately ten years of "relevant data" to be able to have at least as many observations as quantities to estimate. At the time of writing, ten years ago the euro had not even been introduced; sterling, the lira, and the French franc were engaging in their periodic bouts of summer madness to try and stay within the bands of the exchange rate mechanism (ERM); credit derivatives were barely in their infancy; East and West Germany had only recently been reunited; collateralized debt obligations, which today trade with notionals of several trillions, had barely been introduced to a few courageous investors; banks were operating under totally different regulatory regimes; and everybody in the United Kingdom was sure that Tim Henman would one day lift the silver salad bowl at Wimbledon. Does this qualify as the "relevant past"?

This line of my critique goes back to one of the points made above: there may well be (and indeed there are) truckloads of clever tricks to help us in our statistical analysis, but we still cannot get something for nothing. There is something much more fundamental, though. When it comes to establishing the joint probability of occurrence of many variables the problems are much deeper than in the single-variable case. What matters in this case is the *codependence* among, not just the pairwise *correlations* between, the excellent underlying random variables. The term "correlation" is so common and it has so widely entered common parlance and nontechnical writing that it has become synonymous in the layperson's mind with codependence. In reality this is not the case, *and is emphatically not so when we look at the tails of distributions.* Correlation properly describes how different variables "move together" only if their distribution belongs to a very special class (called the class of "elliptical distribution"), which has the nice mathematical feature of being a close cousin of the (many-dimensional) normal distribution—as such, these distributions are relatively easy to work with. But the mathematical ubiquity of correlation should not be confused with usefulness in the real world. To give a simple example, the familiar coefficient of correlation cannot distinguish between dependence when the moves are small and dependence when the moves are large; nor can it prescribe that the dependence should only be present when moves are of a certain sign. Yet it is very simple to think of real situations where both these conditions become important. Consider a bond and equity issued by a highly rated company. The bondholders will always be repaid as long as the company is alive when the bond matures, but they do not share in the upside: at most, they will get their money back. The equity holders, on the other hand, are much more sensitive to relatively small pieces of financial information regarding the future profitability of the same firm and are immediately affected by both good and bad news. Now consider a piece of very good news for the company. The equity price is likely to move up significantly. The bond price, since we are dealing with a highly rated company, will be only marginally affected: after all, the bondholders were pretty confident about being paid back before the good news and are only minutely more confident now. So, for equity and bond price changes after very good news, we expect a low degree of correlation. Now consider a run-of-the-mill piece of financial news about the same company. The stock price will be modestly affected (up, if it was good news and down if it was bad), but, again, the bond price will barely change. Instead, the bond price is much more likely to be moved by the supply-and-demand dynamics of the bond market: a bout of fresh bond issuance in the same maturity bracket as the corporate bond we are looking at can be much more relevant to its price than a run-of-the-mill company-specific piece of news. This points again to a low degree of correlation between equity and bond price changes. Finally, think now of a really major piece of bad news concerning the same company: that all-important massive oil field in Krujekistan has been made inaccessible because of a local war; the foreign acquisition everybody was banking on has been scuppered by the intervention of a populist prime minister looking for votes ahead of a difficult election; a massive class-action law suit against the firm has been filed; etc. Not only is this very bad for the future profitability of the firm (and hence for the upside the equity holders were hoping to share in), but it may be so bad that even the bondholders are becoming worried that they may not get their money back. Now both the equity and the bond price move together, and by a large amount. After major negative news we now expect a strong correlation between changes in bond and equity prices. The final upshot is that there is no single degree of codependence—no one number—that can tell us how the two variables move together (or fail to do so) under all these possible combinations of good and bad, large and small pieces of news.

This is by no means a far-fetched example, and we can find literally dozens of similar situations in different walks of life with a moment's thought. What is the dependence, for instance, between driving visibility and the probability of having an accident? Probably very low, or almost zero, for reasonably good visibility conditions. Under these run-of-the-mill conditions, other variables, such as the speed of the vehicle or its roadworthiness, are likely to be much more important. But as the fog becomes thicker or the snowfall more severe, the probability of having an accident becomes strongly dependent on the visibility conditions. Again, a one-size-fits-all measure of dependence just does not make sense.

In all these cases, the familiar correlation coefficient does a very poor job at explaining how different variables move together. Unsurprisingly, this is particularly true when we are dealing with the dependence among rare events, i.e., with what is called tail dependence. So why are we clinging to this inadequate concept? Old jokes about drunk men looking for their keys at night by lampposts spring to mind. The correlation coefficient is easy to understand,* it is easy to calculate, and it is one of the very few measures of dependence that nicely decomposes the problem into a series of pairwise links between variables—an advantage not to be sniffed at when dealing with 10,000 random variables. None of these virtues, however, makes it more suitable to deal with high percentiles of many-dimensional joint distributions.

And there are still more problems. So far we have looked at the codependence among *different* variables at the *same* time. Just as important, though, is the correlation among changes in the *same* variable at *different* times. In reality, both "versions"

---

*Perhaps I should say that most people believe that they understand it easily. This is not necessarily always the case, as the following exchange reveals:

> Among nine big economies, stock market correlations have averaged around 0.5 since the 1960s. In other words, for every 1 per cent rise (fall) in, say, American prices, share prices in the other markets typically rise (fall) by 0.5 per cent.
>
> *The Economist*, November 8, 1997

> A correlation of 0.5 does not indicate that a return from stockmarket A will be 50% of stockmarket B's return, or vice-versa.... A correlation of 0.5 shows that 50% of the time the return of stockmarket A will be positively correlated with the return of stockmarket B, and 50% of the time it will not.
>
> Letter to *The Economist*, November 22, 1997

My thanks to a referee for pointing this out.

of codependence matter a lot for risk management. A wealth of empirical studies, for instance, carried out not only on financial time series but also on physical (e.g., geological or hydrological) phenomena show that the very largest occurrences display a double signature: not only are these events exceptionally large, they also display a marked change in the nature of their dependence. "Amplification and altered codependence" is the technical term that describes this state of affairs, and the breakdown in the usual dependence occurs both across variables at the same time and for the same variables at different times. A couple of vivid examples can drive the point home. During October 1987 the U.S. Dow equity price index fell by approximately 30% over three days. Irrespective of how the real losses were accumulated over the three days, if the returns were independent, the combination of losses with the highest probability of occurrence would be three losses of 10% each. Given the volatility of the Dow index at the time of the crash and for a distribution that fits the run-of-the-mill price changes well, the probability of a single 10% fall is approximately 1/1,000, i.e., such a fall should occur once every four years. Not a common event, for sure, but not a "perfect storm" either. However, the probability of three consecutive independent losses of 10% each is approximately 1/1,000,000,000, i.e., it should occur once every 4,000,000 years. And this is for the "most likely" combination of losses to produce a combined fall of 30% over three trading days. Any other combination (including the one that actually occurred during the days spanning Black Monday) will have an even lower probability of occurrence. This is taken by many researchers as a strong indication that, when exceptional events occur, the correlation (in this case, over time) of returns changes dramatically. If we are looking at the tails of distributions, the correlation of returns over time that we estimate in normal conditions (with plentiful observations) is of no help at all just when we need it.*

---

*For a general description of these phenomena, see D. Sornette (2004), *Critical Phenomena in the Physical Sciences* (Springer). For more specific applications to financial phenomena see Sornette, *Why Stock Markets Crash*.

During periods of intense financial turmoil the same dramatic change in the nature of the correlation, but this time across different risk factors, also applies. The most striking example is what happened in 1998 to the hedge fund Long Term Capital Management. They had a variety of trades on their books that, under normal conditions, should display little or no correlation among themselves. The trades spanned the credit, interest-rate, equity, foreign exchange, and many other more exoteric markets. In the fall of 1997 a series of financial events began to unravel, starting with the currency crises in emerging countries in Southeast Asia and ending with the Russian default in the summer of 1998. Very soon in many different markets all the "dials" began to point either decidedly upwards or markedly downwards: all safe and liquid securities, of whichever nature, began to perform exceptionally well, and all complex, illiquid, or exoteric securities simultaneously began to perform just as exceptionally badly. The hedge fund Long Term Capital Management was housed at the time in an unassuming building overlooking the picturesque and sleepy Greenwich harbor: a most unlikely place, in the eyes of a casual passerby, for a near-meltdown in the world financial markets to originate from. Yet the financial ripples from this tiny outfit in an idyllic Connecticut harbor into international markets became so wild and unpredictable that the Federal Reserve decided to step in and coordinate the actions of some twenty large international banks to make sure that the fallout of its near-collapse did not cause the infamous systemic contagion.

A posteriori, it was easy to recognize that a "latent" factor (liquidity) was driving all the trading action during this bout of late-summer market madness. But liquidity, under normal market conditions, has a relatively limited impact on prices. Unfortunately, periods of normal market conditions are just those when the vast majority of the data required to estimate the correlation coefficients are collected. Again, during exceptional periods, event amplification and altered dependence sets in.

There is a fascinating literature in this area. The recurrence of this "signature" is so prevalent that it has even been proposed that, deep down, there may be similar underlying mechanisms driving the "perfect storms" in the financial and physical world. The thesis is intriguing, and Didier Sornette (see the footnote on p. 178) presents a fascinating account of the theory. Whether one buys into this grand unified explanation or not, the incontrovertible empirical fact remains that when moves are exceptionally large we are often in an altogether different regime, during which all kinds of normal structural features (such as codependence) break down.

As if from a broken record, you can again hear the same warning, this time amplified: if I want to assign meaningful probabilities to very rare events, I cannot escape the link between the frequency of data collection, the relevance of the data, and the rarity of the event in question. And if the event I am interested in depends on the codependence among very many variables, the complexity of the problem literally explodes. Very rare events are not just bigger cousins of normal occurrences, they belong to a different species. We cannot estimate the size of giraffes by constructing a careful distribution of the sizes of hamsters. And we cannot guess the coordinated collective behavior of migrating wildebeests by studying how cows grazing in the field move about (even if cows, from a distance, can look a bit like wildebeests).

This is all very relevant for risk management, and for the current high-percentile school of thought in financial regulation. In the end, the reason why I have stressed so much the complexities associated with estimating the true dependence among financial variables is very practical. We may not like hearing it, but dependence in general, and *tail* dependence in particular, is extremely important in determining the highest percentiles of a loss distribution. The higher the percentile, the bigger the impact. And if we want to concentrate on the true, fundamental, underlying variables (on the risk factors, not on the losses that come from changes in risk factors and from positions), there is no getting away from the problem of estimating their true codependence (not just their one-size-fits-all correlation). To some extent, this can be done in a meaningful manner. But, once again, by focusing on impossibly high percentiles we are making our already-not-so-simple problems even harder. So, if the reader were to take away from this book three or four important "messages," here is one: whenever you find—in a piece of financial regulation, in the sleek brochure of a software vendor, in a technical paper produced by a quant—references to very high percentiles, please ask some commonsensical questions to make yourself happy that such statements about once-in-a-blue-moon events can meaningfully be made. In particular, do not forget to ask some simple questions about codependence as well. In short, remember the incredulous Surly, from the opening quote, when he avowed:

Faith, I have a humour, I would not willingly be gull'd.

CHAPTER 8

WHICH TYPE OF PROBABILITY
MATTERS IN RISK MANAGEMENT?

THE PROBABILITY SQUARE

Whoever reflects on four things, it were better he had never been born.

> *Talmud, Hagigah,* 2.1, quoted in Umberto Eco's *Foucault's Pendulum,*
> a transparent reference to the four corners of the
> probability square discussed in this chapter.

This is a short but important chapter, because we are beginning to look at what practical insight the general ideas we have developed in the previous chapters can provide.

We have seen in chapter 2 that there is more than one type of probability. Or, to be more precise, I have tried to explain that the "traditional" (frequentist) probability, the one we learn about in Statistics 101 (and the only one that regulators and practitioners seem to talk about when they deal with financial risk management), is actually a special case of a wider class of probability, the Bayesian or subjective one. Frequentist probability, as we saw, rather than living in a world of its own, lies at one end of the probability spectrum, which has purely subjective probability at the opposite end. I have also tried to explain that most real-world applications call for a judicious mix of two sources of information: one that is "data related" and one that is "model related." In all except some very special and artificial cases, it would be silly not to make heavy use of what the data tell us. But it would be just as "irrational of us to ignore other information based on the experience or insights—also called *priors* or *preknowledge*—of investors, statisticians and financial economists."* In general, acknowledging the importance of prior information in statistical analysis calls for a subtler, less mechanical, and more nuanced use of "the data."

Therefore, for the purpose of this book the really important question is not whether we should use one type of probability or the other. Rather, we should ask ourselves questions like, where, on this spectrum, is the probability of relevance for risk management? Is it close to the frequentist end of the spectrum or to the subjective end? Is the extra complexity called for by the Bayesian approach really necessary, or can we get away with the simpler (or, at least, more familiar) frequentist tools? I will argue that the answers to all of these questions are, largely, "it depends," and that, once again, the criterion that will allow us to judge where we stand on the probability spectrum is given by the probability square that I have already mentioned in chapter 7: as you will recall, its four corners were the frequency of data collection, the time homogeneity of the phenomenon at hand, the rarity of the event we are interested in (the percentile level), and the time horizon of our prediction. Since understanding this square is crucial for our discussion, let us remind ourselves of the interplay among these four factors.

At the heart of the problem is the fact that to find *relevant* data we must look *selectively* at the past. The more the phenomenon we are interested in is time homogeneous (a fancy way of saying that it does not change over time), the further back we can go in our historical records confident that the data we are finding are

*B. Scherer (2002), Bayesian analysis and portfolio choice, in *Portfolio Construction and Risk Budgeting*, chapter 4 (London: Risk Books); Scherer's emphasis.

relevant (assuming, that is, that we are blessed with such richness of information). Plentiful relevant information means that
we have to rely less on our prior beliefs: the evidence "speaks for
itself." Time-homogeneous phenomena can therefore be handled
relatively easily by frequentist techniques (as long as, of course,
we have enough data). This is one corner of our square.

How far back into the past I am able to confidently gaze is
not the whole story, however. If what I am interested in is having
at my disposal a lot of relevant data, the more frequently I can
collect data, the more records I will have without having to go
too far back into the past (without running out of empirical data
points).[1] Since what ultimately matters is the amount of relevant
data, a high frequency of data collection counts as another tick in
the frequentist box.

For a given frequency of data collection, making predictions
about what happens on average once every 10, 100, 1,000, ...,
1,000,000 data points—the percentile we are interested in—clearly
also affects the statistical power of our available data. Give or take
an improvement by a factor of two-to-five that clever statistical
techniques can buy us, if I want to say something about events
that occur once every 1,000 data collection intervals, I will roughly
need a number of relevant observations of the order of 1,000. No
matter how clever, no statistical technique *by itself* (i.e., without
the help of an "external" model) will be ale to tell me much about
what happens once in 5,000 days from the information collected
over 10 days, or even over 100 days. Of course, if I supplement the
data with a *fully calibrated* structural model about the phenomenon
I am looking at, I may be able to pull off such a feat. But, as Scherer
reminds us, "confining ourselves to the information within a sample will not allow us to tackle the effect of the uncertainty in the
parameters"* in a statistical problem. More specifically, just looking at the information in a given sample will not allow us to test
the appropriateness of the structural model that is supposed to
leapfrog the gap from the 90th to, say, the 99.9th percentile. So,

---

*Scherer, Portfolio resampling and estimation error, in *Portfolio Construction
and Risk Budgeting*, chapter 2.

the higher the percentile, the more difficult it becomes to apply strictly frequentist techniques. (This sentence should be kept in mind in the next chapter when we discuss economic capital.) This is the third corner of our probability square.

Finally, even if I collect data every minute (and therefore have zillions of data points), but I want to make predictions about what happens every year, what I can certainly and "safely" talk about comes from the number of independent, nonoverlapping, *years* of data that I have at my disposal—barring, again, the use of an exogenous structural model that tells me if, and to what extent, the mechanisms producing yearly data are relevant in generating the minute-by-minute data. The validation of this structural model poses the same questions mentioned above. So, estimating the 99th percentile for *daily* price moves is an altogether different matter from estimating the same percentile for *yearly* moves. The time horizon over which our predictions must be made—the fourth corner of the square—therefore also affects to what extent a frequentist approach makes sense.

The square has been closed and the interplay among the four factors, under the unifying requirement of providing *relevant* information, has become evident. So, if the phenomenon I want to investigate is very time homogeneous, if I can collect data very frequently, if what I am interested in happens not too rarely, and if the horizon of my statistical prediction is short, I am clearly in Frequentist Land. I do not need a lot of prior information to make robust and precise predictions,* because, just looking at my relatively recent record will give me a lot of relevant data. It is relevant almost by definition because, *over the timescale of the prediction horizon*, I have assumed that the phenomenon changes very slowly. I am therefore in Jaynes's proscribed (but also statistically blessed) situation of "independent repetitions of a 'random experiment' but no relevant prior information."[†]

---

*Even if I *did* have strong prior beliefs, the weight of such plentiful information will ultimately become dominant anyway. Bayesianism does not "dislike" frequentist information: it only makes sure that it is used correctly.

[†]Jaynes, *Probability Theory: The Logic of Science*.

At the opposite end of the spectrum, if I am interested in the 99.97th percentile of the distribution of one-year events for a phenomenon that can change with cycles of approximately five to ten years and about which I have only a few dozen independent data points (sound familiar?), it is clear that I am firmly in Bayesian Land and that my prior information will have a lot more weight in arriving at the final answer than my meager data set can provide. And as for this final answer, it is clear that no Bayesian magic will create certainty and information out of thin air. Recall that the outcome of a "proper" Bayesian analysis is a full probability distribution for the possible values of the parameter I want to estimate (the percentile, in this case). If the conditions for applicability of frequentist statistics are met, I may obtain for this Bayesian posterior a very sharp distribution (i.e., a distribution different from zero over a narrow range of possible values). But only rarely will I be in this lucky situation. If the phenomenon is time-varying, if the relevant data are scarce, if the required percentile is high or the prediction period long, the posterior distribution will be spread over a very large range of values.* The width of this distribution is just a measure of our unavoidable ignorance. This is how Bayesian analysis keeps us honest. We may well choose some parameter of this diffuse distribution (say, the mean, the mode, the median, etc.) as *the* value we are looking for, but the underlying degree of uncertainty has not gone away.

With this brief discussion clear in our minds, let us look in turn at the management of market risk and credit risk and let us try to see where each sits along the probability spectrum.

SHORT HORIZONS: MARKET RISK

Very often the term "market risk" refers to the risk of loss associated with holding securities on the so-called trading book. Roughly speaking, trading-book valuation applies when there is

---

*Unless, of course, my prior belief was very strong (basically, unless I knew the answer before I asked the question).

no a priori intention to hold the securities for the long term. This is indeed the meaning of the term I will implicitly use in this section. These securities may end up being held on the trading book of a financial institution for an extended period of time—weeks, months, or perhaps even longer—but every day the decision as to whether the position should be held or closed is made, as it were, afresh, and at any point in time it must be possible to enter or exit the trade with relatively small transaction costs.

If this is the case, the relevant measure of the value of a security is indeed its market value, i.e., the price a market participant would be willing to pay to acquire it or the price they would want to receive to sell it. (In market jargon this is called the mark-to-market value of the security.) Why is this? Simply because, since I may decide to reverse my current position in the next five minutes, what matters for its valuation is the price that a counterparty would be willing to pay in the next five minutes, not (necessarily) its "intrinsic," "true," or "fundamental" value. Of course, if you also believe that markets are always perfectly efficient, the market price and the fundamental value are one and the same thing, and you do not need to worry about the distinction. This need not be the case, however, if you think that markets may not always correctly reflect fundamentals. Be that as it may, in the trading-book world you do not have the luxury of being overly concerned about whether this identification of value and price is correct: you simply do not have a choice. If you want the flexibility that comes from being able to buy and sell your securities whenever you want, you must value them at market value—whether markets are informationally efficient and whether prices truly reflect fundamentals is neither here nor there.[2]

The upshot of this preamble is that the risk we are concerned about in this section is associated with potential losses from the rapidly varying prices of the trading-book securities. The frequencies of actually visible transactions clearly vary from asset class to asset class: for some not-so-liquid bonds only a handful of bona fide transactions may be recorded every week; at the other end of the frequency spectrum, you can observe on any trader's screen the tic-by-tic, second-by-second moves of any of the major foreign exchange pairs, say $/yen or $/euro. For most securities the frequency with which real prices are updated is in between these two extremes.

For those market risk factors whose changes are visible at frequencies higher, and sometimes *much* higher, than daily, the plentitude of data appears to make for a statistician's paradise. One must be careful not to get carried away, however, by this embarrassment of riches, because it is debatable whether, and to what extent, the statistical properties of the price changes are timescale invariant. It is *not* a model-independent truism, in other words, that the millions of data records collected at minute-by-minute, or even at transaction-by-transaction, frequency will in the end allow us to say something meaningful about the very high percentiles of, say, the daily or monthly returns. How can that be? Because, even if I have 10,000 second-by-second data records, these only cover a time span of less than three hours. Only an external structural model will tell me how these (very finely populated) three-hour patches can be aggregated into daily or weekly returns. And how did we validate *that* model?

Be that as it may, it would be churlish to complain too much about data paucity in the market arena: as far as the frequency of data collection is concerned, market risk is as good as it gets for a financial risk manager. The frequency corner of the probability square therefore often gets a big tick.

Good and abundant data does not mean perfect and infinite *relevant* data, however. Let us get a feel for the types of statistical questions that it is meaningful to ask in the market risk arena. The features of market returns certainly change over time, and do so for a variety of reasons: because of financial innovation, for instance, or because of changes in the institutional or regulatory setup. In general, strong evidence should always be supplied that the statistical features of any price series stretching over more than about five years have not changed substantially over this time period. And for markets that have developed recently and explosively (such as markets in credit derivatives), even five years takes us back, so to speak, to the early Jurassic period. So, in general it may well be the case that a relatively long time series is still relevant today, but it should not be taken for granted without many probing questions.

What does this entail? Let us try a simple back-of-the-envelope calculation. Let us take ten years as a very optimistic but workable order-of-magnitude estimate of the time period over which we can hope that time homogeneity applies. As trading books are marked to market daily, one day would be a reasonable time horizon for a statistical question. With 252 trading days per year, this gives us approximately 2,500 data points to play with.

Suppose that we are interested in the 99th, one-day percentile of the profit-and-loss distribution arising from a single risk factor. I can subdivide my 2,500 points into 25 blocks of 100 observations each. The worst outcome in each block gives me one estimate of the 99th percentile. Again assuming time homogeneity over this period, this would give us 25 independent realizations of the percentile we are trying to estimate. If we make some heroic assumptions about the distribution of this percentile estimate, its value could therefore be known with an uncertainty of plus or minus 20%. Given the type of question asked (i.e., given the percentile and the time horizon) and since we have been able to repeat the "experiment" 2,500 times under conditions that we have deemed to be sufficiently "identical," in this as-good-as-it-gets scenario an almost-strictly-frequentist approach makes quite a lot of sense.

It does not take much to spoil this reassuring picture. The regulators, for instance, are interested in percentile estimation for prudential capital purposes. Therefore, they reasonably require that we should focus our attention on price moves that occur in situations of market distress. In these turbulent days, liquidity (the ability to buy or sell a security close to the book value) may be significantly reduced. If, under normal market conditions, it takes one day to "digest" a typical-size market position without "moving the market," it may well take ten days to do so in times of turmoil. So, for regulatory purposes, banks are required to calculate the 99th percentile over a ten-day holding period. This apparently mild, and certainly reasonable, request has the immediate effect of reducing the number of independent data blocks obtainable from our ideal data set from 25 to 2.5. With the same assumptions above about the distribution of the percentile estimate, my uncertainty is now plus or minus 63%. Assuming that I do have the data at my disposal, if I want to reduce this uncertainty, I must dig deeper into the past. As I do so, however, I must recognize that expert judgement about the relevance of these ancient data becomes more and more important.

I could, however, go down a different route that may or may not give me a more precise estimate, depending on the case. I could enrich the purely statistical (data-based) information with prior information. For instance, I could first estimate using purely frequentist methods the *90th*, ten-day percentile (for which I again have sufficient points for a reliable frequentist estimate). Then I could try to deduce what the 99th, ten-day percentile *should* be if a given structural model applied.* My final estimate of the 99th, ten-day percentile would then be given by a combination of my prior knowledge and the "experimental" data. The relative importance given to the two components would depend on the confidence I have in my structural prior and on the precision and relevance of my "experimental" data.

The flexibility and generality of a Bayesian approach is evident. With some obvious modifications, I could in fact also have engaged in the same three-step tango (prior belief, evidence, and posterior) in the case of the estimation of the 99th, *one-day* percentile. In this case, however, given the wider availability of relevant data, the trust in the data would be greater (but not infinite), and my prior would have modified this information to a lesser extent. The Bayesian approach may be more cumbersome, but it is *always* applicable, and is designed so as to give the same answer as the frequentist method when the latter is appropriate. The reverse, however, is not true: if the conditions of applicability

---

*One such model, for instance, may invoke independence between successive returns.

are not met, there is only so much blood we can squeeze from a frequentist stone.

In closing this section about the management of short-horizon market risk, a last word of caution is in order. Even in this relatively benign environment, frequentist techniques can easily run aground. This can happen, for instance, in those markets where the price movements can be relatively (and sometimes extremely) well-behaved and apparently predictable for a very long time but then undergo sudden and massive lurches. Prices of emerging-market bonds, or of pegged currencies, often behave this way. Prices of single stocks (as opposed to stock indices) can also display a similar discontinuous behavior. This poses interesting questions about what data one should use—and about what one should do with these data. Suppose we are looking at the equity price of a technology company that has not defaulted (yet). The very fact that we are trading this stock today means that, no matter how far back we look, this particular company never defaulted in the past.* However, part of the risk premium reflected in its price is due to the fact that it may well default in the next few months. Exactly the same considerations apply to the price of an emerging-market bond, whose juicy yield would be difficult to rationalize if the possibility of currency devaluation or debt default were not real. What use, then, is the time series of the company's or the emerging-market bond's past price moves for assessing the probability of the event I am arguably most interested in, i.e., the company's default or the emerging-market bond's devaluation? A frequentist would not even know where to begin.[3] A statistician who regards probability as degree of belief could at least take a reasonable stab at the problem. For instance, he may want to look at the time series of similar companies or emerging-market bonds that in the past *did* default or suffered devaluation. But in doing so he will have to make a courageous call as to what constitutes a "similar" company or emerging market. If I want to assess the risk of investing in freely

---

*To keep matters simple we will not consider debt restructuring or chapter 11 in this discussion.

floating rubles in 2007, should I look back at the history of the ruble currency in 1998, when it was pegged? Or does it make more sense to look at an altogether different currency but one that at least shares the feature of being freely floating? (Remember, by the way, the example about the weather prediction on Cape Cod. Did we decide to use Boston or Long Island data in the end?)

The upshot of this discussion is that it takes surprisingly little to spoil the rather delicate hothouse conditions under which frequentist statistics flourish. And the more we move into subjective-probability territory, the less speaking about extremely precise probabilities makes sense—no more sense than saying that the probability of the next president of the United States being a Democrat is 50.023%. If this is the case, how would *you* calculate the 99.97th loss percentile of a poorly diversified portfolio of emerging-market bonds?

LONG-HORIZONS: CREDIT RISK, ASSET-AND-LIABILITY MANAGEMENT, ETC.

As we move away from the fast-paced trading book, we enter a very different world where assets and securities are held for the long term—in the case of loans and debt obligations, often until maturity. This is the traditional banking world where loans were advanced to borrowers and typically were held on the bank's balance sheet (i.e., remained "the property of the bank") until their maturity. This state of affairs clearly generates a different value dynamics and a different interplay between the fundamental value (which will be realized over the life of the security) and the day-to-day vagaries of the supply-and-demand-buffeted price. Recall that a mark-to-market valuation reflects the value that my asset would fetch *today* in the market. But if it is my declared intention to hold on to a bond or a loan until its maturity, it becomes debatable whether a mark-to-market valuation is still appropriate.* Be that as it may, the relevant observation for our discussion is that, given the buy-and-hold nature of the banking book, speaking about prediction horizons of days or weeks no longer makes a lot of sense.

This seemingly technical observation has a major impact on the nature of our statistical prediction problem. Suppose that we want to create our profit-and-loss distribution in order to assess the risk profile of our long-term portfolio. This is all well and good, but over what period? If I do not mark-to-market my securities, the one-day profit-and-loss distribution would look very peculiar indeed: there would be a cumulative probability of close to one, corresponding to zero unexpected changes in book value, and a very minute probability mass corresponding to the losses that my portfolio would incur due to defaults or impairments *that happen between today and tomorrow*. So, in order to make sense, a reasonable profit-and-loss distribution would have to record the changes in value over much longer periods, of the order of, say, one year. But if we are interested in value changes that occur over periods of this approximate length, all the dials point away from the frequentist corner of the quadrant: the sampling frequency is now much lower (how quickly is the information about the creditworthiness of a borrower updated?); as a consequence I have far fewer data points; and even if fresh credit information was available, say, monthly, this would have to be aggregated into yearly blocks, further reducing the availability of useful points. Finally, in the desperate attempt to collect more and more data I would have to look further and further back into the past: but credit data collected in, say, the depths of the 1991 U.S. recession would hardly be relevant for the benign environment of 2005. All these factors point to the fact that, in our statistical estimate, we must rely much more heavily than in the market-risk case on subjective, expert knowledge. Bayesian analysis, however, is no magic wand

---

*As I said, only if markets are perfectly efficient is the mark-to-market value always "superior." But even if you think that markets are always efficient, and that mark-to-market therefore *is* always intrinsically superior, you may want to ponder the relevance of a (correctly and efficiently priced) liquidity premium on the price of a bond that will not be sold before it matures.

that can create certainty and precision out of uncertainty: Bayesian analysis will only give sharp predictions if we are very sure about our prior understanding of the phenomenon, or if the evidence by itself speaks volumes. If our expert knowledge is fuzzy, and the available data are scarce and of dubious relevance, Bayesian techniques simply force us to face up to the fact that some quantities can only be predicted with very great uncertainty. Bayesian techniques only make precise the intuitive statement that, if I have ten relevant pieces of information, statements about events that happen once every thousand years should be looked at with enormous suspicion. Unfortunately, when practitioners or regulators talk about the 99.9th (or, sometimes, even about the 99.97th!) percentile for a one-year horizon they are squarely in these extremely misty and fuzzy regions of statistical enquiry.

Is an estimate, however rough, not better than no estimate at all, though? Are we not somewhat richer if we have a very imprecise estimate than if we have none? Indeed it is, and indeed we are, but only if we use these numbers wisely and we make an almost superhuman effort to overcome the temptation of "infinite precision." I have already touched upon this point in a rather theoretical context (chapter 2), but let me explain what I mean again with a more practical application in mind.

Once frequentists accept (at a given statistical level of confidence) the point estimate of a quantity (say, a percentile), they tend to act as if the estimated number were *the* true value of the parameter. Remember that, for a frequentist, a coin cannot have a 40% chance of being biased. It does not make sense to say that the economy is 60% in a recession. Either the coin is fair or it is biased. Either we are in a recession or we are not. We simply accept or reject these black-or-white statements at a certain confidence level. If we have had elementary statistical training, this way of looking at the nature of uncertain phenomena has become ingrained in our statistical psyche by exposure and repetition. But this is *not* the only way that statistical information can be used. More than that: I believe that this is *not* the best that one can do given the information. A Bayesian approach automatically tells us that a parameter (say, a percentile) has a whole distribution of possible values attached to it, and that extracting a single number out of this distribution (as I suggested above, the average, the median, the mode, or whatever) is a possibly sensible, but always arbitrary, procedure. No single number distilled form the posterior distribution is a *primus inter pares*: only the full posterior distribution enjoys this privileged status, and it is our choice what use to make of it.

The perspective is different for a frequentist. He begins by assuming that, ontologically, the "true" nature of a phenomenon is what is. He then attempts to obtain a point estimate of this Platonic true value, and looks in the estimators he devises for nice properties such as efficiency, unbiasedness, etc. This philosophical belief in the uniqueness of the "true" value makes a big conceptual difference. For all the uncertainty associated with the estimation, the outcome of an unbiased estimator *has* a privileged position among all the other possible values: it is our best estimate of the true value of, say, the biasedness of a given coin, the state of the economy, or the percentile we were looking for. A corollary of this attitude is that, when it comes to the detection of statistical effects (whether the coin is biased, say, or whether the risk premium is zero), frequentists will arbitrarily choose a significance level and will then consider their estimates either significant, and hence perfectly true, or insignificant, in which case they are rejected.

This "philosophical" attitude to statistical estimation does not logically imply the assumption that the probabilities, variances, correlations, and expected returns, etc., are perfectly known to the investor or the risk manager, but it does make the assumption much easier to accept. So, in traditional portfolio optimization, capital budgeting, and risk management (and game theory and utility theory) the "innocuous" assumption is almost universally made that the true parameters (say, the variances and correlations or the objective probabilities) are perfectly known to the asset allocator. In Markowitz's *Portfolio Selection* bible, for instance, the possibility that all the probabilities attaching to the different outcomes may *not* be perfectly known only makes its appearance on p. 257 of a 303-page book—by which time the assumption that the objective probabilities are perfectly known has become solidly embedded in the psyche of the reader.

Is this really so bad? Is making use of our best estimate as if it were the *one* true value not the best we can do? Emphatically, no. This is where the almost superhuman effort in self-restraint I mentioned above must kick in (and this is why I find an unreflective use of frequentist thinking not just ineffective but outright dangerous). We have already encountered a thought experiment concerning repeated coin tossing with a biased coin. We saw that adding a bit of uncertainty to our knowledge about the degree of biasedness of the coin changed our behavior radically, not at the margin. Similarly, it is well-known to asset managers that a naive application of the Markowitz portfolio optimization technique (an application, that is, in which we assume that all the entries of the covariance matrix are known with absolute precision) ends up acting as a noise amplifier and producing unstable asset allocations.

Perhaps there is one way out. We were forced to use long-horizon projections because we did not want to use a mark-to-market valuation for our long-term portfolio. This is the root cause of the problems we have seen so far (and of other problems that we discuss below). Why not force the portfolio manager to use mark-to-market valuation, then? A full answer to this question would take us on a very long detour as we would have to deal with market efficiency, the effect of liquidity on prices, long-term forecastability, market segmentation, prudential regulation, etc. I will simply point out that if a portfolio manager conducts his business with regard to a set of metrics (say, the income produced by his portfolio), one can easily create havoc by forcing on him risk-management practices based on a different set of value indicators (e.g., the mark-to-market valuation of the same portfolio).

THE PROBLEM WITH THE TREND

The discussion so far has implicitly focused on the uncertain (stochastic) component of price moves. In reality, one should take into account the trend (deterministic) component as well. What do I mean by "trend"? Whenever we have to estimate whether, on the whole, interest rates will be falling or rising; whether we are entering an inflationary or a deflationary period; whether over the next few years the U.S. dollar will fall or retain its value; whether equity markets will perform well or poorly—whenever, in short, we make statements about the long-term future level of some price or rate, we are really making a statement about its expected future trend. I will deal with this topic in some detail in chapter 10, and, for this reason, the present treatment is brief. This does not mean, however, that the issue is not very important.

Three simple points are worth making at this early stage. The first is that, in the presence of reasonable statistical noise, estimating a trend from historical data is much more difficult than estimating the "volatility." So, despite the fact that we often call the trend term "deterministic," we should not forget that our uncertainty about it can be very substantial.

The second point is that the longer the time horizon over which we want to make a prediction, the greater the importance of the (comparatively more uncertain) trend term over the volatility component. For a given portfolio, the uncertainty in the "width" of the distribution of its future values (the stochastic part) does grow with the prediction horizon, but the uncertainty in its location (determined by the trend) grows even more: my most likely losses over a five-year period may well span a range of, say, $60 million— this is the type of information the stochastic component gives me; but is this fan of likely values centered around a future loss of $50 or around a gain of $200? This "location" piece of information is mainly determined by the trend. In the end, the trend will prevail over (almost) everything.

The third point is that since long-term portfolios are held, well, for the long-term, they fall squarely in the class of portfolios where the difficult-to-determine trend matters most.

Taken together, these three observations tell us that, when we try to make predictions about the riskiness of long-term portfolios our approach should be much more heavily reliant on subjective probability than on frequentist probability. Do *you* expect to find in past data alone the answer as to whether the equity market will rise or fall over the next twelve, or twenty-four, or sixty months?

In short, the frequency with which we can update the value of a long-term portfolio (if we do not mark it to market), the length of the projection horizon of interest for these portfolios, the difficulty in estimating the trend and its high dependence on our models and prior beliefs, the importance of the trend itself in determining the overall portfolio performance—all these factors strongly suggest that a subjective-probability approach is the appropriate one. If this is the case, speaking of "sharp" high percentiles (or other statistical measures) does not make a lot of sense. In our probability square we are located, in a way, in the corner diametrically opposite the one occupied by highly liquid, marked-to-market assets held for short periods of time. Why does this matter? Because asking the same probabilistic question (e.g., what is the 99th percentile?) can make good sense in one case but be close to nonsense in the other. This may seem too obvious even to state: surely, the greatest long-term loss or gain from a fixed-income investment portfolio (hence the greatest risk associated with it) will depend on whether rates will rise or fall. Everything else should be pretty much icing on the cake. This may indeed sound obvious, but let us not forget that a variety of high-percentile-based, something-or-other-at-risk approaches (liquidity-at-risk, income-at-risk, etc.) have recently cropped up in more and more bizarre contexts: from the solvency of pension funds to the liquidity management of a bank, to the regulation of the investment portfolios held by insurance companies. The prudential goal is laudable, but the frequentist instrument used to attain it is blunt at best, dangerous at worst.

CHAPTER 9

THE PROMISE OF ECONOMIC CAPITAL

Far better an approximate answer to the *right* question, which is often vague, than an *exact* answer to the wrong question, which can always be made precise.

J. Tukey[*]

If this were play'd upon a stage now,
I could condemn it as an improbable fiction.

Twelfth Night (3.4.127–28)

THE ECONOMIC-CAPITAL VIEW OF THE WORLD

What is economic capital?[1] No single definition has found universal acceptance, but a reasonable, brief definition would probably sound something like, "Economic capital is the amount of capital a bank would *voluntarily* set aside to support its business independent of any regulatory requirement to do so." You may feel rather underwhelmed by this definition. Yet economic capital has been hailed by some as a major breakthrough in the management of the risk and of the strategic decisions of a bank. Surely, there must be more to this dry definition than meets the eye. Are we missing something?

Indeed, as we begin to look below the surface of the definition, we soon realize that it raises more questions than it answers. To

---

[*]J. Tukey (1962), *Annals of Mathematical Statistics* 33:1–67. Quoted in Poirier, *Intermediate Statistics and Econometrics*.

begin with, one important feature of economic capital is that it has often been used in a way that places great emphasis on extremely rare events.* In order to "support their business," some private banks have *voluntarily* attempted to link their risk-management decisions to the estimation of extremely high percentiles of loss distributions (we are often talking here about events happening once every several thousand years). Why did this happen? Why have some private banks voluntarily devoted the best part of their risk-management efforts (and budgets) to the estimation of statistical quantities that are of relevance only in extremis? Is this reasonable?

To understand this, and whether the economic-capital project as a whole is reasonable, a good place to start is to look at how it is built. Since virtually all the implementations of economic capital I can think of make use of a profit-and-loss distribution, we should look at what the link is between these distributions and "the amount of capital a bank would *voluntarily* set aside to support its business."

Let us refresh our memory about profit-and-loss distributions. As a first step, we should first of all construct a curve that associates to each possible future gain or loss produced by the *current* business mix (over a given period) its probability of occurrence. Recall that this is not a graph of actual past profits and losses; rather it depicts what profits or losses the current positions would generate if subjected to the price moves that occurred in the past. So, from figure 4.1, we read that our current business setup gives rise to a probability of 10% of making a gain greater than $30,000,000 and a probability of 20% of making a loss greater than $20,000,000. We have already encountered this curve, which we called the profit-and-loss probability distribution. We noticed that it conveyed a lot of information but that it was not clear how to "condense" it into a synthetic measure so as to help us with decision making. You may want to revisit the discussion in chapter 4

---

*The regulators have certainly encouraged this usage, but it would be unfair to claim that this practice has been forced down the throats of all banks.

on this point. This is just where the economic-capital approach promises to help us.

The mix of businesses of a bank is made up of risky activities. To fix ideas, let us imagine that we, the bank, have lent money (perhaps in the form of corporate bonds) to 100 different companies. The interest we get from these loans is, of course, higher than if we had lent the same amount of money to the Treasury because some of these companies may default before the maturity of the loan and we need to be compensated for the losses that these defaults will produce. So, even if all the loans pay us 5% more than the rate of interest on comparable riskless Treasury bonds, we cannot reasonably expect that all of this 5% will be crystallized as profit. By virtue of the fact that these companies are risky, we expect, on the basis of statistical information about past defaults of similar companies, that some of our monies will be lost (much as was the case with Bernoulli's wares on the pirate-infested seas). For obvious reasons, we call this amount of money that we can expect to lose the "expected loss."

So far, so good. Now things get a bit more tricky. Despite the fact that economic capital promises to deliver a lot more, let us start from the prudential question that naturally arises in the context of capital: how much money (capital) should we set aside to safeguard the viability of our business even in a difficult business environment. Clearly, if we wanted to set aside money against *any* possible eventuality, we would need an infinite amount of capital—not a very practical or useful place to start. To make some progress we can go back to the example above where we lent to 100 different companies. If things should so turn out that we will incur exactly the expected losses, then we would not need to set anything aside at all today. We would in fact probably be making a small profit. This is because, when we accepted to extend the bank's money to the risky companies, we already knew that some were expected to default and we built this knowledge—plus, presumably, some profit—into the interest margin (5% above the riskless rate) that we charged.

It is because of the distressing habit that events have of not unfolding according to plan A that we need to set some extra money aside: a capital buffer.* So the next question is, how much money should we, the bank, set aside for a (very) rainy day?

The question is not as simple as it seems, because more does not necessarily mean better. Not, at least, in everybody's eyes. Apart from the regulators, two very different sets of players have an interest in the performance of a bank: those who have lent money to it (the bondholders); and those who have directly invested in it (the equity holders). To some extent their desires are aligned, at least in the limited sense that both will rejoice if things go well for the bank and it makes a lot of profit. Note, however, that if things go *extremely* well for the bank, the bondholders soon stop feeling proportionately happier, because their maximum gain (their upside) is limited to getting back all the money they lent plus the interest. The dream of every equity holder, on the other hand, is that every fledgling company he has invested in will turn out to be another Microsoft. If this dream comes true, he will fully benefit, dollar for dollar, in the upside, pro rata with the magnitude of his investment.

Unfortunately, in order to have some hope in exceptional returns one has to accept exceptional risks—something that the bondholders are not too keen on ("steady as she goes" is *their* preferred mode of operation). On the other hand, unless those boring bondholders are convinced to lend their money, it would be very expensive to finance in the future all the sexy projects the equity holders want to embark upon.[2] A balance must be struck. The bank must hold enough capital so that the probability of default is remote (and so as to please and entice the bondholders); not too much "fallow" capital should be set aside, though, if the equity holders want to have hope in a decent return.

---

*By the way, if we are a bank, for all the "systemic" reasons discussed above the regulators would want this safety margin to be very considerable indeed; but, for the moment, we will leave the regulators aside and concentrate on what the bank would choose to do of its own accord (i.e., if it were an unregulated entity).

This is where the rating agencies come in. Rating agencies are institutions that express an opinion about the ability of a bank to repay the money it has borrowed (to repay principal and interest in a timely fashion, as the expression goes). They express this opinion by means of a letter-based system, ranging from AAA for the most reliable companies down to C, through AA, A, BBB, etc. Note that a AAA rating does not necessarily mean that the company is expected to post stellar returns. Actually, AAA companies are very unlikely to have extremely exciting prospects ahead of them. The high rating is simply an indicator of the firm's ability to repay debt. It is therefore a signal of great importance *for the bondholders*.

Now, the rating agencies have been granting their ratings for a long time—as a matter of fact for much longer than the expression "economic capital" has been around. They have been doing so by using a number of qualitative and quantitative criteria of their own choosing,* with a view to assessing the ability of the company to repay its debt. This practice has been going on for so long that the companies that the rating agencies have grouped together on the basis of their rating (all AA companies, say) have acquired an identity of their own. Irrespective of whether they are active in mining, construction, or finance they have something important in common. They are all AA firms.

As such, they have been scrutinized by investors for a very long time. Thanks to this careful scrutiny, investors have been able to assess the frequency of default over a given period of time (a year, say). Tables have been built that report the observed frequencies with which firms which were of a given rating at a given point in time have defaulted or changed rating *in the following twelve months*. One natural and apparently innocuous step in the

---

*"Given the nature of ... ratings, qualitative factors *can have a weight of more than 50% of the total rating analysis*. Examples of qualitative factors include industry risk and trends; competitive advantages and disadvantages; management quality; expected parent or state support; legal and financial structure" (my emphasis), from B. O'Sullivan and I. Weston (2006), Challenges in validating rating systems for IRB under Basel II, gtnews article, October 2006 (Standard & Poor's).

reasoning has then been to associate the observed *past frequency* of default for each cohort (say AA companies) with the *current probability* of default of AA-rated firms. This identification is far from straightforward but let us accept the reasoning for the moment. Even as we accept this identification (past frequency equals current probability), let us recall, however, that the rating agencies do not say that a AA rating means that the probability of default over a year of a AA firm is 0.03%. The imputed probability of default is a byproduct, arrived at by an a posteriori observation carried out by third parties, who simply group together companies identically rated by the agencies and observe their ex post frequency of default. And as for the criteria employed by the agencies to arrive at the rating, once again I must stress that they are only concerned with the ability of a firm to repay its debt. They do not directly take into account the profitability of the firm—or, more precisely, they only do so to the extent that better profitability enhances the ability to repay debt: an unkind analogy is that of a slave master who cares about the well-being of his slaves only to the extent that they can be productive.

This may be enough for those who have lent money to the bank (i.e., for the bondholders), and who therefore do not share in the exceptional upside. Give or take some extra safety factor, this logic also suits the regulators well—who, as we have seen, should mainly care about banks not creating havoc in the real economy by going bust. But what about the equity holders? Two companies with very different profitability prospects but with the same ability to repay their debt will be granted the same rating by the agencies. Given this rating, a small army of statisticians may well be able to calculate their respective probabilities of defaulting. This is all well and good, but those investors who do benefit from the upside, i.e., the equity holders, will assign very different values to the two companies. Why should the shareholders want the desirability of projects to be assessed just on the basis of the probability of not going bust (i.e., just on the ability to repay the debt holders)? How can one link (and why *should* one link) this remote probability of default to the desirability of an investment project? Where does economic capital come into investment (as opposed to prudential) decisions? Why should one care about return on *economic* capital? To understand why one should care, we must look more closely at what economic capital is.

As discussed in chapter 3, deciding how to choose among risky investment alternatives has always been at the core of decision making in financial institutions. The most intuitively obvious criterion in making these choices is by looking at what return we expect to make from a given investment. Indeed, if we read the financial section of the Sunday papers, with their emphasis on "star performers," "best-managed funds," etc., it would seem that little else is required to make a good investment decision. In short, shoot for the stars.

The first fly in the ointment is that, according to Finance 101, some investments *should* yield more, not because they are superior, but simply because they are riskier.* Take, for instance, a bond that was issued in 2005 by the Iraqi government. It was priced at the time of issue to yield approximately 10% above the riskless rate. Only the courageous investors who bought it will be able to tell, when the bond matures, whether it has proved to be a good investment or not. But, if the bond does indeed turn out to be a good investment, it will *not* be simply because it yielded (a lot) more than a U.S. Treasury bond (around 4% at the time). It may all sound too obvious even to mention, but, if we accept this, we are already streets ahead of the Sunday papers.

So, the task ahead is to assess the desirability of an investment by taking into account both its return and its risk. It all sounds very natural, and, so far, theory and common sense (or common practice) have not parted company. The second fly in the ointment, however, is that there is no single measure of risk, as we have seen. Some very influential, but also very assumption-laden, theories may well suggest equating risk with variance of returns. As we discussed in chapter 3, however, this is not a "truth," it

---

*To be more precise, they should yield more, according to finance theory, if the payouts covary with future consumption. See the discussion in chapter 3 on this point, or, for far greater detail and insight, see Cochrane, *Asset Pricing*.

is a conclusion drawn from some strong, possibly appealing, but sometimes certainly inappropriate assumptions. Whichever definition we choose for risk, and whatever route we employ to capture it in a quantitative measure, we will need this adjustment term in our decision rule or we will all end up stuffing our portfolios with high-yielding Iraqi bonds.

The third problem is as follows. If I buy shares, or a bond, in some company, I have to part with some money today in the hope of receiving a payoff in the future. Calculating the return associated with any future outcome of the payoff is a straightforward matter, simply requiring us to divide each future payoff by the initial investment. (The *probability* of each future payoff may well be very difficult to estimate, but this is a different issue and one that is best left aside for the moment.) But what if instead I enter a derivatives contract today, which often requires no initial outlay of money? We do not need to be derivatives experts to understand what the problem is: think of the derivative as a bet where you can make or lose a lot of money, *but one which does not require setting aside any money for security today.* Suppose that the bet is on the outcome of a single toss of a fair coin. If the coin lands "heads" you make $1,400,000; if it lands "tails" you lose $1,000,000. If the coin is fair you expect to make a gain of $200,000, but what is your *return*?* Since, unlike in the case of the bond or the share, you did not part with any money today, what should you divide your expected payoffs by to obtain the return? Rather awkwardly, if you divide by zero, you would get an infinite return. Is this bet on a coin therefore infinitely better than a stock market investment, from which you expect to make, say, a 20% return? Something does not sound quite right.

Let us inject some degree of realism into the coin-flipping example. The friend with whom you have entered the bet is of a rather untrusting nature, and harbors some doubts as to whether, if you were to lose the bet, you would actually be able to pay the $1,000,000. He may therefore require you to set aside (to "park" with a trustworthy third party) at least part of his potential win,

---

*Recall that (gross) return is defined as final payoff divided by initial outlay.

say $800,000. So, if you want to play this game, this will not really cost you zero today: even if you have not technically "spent" the money, but simply lodged it as security, you still have to part with $800,000 just to enter the betting game. Perhaps we can calculate the *return* on the bet (on the derivative contract) by dividing the expected gain by the "capital" you have been required to set aside ($800,000). If we do this, your return (12.5%) is a number that can now be more meaningfully compared with the stock market investment: in both cases you divide each possible future payoff by the amount that, for whatever reason (purchase in one case, security in the other), you had to part with today. This manner of putting on the same footing funded investments (for which you have to pay a purchase price up front) and unfunded investments ("bets," or derivatives in general, where the money is required so that you will be able to make good on your commitments if things turn sour) seems promising. Can we pursue the reasoning a bit further?

How did we arrive at the amount of money ($800,000) that you had to set aside? Perhaps there was a rule, set out by a "regulator of bets," that said: "Thou shall set aside $800,000 for every $1,000,000 you stand to lose." If you set aside this amount of money because of this rule, you are implicitly calculating your return on *regulatory* capital.

But was the amount you were required to set aside reasonable? To answer the question, let us pursue the analogy between entering a derivative contract and entering a bet, but let us make it a bit more realistic. Suppose that you were engaged not in one, but in 100 identical bets with a single friend. You may, of course, lose every single bet, but, since we assumed that the coin was fair, this would be a very unlikely event. In theory, your friend could, of course, ask that you set aside the maximum amount you could theoretically lose, i.e., $100,000,000. (By the way, if the coin is fair the probability of you incurring such a loss is approximately 1 in 10^{31}: not a terribly likely event, especially if you think that the total number of particles in the universe is estimated to be about 10^{64}.) In reality, it is more likely that the counterparty to the bets will require you to set aside an amount of money linked to a "bad but plausible scenario," say, $35,000,000, corresponding to 65 losses out of 100 (the probability of you losing that amount of money or more is still less than 0.2%). Whatever number your friend might settle on, he will link in some way the capital you have to set aside, and that you will use to calculate your return, with the riskiness of the bet.

One last small twist in the coin/derivative story: suppose that you have realized that unless your friend feels that you have chosen to set aside an adequate amount of capital he will not be willing to play the betting game with you. If this is the case, you may well *voluntarily* choose to set aside enough capital to give your friend sufficient confidence that he will get his money if and when it comes due to him. And, by the way, you may have different bets with many different friends. These friends do not all necessarily have the same risk aversion: some would like more safety capital, and some less. By setting different amounts of capital aside you automatically vary the number of friends willing to enter the betting game with you. So, if you set aside $35,000,000, virtually everyone will be ready to enter bets with you—your "rating" is AAA. But if you set aside only $30,000,000, the probability of your losses exceeding your wins is more than ten times larger: perhaps your rating has slipped to AA. And so on. Note also that, as you set aside less capital, your return on capital per bet increases, but, unfortunately, fewer people are ready to take on your "credit risk." Your *total* return will therefore depend not just on the attractiveness of the single bet, but also on the number of friends willing to enter these bets with you. There may therefore be an optimal amount of capital that maximizes your *total* return (not the return per trade). This is what we meant before when we said that an institution will, in general, want to present itself to the outside world as of a certain chosen credit standing.

As we move from betting to derivatives transactions, the amount of capital that you would voluntarily choose to set aside independent of any regulatory constraint in order to entice counterparties to enter unfunded transactions with you is just economic capital. Of course, this reasoning need not be limited to derivatives transactions. If I lent money to a corporation, I also stand the chance of losing money. It is when it comes to comparing *returns* from the derivative transaction (the unfunded bet) and lending (the funded transaction) that the economic-capital approach provides a unified conceptual framework: if we are concerned with keeping the regulators-of-bets-and-loans happy, the relevant return is the return on regulatory capital; if we are concerned with keeping happy those who may have to lend us money tomorrow (the bondholders and the counterparties in derivatives transactions), we should be concerned with economic capital. The universe of lending friends that we want to be able to tap in the future will dictate our preferred rating (AAA, AA, A, etc.), i.e., the creditworthiness we will be required to "signal" to the market.*

Now comes the last step in the reasoning. The chosen degree of "projected creditworthiness" will indirectly dictate what percentile of the profit-and-loss distribution we should be concerned with—as you recall, this logical step, admittedly the weakest, comes from the identification of the observed *past frequency* of default of, say, AA-rated financial institutions with their *current probability* of defaulting. The advantage of the economic-capital approach is that all these different sets of initiatives (funded or unfunded) can now be looked at in a unified fashion.

We now understand where the 99.97th percentile that we have encountered several times in this book originally came from: by looking at the whole universe of AA-rated firms over a very long period of time, the empirical frequency of default over a one-year period has been estimated to be roughly one in three thousand. Hence, the economic-capital line of reasoning says, if you *want* to belong to the AA club, you should voluntarily *choose* to set aside enough capital to cover adverse events with that likelihood of occurrence. In calculating the extra return from each possible business initiative you should therefore divide the expected payoffs

---

*It is for this reason that banks often keep more capital than strictly required by regulators.

by the amount of incremental economic capital that that initiative requires.

Looked at from this perspective, *return* on economic capital would therefore seem a very sensible way to assess the desirability of different business initiatives. Indeed, the whole approach sounds both logical and elegant. Unfortunately, elegant theories tend to have a hold on human minds that at times goes beyond what a hard-nosed critique would recommend. To see to what extent the economic-capital idea can deliver what it promises we have to look in some detail at how the whole approach works in practice.

How would we go about calculating these returns on economic capital? Suppose that we are considering adding a new business, from a few candidate initiatives, to our current mix of businesses. The first step, which we have already carried out, is to build the profit-and-loss distribution for the current set of businesses. We then build, one at a time, a number of similar curves, each one including the current mix of businesses and one of the candidate business initiatives being examined. I must stress that each curve is obtained by assigning a probability to the expected profits and losses of the current business mix *plus one at a time of the new proposed businesses.* So, there will be a profit-and-loss distribution associated with the current mix of businesses plus, say, a new fixed-income initiative; another associated with the current mix of businesses plus a new equity "trade"; and so on.

If correctly built, the resulting distributions will therefore automatically "know" about the interaction between each new business and the existing mix. So, a business initiative that, on a stand-alone basis (e.g., using the discounted-cash-flow method), might have looked attractive, may now be shown to produce losses just in those states of the world where our existing business activities are also losing money. This could make us change our minds about the desirability of the new business, even if looked at in isolation we might have rather liked it. Conversely, a business initiative that, on a stand-alone basis, did not appear particularly exciting may be revealed by the economic-capital type of analysis to do rather well just when the other lines of business are doing poorly. Again, armed with this new information we may well look at the new business in a different light.

At first blush, and assuming that these distribution curves can be reliably built (a big assumptions that we will discuss later), the return-on-economic-capital approach appears not only reasonable but very appealing. As informative as they are, by themselves the profit-and-loss distributions for well diversified and poorly diversified businesses presented above do not automatically solve the decision-making problem we started with. What trade-off should we make between expected return and diversification?* How much expected return should we give up to reduce "risk"? 1%? 2%? 5%? How much extra risk are we going to accept for an extra 2% in expected return? And, above all, what do we mean by risk?

This is exactly where the rule to maximize return on economic capital comes in. First, the CFO of a bank will weigh and choose among the financing opportunities available to his firm—his preferred mix of debt and equity financing to raise the money he needs. He will then endeavor to signal this to the market, i.e., to the prospective equity investors and bondholders. So, a particular bank may decide to project itself as a "safe" bank: as a bank with a AA rating, say. At the time of writing, the probability of a company rated AA at the beginning of a year still being alive at the end of that year is 99.97%. Let us therefore choose the 99.97th percentile as the economic capital for our bank. The world will observe this, and will conclude that I, the bank, *intend to remain* a AA-rated bank. By managing my business this way, I will reinforce the message that I am a bank of *that* particular degree of stability, I will remove at least some of the investor's doubts

---

*In some rare cases comparing profit-and-loss distributions *can* tell the whole story. This is when, for all levels of the cumulative probability, one distribution is better than ("dominates") the other. Dominated portfolios are in practice extremely rare—indeed, in an arbitrage-free world they could not exist, however fleetingly.

as to what I am doing with their money, and I will add consistency to my investment process, i.e., I will only engage in those projects that are consistent with my desired and freely chosen rating and that provide an acceptable return on the capital required to maintain such a rating. It all sounds very sensible and, as I said, appealing.

Appealing it certainly is, but how feasible is it? Let us look at what we have done in some detail. Let us start from the magic 99.97th percentile. This value may well have been derived from the observed frequency of default within a year of AA-rated firms. But, given the rarity of such an event, nothing can convince me that this frequency was not obtained from a very, very small number of actual defaults—perhaps as few as two or three. Perhaps those defaults occurred during a severe economic downturn, but we now find ourselves in a benign economic environment. So, the observed *past frequency* of default may well be three in ten thousand, but the true *current probability* of default could very easily lie anywhere between one and five.* If the "true" number of defaults that we should expect were one, we would be talking about the 99.99th percentile; if it were five, the appropriate percentile would be the 99.95th.

"What are a few nines between friends?" one might ask. Unfortunately, as in the old joke about the budget deficit ("A billion here, a billion there, and soon you begin to talk about some real money"), a nine here, a nine there, and soon you are talking about very different amounts of capital. Let us get a feel for the numbers. Even assuming the most benign distribution of all, i.e., the non-fat-tailed normal distribution, the "economic capital" associated with the 99.95th percentile is 20% lower than the capital for the 99.99th percentile. It may not seem to amount to much, but since these numbers enter the denominator when we calculate the return on capital, this difference can completely alter our investment decision. Suppose the expected payoff from a risky investment with a volatility of 20% is twice the initial outlay of

---

*If you are a frequentist, of course, this sentence is heresy, as there is only one true probability of default. We will not go into that.

money. On a stand-alone basis, the return on capital can be 13%, 4%, or 1.5%, depending on whether I am looking at the 99.5th, 99.9th, or 99.97th percentile, respectively—and all these numbers are about as plausible for the chosen rating.

This, unfortunately, is not nit-picking. When we are that far out in the tails, apparently small differences in comfort level (say, between the 99.95th and the 99.99th percentile) can make a very large difference in the ratios we construct. Recall that we never said that the bondholders, the equity holders, or even the rating agencies started by demanding that the probability of survival per annum should be, say, 99.97%. This number dropped out as a byproduct of a rating, i.e., of an independent set of (largely judgmental and qualitative) criteria to assess a firm's ability to repay debt.* It is a doubtful "reconstruction of history" to claim that investors and bondholders *required* that probability to start with. Indeed it would be extremely surprising if this were the case because, as we discussed in chapter 2, human beings are *cognitively* very poor at making decisions based on such low probabilities. So, looking at return on economic capital can make sense, but, unless we are careful, the results we obtain can strongly depend on the percentile we choose. And the route by which this particular choice was made (i.e., the reverse engineering of a probability from a frequency of defaults, and of the latter from a rating) was ingenious, but not exactly very robust.

"You worry too much," you may rebut, "As long as you always use the *same* percentile, you will be comparing apples with apples: the return you compute may be 'wrong' (in some sense), but the errors will cancel out. Your *ordering* of investments would not change." Unfortunately, things are not so simple. This objection may be valid in this form if you only compared unfunded (off-balance-sheet) transactions, i.e., transactions for which you have to advance no money up front. Unfortunately, in reality you have to compare returns from "bets" with returns from funded transactions (say, lending money to a risky counterparty or buying some

---

*See again the footnote on p. 203 regarding the weight of subjective criteria in assigning a rating.

equity investment), for which you *do* have to part with "real" money up front. Let us see how these two types of investments interact when it comes to overall economic capital—and hence to their expected return on economic capital.

To simplify matters, suppose that you are considering two investments, one funded (buying a risky bond) and one unfunded (entering a bet). You have paid $100 for the bond today and, if everything goes well (i.e., if the issuer of the bond does not default), you will get $110 at the end of the period (say, one year). You have also entered a bet that will settle at the end of the same period. According to the terms of this bet there is a 50% chance that you may lose $100 at the end of the year. If you advanced the money on the funded transaction from money you already have (i.e., not from borrowed money), no one else apart from you will have to worry about the bond defaulting. In other words, you would not have to set any additional capital aside: you have already parted with your "economic capital," in the form of the money you have advanced to the borrower. If you only entered the bet, on the other hand, you may be required to set aside $100 in economic capital to give confidence to the counterparty that you will pay up if you lose. But what about the economic capital required if you entered *both* transactions? Let us see how things could pan out. If you could count on the bond issuer paying you back, you would not need to set any extra money aside, because the final proceeds from the bond ($110) would more than guarantee your ability to pay up if the bet turned sour. If repayment of the bond, however, is uncertain (and it is very likely to be: how else did you get a 10% return, after all?), then your counterparty on the bet transaction will be less than certain of getting his money back. The amount of "economic capital" you will want to set aside therefore becomes a complex function of the probability of losing the bet, the probability of the bond being repaid with interest, *and of the interaction between the two probabilities* (i.e., of the joint probability). To appreciate where this "interaction term" comes from think, for instance, of the bet, "the issuer of the bond will pay me back": you will lose the bet just when you have no money from the bond to pay the bet!*

The important point is that the economic capital required to support a set of unfunded transactions not only depends on the probability of losing your bets, but is also a rather complex function of the probability of default in the funded transactions you have already entered and of the (statistical) dependence between the two. If you have lent money to the Treasury, it may yield a lot less than an Iraqi bond, i.e., on a stand-alone basis it may show a pretty poor return on economic capital. However, since you are guaranteed to get your money back, you will be required to set aside less extra money to "support" the risky unfunded bets you have entered. Also your creditors will sleep better at night, and may therefore be more willing to advance the money you require for your next project.

Of course, a perfectly functioning economic-capital engine would automatically "know" about all of this. However, the investment decisions suggested by maximizing return on economic capital *do* depend on the precise level of safety chosen: for instance, derivatives transactions with *potentially* unlimited downside become progressively more penalized over lending transactions as the percentile increases. And this precise level of safety (99.97? 99.9? 99.99?) is a very weak link in the chain of reasoning. This is another reason why a few nines (between friends) can make a big difference: any change in percentile level can alter the ranking of investment returns, both between funded and unfunded ones and among funded ones.

There is one more important problem with the return-on-economic-capital approach. Like most problems that arise with a complex but reasonable theory, it is not insurmountable, but it should not be ignored. Its roots go to the core of the discussions we had about relevant data in the first three chapters.

---

*Readers familiar with capital markets will immediately recognize that what you have done is to buy a bond and to sell protection on the same bond via a credit default swap.

We know that what matters in calculating the return on economic capital is the *excess* capital generated by a given candidate initiative. This is the quantity by which the expected excess payoffs should be divided. This excess capital depends on all the other existing business initiatives and interacts with them in a complex way. The far tail of the overall profit-and-loss distribution will in fact depend not only on the tails of the individual risk factors affecting the new candidate initiative, but also on the codependence among all the risk factors. We have seen in chapter 6 that codependence is not the same thing as correlation. And we have also seen that most of the statistical information we have pertains, by definition, to the body of the distribution, not the tails (that is why the body is the body and not the tail, after all). This is particularly worrying, because when exceptional events occur it is well-known that the nature of codependence changes dramatically, as any trader who lived through the market events of 1998 can testify: all of a sudden, strategies as apparently "uncorrelated" as swap spread trades, equity-merger arbitrage, positions in equity volatility, emerging-market bets, holding of safe but illiquid mortgage bonds, and many other trades suddenly displayed an unexpected, but extremely strong, degree of codependence. It was this unexpected, and unexpectedly strong, codependence that effectively sank the legendary hedge fund Long Term Capital Management. Therefore, if we want to look at the extreme tails of a profit-and-loss distribution, we should try to estimate the codependence that prevails not during normal market conditions but when exceptionally large and rare price moves occur.

As usual, there are sophisticated statistical techniques that allow us to take a stab at solving the problem. Unsurprisingly, in doing so we encounter (in spades) all the problems we have already discussed in the estimation of the tails of single-factor distributions: paucity of data, lack of a reliable structural model that would allow us to extrapolate confidently, dubious relevance of very ancient data (even if they are available), etc. But we are also faced with new problems stemming from the fact that we are now trying to disentangle a multitude of cross-dependencies that only in textbook cases can be decomposed into pairwise terms.

As a consequence of this we are faced with a trebly difficult task. First, when we set out to describe the dependence of several variables our task has become infinitely more complex (for each pair of risk factors we need at least *a whole function*, not a single number, to describe both their body and tail dependence*). Second, when we look far out in the tails, by definition we have very few data points and our results become more sensitive than ever to parameter uncertainty. Third, we are still faced with the usual cognitive difficulty of not knowing how one should "behaviorally" deal with low-probability but potentially catastrophic events. As a consequence, assessing the desirability of an investment by looking at the return on economic capital may well sound like an appealing idea, but, by looking at the very far tails, we are making our task very difficult indeed—and the farther out we want to move in percentile land, the more difficult our task becomes.

The reader might think that what I have said is so obvious that everybody in the field should wholeheartedly agree with it. This is unfortunately far from being the case. Here is one example, from the many I could have chosen, that comes from an article that recently appeared in a refereed journal.

The authors, two consultants who have "conducted economic capital projects for both large and small banks in Europe," set themselves the task of estimating the 99.95th percentile of the yearly loss distribution for a corporate loan portfolio. Let us remind ourselves that this means that they intended to estimate a loss from a loan portfolio that would have been exceeded only once since the birth of Christ (give or take a few years). They employ a variety of statistical techniques (standard Gaussian distributions, correlation matrices, and regression coefficients, of course, but also somewhat fancier stuff, like Beta distributions and their inverses). The equations and acronyms flow effortlessly in their paper, but when it comes to the crucial empirical question of where they are going to find sufficient relevant data to estimate

---

*For quantitative readers, this function is, of course, the copula function.

once-in-two-thousand-years events the answer the authors give is as follows: "we deem a period of five years to be a relevant regime for the economic circumstances over the next year." Since the authors wrote this article toward the end of 2006, their data set fails to include not only the Black Death, the Thirty Years' War, the Barbarian invasions, and the fall of the Roman Empire, but even the economic recession of 1991—*the only meaningful recession in the last twenty years.* I find it astonishing that this seemed to worry neither the authors nor the referee. Needless to say, to bridge the gap between what happened (or, rather, did not happen) five years ago and the famous corporate loan book crises of the Paleochristian era, Monte Carlo simulations ride valiantly to the rescue: "After, say, 1 million iterations, economic capital can be determined with the help of the 99.95th percentile of the expected loss." The precision of the author's estimate is equally staggering: the loss is not €110 million—it is €109.7 million!

It would be cheap of me to criticize one particular paper were it not for the fact that similar arguments can be found by the dozen in the current risk-management literature. I recently challenged a journal reviewer as to why so many technically correct, but ultimately meaningless, papers similar to this one get past the peer-review process. The answer I received was that this type of approach has by now become so widespread that it would be unfair ("churlish" was the word used) to penalize a particular submitting author for the sins of the whole community. This is not a healthy state of affairs.

In short, the main reason why economic capital has become so popular is that it seems to offer an answer to the question of what we are supposed to do with the pre- and post-new-business profit-and-loss distributions—and, as we have seen, this question is a really tough one. These curves do contain a lot of information.* One may even say that, from the statistical point of view, they

---

*Incidentally, the production of these nice curves does not come cheap: for a large international bank, the cost of pulling together in a meaningful manner all the pieces of information needed for the task can easily run into the tens of millions of dollars. I am personally aware of a large American bank whose total bill was a number with eight trailing zeros after the first significant figure.

contain *all* the relevant information at hand. But how can we tease a simple decision rule out of them? Looking at return on capital provides an appealing tool to extract from these complex curves one such relatively simple decision rule. We should not forget, however, how the sausage was made: in particular, we should not forget that the weakest link in the chain, i.e., the choice of the precise percentile, can make a big difference not only to our final ranking of returns, but, ultimately, to the very meaningfulness of the question we are trying to answer.

THE BIGGER PICTURE

It is time to set the discussion of economic capital in the wider framework of the topics covered so far. We can go back to the example of entering a coin-flipping bet and simultaneously purchasing a bond. We started that discussion by assuming that we can establish exactly the probability of the bond defaulting, the probability of you winning the bet, and the dependence between the two events. We have discussed at length that the validity of this assumption of perfect knowledge is far from obvious and that, unfortunately, the answer is not "all in the data." This becomes more valid the rarer the events we are looking at: by their very paucity they make any (frequentist) approach based purely on data observation more dubious and increase the importance of our nondata, model-driven judgement. Indeed, the rarer the events and the lower the probabilities, the more dubious a purely frequentist answer becomes:

> A prediction based on past observations is a subjective judgement inferred from the available data and the belief that nothing else about the problem will change in an unexpected way. … This is our contextual information. Every time we infer that some property of some random sequence will also hold in the future, we are making an educated—but subjective—judgement of this type. This is exactly the problem faced by [financial] institutions, which always have limited information

on obligors and often need to aggregate historical data to obtain meaningful estimates of default probabilities.*

We have also seen that when probabilities and correlations become "fuzzy" rather than sharp and perfectly known, the decisions we reach can change dramatically, not just at the margin. The reader could revisit the example about betting on a thousand coin tosses when the coin is known with certainty to be biased in our favor but when there is some reasonable uncertainty about the biasedness of the coin (without changing the central estimate). In this case we saw in chapter 2 that, because of the uncertainty in one parameter, we did not simply bet a bit less: our anticipated behavior changed completely.[3]

Looking at the problem from a different angle, we saw that, at a cognitive level, human beings can be both surprisingly good and very poor at making decisions under uncertainty. They can display an uncanny ability to use their System I mechanisms to arrive at better-than-fair assessments of medium-to-high-probability events. But they fail miserably (and sometimes even in comical ways) when the probabilities in question become extremely low. Therefore, when we speak about events whose probabilities of occurrence are of the order of one in a thousand or ten thousand years, we are fully and exclusively relying on our System II mechanisms. In other words, if we based our choices only on the return rankings produced by a very-high-percentile economic-capital engine, we would be placing an awful lot of reliance on the precise workings of a pretty dark grey (if not outright black) box. To top it all off, the task is not made any easier by the fact that these System II mechanisms have to rely on calculations that are very sensitive indeed to parameter uncertainty.

Despite its opaqueness and its sensitivity to parameter uncertainty, the rule to maximize return on economic capital does have some important and appealing features: to start with, it gets the business community out of the decisional impasse generated by

*J. Sobehart (2005), Estimating default probabilities: the value of contextual information, Citigroup Working Paper RA-CRA-JRS-091205.

the transcendental contemplation of the profit-and-loss distributions. More importantly, it provides decision makers with one tool broadly linked to the way they choose to (or have to) manage their business: return on *some* capital, be it regulatory or economic, is something they just cannot ignore. Also, entering any risky investment does have unavoidable capital implications. Whether these are dealt with by mechanistic rules (such as the ratios that make use of risk-weighted assets) or by an all-singing, all-dancing economic-capital engine is not a fundamental choice between radically different ways of looking at a business proposition. Rather, the choice of the particular decisional tool embodies a trade-off between several factors, such as the transparency of the output, the reasonableness of the assumptions, the reliability and robustness of the results and, last but not least, the cost in arriving at the decision. Any reasonable piece of information can be of use in making a complex choice. As we have seen, the trick is to use our decisional silver bullets wisely.

In my opinion, if applied to significantly lower percentiles (of the order of 90% or below, say), economic-capital reasoning is much more intuitive, robust, and cognitively resonant—in short, much more appealing. It will not contain all the answers we need, but what it tells us can make sense and be useful. I am encouraged by the discovery that, at the time of writing, a major and sophisticated European bank has joined the ranks of those banks that deploy an economic-capital engine to manage their risk, but that it does so by focusing on the 75th percentile of the yearly profit-and-loss distribution (i.e., by looking at events of a severity that should be experienced, on average, once every *four* years).

Admittedly, such "low" percentiles would not automatically satisfy the AA-rating criterion. But recall that these ratings are not given by looking at probabilities of current default to start with; rather, the default probabilities are derived by looking at the past default frequencies of cohorts of similarly rated entities. Therefore, a multiplicative safety factor ("metaphorically" intended to translate the 90th or lower percentile to the desired level of confidence) would be both simple and transparent. There is, of course, a strong precedent in regulatory practice in this respect. When the regulators first associated the capital to be set aside to cover for market risk losses with the Value-at-Risk metric, they required the computation of a somewhat reasonable percentile (the 99th, one-day percentile). They then stipulated that this number should be multiplied by a factor of three—an inelegant patch, perhaps, meant to cover a multitude of modeling and statistical sins, but a reasonable and sensible one nonetheless. If we want to use return on economic capital to rank investments, a fixed multiplicative factor like this would have the advantage of not altering their ordering. There will be more about this in the final pages of this book.

In conclusion, if the uncertainty in the parameters is taken into account, if the percentile is not chosen to be ridiculously high, if, in sum, we use common sense, economic capital *can* provide one useful decisional tool. If it is judiciously used, it can help a bank reach the investment decisions it has to make. Perhaps it can even become one of our silver bullets, but it is no panacea. With Montale, we still do not have the magic formula capable of opening to us decisional worlds.

CHAPTER 10

WHAT CAN WE DO INSTEAD?

It is in vain to speak of cures, or think of remedies, until such
time as we have considered of the causes. ... He is happy that
can perform this aright.

Robert Burton*

It's a nice idea in practice, but it will never work in theory.

A joke often told about economists†

THE DIFFERENT FACES OF RISK MANAGEMENT

Criticizing something is always considerably easier than proposing a constructive alternative. Indeed, it is so much easier that it
would be unfair of me not to try and offer some proposals as to
what one could do instead, thus laying myself open to someone
else's criticism.‡

My starting point is somewhat different from the currently
received wisdom, i.e., the motherhood-and-apple-pie statement
that great advantages will be reaped by aligning prudential regulation with the "best risk-management practice" actually imple-
mented by financial institutions. Regulators, according to this

---

*R. Burton (2001), *The Anatomy of Melancholy* (New York Review Books Clas-
sics).

†Quoted in Coyle, *The Soulful Science*.

‡As usual, I have tried to keep the tone as discursive as possible, but, especially in the second part of the chapter, the reader who does not have some knowledge of financial markets and risk management may find the going somewhat
tougher than in the rest of the book.

view, should take inspiration for their *rules* from the industry's risk-management *practices*. This approach may appear both intuitive and laudable, but it is not obvious to me that it is necessarily such a good idea. Both private firms and regulators are of course concerned with the management of financial risk, but they are interested for very different reasons. The following quote from the opening pages of the 2005 *Financial Stability Review* published by the Bank of England* makes the point clearly:

> Private firms cannot be expected voluntarily to take full account of the possible consequences of spillovers from their actions for the overall stability of the financial system as a whole, unless their incentives are altered. Hence there is a potential role for policy makers in influencing incentives appropriately and in some cases constraining private action.[1]

If banks and regulators are driven by different motives, *they should also use different tools*.[2] To the extent that *systemic* risk is the concern of regulators, they should have no obvious role to play in actively managing the day-to-day affairs of the bank[†] (nor do they have special knowledge that would allow them to do so better than the bank's managers themselves). So, it does make sense for regulators to require "safety buffers," but these should be designed to prevent only extreme negative events.

One way of doing this (but by no means the only way) is for regulators to measure and monitor banks' losses at very, very high percentiles, and to equate prudential capital to these high percentiles. If it could be estimated reliably, the extreme-percentile approach may make sense for the ultimate gatekeepers of financial stability. Such an approach would, however, be of dubious use to the managers of a private bank: there are a host of unpleasant events short of total default that private-firm risk managers should worry about.[3] By and large, these are all the nasty surprises (well, short of default) that occur over timescales not too

---

Financial Stability Review, Bank of England (June 2005, issue 18, p. 3).

[†]Of course, regulators may have wider mandates than preventing systemic risk—such as, for instance, protecting the consumer. In this domain the enlightened interference of regulators with the affairs of a bank is right and proper.

dissimilar to the frequency with which substantive new information about the firm's performance is provided to investors. If investors think in terms of, say, annual or semiannual reports, the CEO of a bank may want to organize his business in such a way that he will have a chance somewhere in the region of one-in-twenty to one-in-fifty of having to stand up and deliver some pretty disappointing news to analysts and shareholders. Of course, if the CEO decides that he will *never, ever* give such disappointing earnings reports, his business is likely to be so staid and boring that he is more likely to disappoint investors from the returns side. But if, on the other hand, results are too noisy, the estimation curse kicks in, and his share price may begin to suffer from the Goldman Sachs syndrome that we discussed in the closing pages of chapter 5. Indeed, one of the main tasks of CEOs and CFOs is to find the right trade-off between perceived risk (and the accompanying degree of opaqueness) and the expected returns; all of this while keeping their financing options open, i.e., keeping their future bondholders happy.

If we accept this, this brings me to the first suggestion of this chapter. A variety of decisional tools and risk indicators will have to be used by private-firm mangers and regulators: no single metric (economic capital, VaR, more-or-less risk-adjusted return on equity, etc.) will be able *by itself* to tell the full story. All of these tools, if confidently and robustly estimated, will provide some help in reaching sound decisions, but none will, or should, constitute the be all and end all of risk management or decision making. For this reason, in the rest of the chapter I will clearly split my suggestions between recommendations for risk managers and for regulators.

WHAT CAN PRIVATE-FIRM RISK MANAGERS DO?

Here is a preview of the approach I suggest for private-firm risk managers.

We start from a risky initiative: this could be a trade, the proposal to invest in a new business line, to lend money to a particular borrower, to purchase a risky security, etc. Given this risky initiative (for brevity, the "trade" in the following), we analyze its expected return and its risk *separately*. I will explain the reasons for doing so in the next section.

When we look at the risk part of the equation, we may want to build the profit-and-loss distribution associated with the "trade," as we discussed in the previous chapters. When we choose to do so, we identify a handful of critical indicators associated with it.[4] These will be indicators that, empirically, appear to be associated with the way we react to risk: they will be pointers, for instance, that allow us to understand whether we are selling lottery tickets, buying insurance, or rolling dice. These will be our silver bullets.

We will *not* combine the special indicators thus identified into a single "decision indicator"—yet another magic formula. Instead, we stick to our view that choices come first (and only from these, if one really wants to, can one distil a utility function or a decisional rule). What we try to attain is some help and guidance in making these choices. "Help and guidance" often translates into "decisional consistency": we will highlight certain critical behavioral responses to risk in relatively simple situations, and try to use these insights for the real-life problems we are faced with. A variety of risk indicators (of which economic capital may well be one) can help us. It is not an easy task.

Finally, we will not limit ourselves to studying the profit-and-loss distribution. We may want to make use of scenario or survivability analyses. It may well be the case that we will not be able to assign a sharp probability to these scenarios. We should not feel bad about this (we should not feel that we are engaged in second-class risk management) and we should not think that our control of risk will necessarily be less effective.

It is clearly a modest approach. It does not promise a "revolutionary new way to look at risk." It should reflect, however, the way risk management is actually carried out in banks. The following subsections flesh out this program.

Risk and Return: A Separate or a "Holistic" Approach?

Since risk and return are the cornerstones of modern finance, this is surely a good place to start. Should we look at these two components separately or in a combined fashion (as common sense would suggest)?

My views on this are somewhat at odds with much of current conventional "industry best practice," which seems to place a very high reliance on the construction of profit-and-loss distributions (built using frequentist techniques) in order to answer *in one fell swoop* the fundamental question in investment decisions: does this initiative give a good return for the risk it entails? Once you have built these profit-and-loss profiles, this view recommends, read off from this all-informative graph, *both* the expected return from a project *and* your favorite proxies for its risk (variance, 99.9th percentile, omega function, skewness, you name it). Reach your decisions accordingly. Above all, reach your decisions "holistically" (perhaps even at an enterprise-wide level), where "holistically," as far as I can understand, means that you should use the same tool (the profit-and-loss distribution) to assess both the profitability of the "trade" and its risk.

I have serious reservations about this program. I believe that it is more effective to use different tools in conducting the analyses of the expected return and of the risk of a proposed initiative. More precisely, I intend to argue as follows:

- Statistical (frequentist) analysis of data plays a different role when we analyze return and when we assess risk.
- Statistical (frequentist) analysis of publicly available data is of little use *in itself* to assess the return characteristics of a project (i.e., to tell us whether we expect to make money from the project).
- When it comes to the assessment of the *risk* associated with a given initiative, statistical (frequentist) analysis of historical data often becomes more relevant and useful.

- Different "types of" probability are therefore of relevance in analyzing return and risk: mainly subjective for the former, more frequentist for the latter.

Since this view is not mainstream, the onus is on me to justify it. This is my line of argument.

Data are obviously useful, indeed essential, in arriving at all good business decisions. But when it comes to estimating the expected return from a "trade," the competitive advantage we hope to reap is most unlikely to be found in publicly available data, no matter how clever we are at using the statistical tools at our disposal.* We may well have religiously kept long histories about hundreds of financial time series. The problem is that our competitors have them as well. If an asset has, say, performed very well in the past, this stellar performance is there for all to observe. Its price will have been bid up to reflect this. It may be debatable whether prices efficiently and immediately incorporate *all* publicly available information, but it would be very surprising if they failed to reflect statistical information that can be distilled from public-domain data. Therefore, market expectations about *future* returns certainly incorporate information about *past* returns (which you, your competitor, and your competitor's dog all have access to)—plus a lot more besides.

Perhaps you may have an informational advantage if you have kept or otherwise obtained better data than your competitors. But do not forget that it is not enough to have better data than the *average* bank: for you to be able to exploit this type of informational advantage you must have better data than the smartest deep-pocketed guy out there.

The view I have presented may seem uncontroversial: it simply restates in a rather roundabout way that chartism does not work—these days, hardly a conclusion one should make a song and dance about. Note, however, that whenever we try to estimate the expected return from a project from its past

---

*Unless, of course, you have at your disposal data that no one else has, or unless you have devised extremely sophisticated and effective statistical tools that no one has discovered yet. Good luck.

performance using the profit-and-loss distribution—as the "holistic" school of thought recommends—this is just what we are doing: we are assuming that the *past* gives us equally useful information about *all* the features of the *future* distribution. I maintain that this is not the case. In particular, frequentist analysis of past data may give us better guidance about the dispersion of a distribution (technically speaking, the second and higher moments) than about its future central location (its first moment). Put more simply, frequentist analysis may tell us a lot more about the risk than about the return. To a significant extent, this goes back to the fundamentally greater difficulty in estimating returns (where the distribution is located) than variance (its dispersion).

What else, then, can give us a competitive advantage when we formulate our views about the returns we are seeking? It can only be something that comes from outside the publicly shared data. In Bayesian terms, this something else is what makes up the prior beliefs (the "model" in the meteorological example of chapter 7) on the basis of which we organize and make sense of the publicly available data. If public information is promptly disseminated to all market participants, and therefore almost instantaneously becomes *common* knowledge, our hopes of engaging in a successful (superior) "trade" can only come from the superiority of our prior beliefs.

These prior beliefs, on the other hand, are not the answer in themselves. Without the information coming from the data, they only tell one part of the story. It is only by efficiently integrating the two components (priors plus evidence) that we can arrive at the best possible decision. And this is where careful statistical analysis of whatever data we, and our competitors, have becomes essential.

My views about estimating returns can therefore be summarized as follows:

- Subjective (Bayesian) probability teaches us how to combine our prior views about a phenomenon (our "prior belief") with new data (the "evidence"), to reach a new, hopefully better, view (the "posterior").

- Given the same "evidence," different prior views (i.e., different individual models to organize facts and information) give rise to different estimates of future expected returns (different posterior beliefs).
- As *public* information is, by definition, *publicly* shared, different views about returns can only come from different prior beliefs.
- Since, when looking at expected returns, money can only be made by drawing conclusions different from "the market's," *one's advantage can only come from one's prior beliefs*.
- Frequentist statistical analysis places all the emphasis on the analysis of the publicly available data, i.e., on the common-knowledge component of the posterior. By itself, it is therefore ill-suited to giving us market-beating (superior) information about returns.

Does this leave any room for statistical analysis then in formulating a view about the return part of a trading decision? Of course it does. Without data, and without good tools to analyze them, we are blind. We *do* need accurate frequentist statistical analysis when formulating a view about expected returns, but only so as not to be at a disadvantage with respect to the market. We need accurate frequentist analysis, in other words, so as not to be punished by the market with near certainty. But this analysis, in itself, will not give us "the edge."

Now, here is the punch line. If you have been convinced by the argument above that subjective probability is the relevant type of probability for assessing returns, but also believe (as I do) that judiciously employed frequentist analysis *is* useful to assess risk, it then follows that *we cannot use the same statistical tools to evaluate the risk and expected reward from a project*. This is where the holistic project runs into trouble. This is why I propose to look at risk and return separately. I explain below how I propose to do so.

Looking at the Return Part of the Equation

Expected return is perhaps the most important piece of information in arriving at an investment decision. For the reasons explained above it is also (and by far) the most difficult one to estimate using "objective" (frequentist) statistical tools. Make no mistake: given enough good data there is no intrinsic impossibility in estimating the drift of a natural noisy phenomenon that is unaffected by our observations and by the actions inspired by these observations. Unfortunately, this is not the situation we are in when dealing with financial time series: as we just discussed, the observation of past performance is one of the determinants for current demand for an asset. Observation alters demand, demand alters price, the change in price modifies the observation. *Au refrain.*

There are more reasons why estimating returns is difficult. When we try to do so, two time frames are of relevance: the length of the historical record at our disposal and the projection horizon (i.e., the horizon of our prediction). Ideally we would like the first to be very long and the second to be very short. Unfortunately, we are in this blessed situation only when dealing with market risk for trading-book positions, but in few other instances of financial or risk-management relevance. Ultimately it all goes back to the discussion in chapter 8, where I explained why it is so much more difficult to estimate trends than volatilities. (Not an unimportant point, after all, because I argued that risk management makes sense for a firm in order to make it easier for external observers to spot the difficult-to-identify trend.) There is no need to repeat the argument here, but the point remains every bit as valid.

This difficulty becomes greater as the time horizon increases. Those romantic ancient Romans used to say that love conquers all. More prosaically, in finance it is true that not love but the trend ultimately prevails over everything. On a century-long chart of equity returns, the 1929 crash and the ten-year Depression that followed appear as little more than a pause in the price progress; 1987's Black Friday is a sneeze; and the dot-com bust barely qualifies as a hiccup. We are fascinated by market crashes and the almost mystical aura that surrounds them. Over short investment horizons, we should well be. But if one is looking twenty or more years ahead, a more relevant (although far less "dramatic") question for equity investment is whether the so-called risk premium (i.e., the extra performance equities are supposed to provide over riskless investments such as Treasury Bills) is two, four, or six percent.[5] Twenty or thirty years are the time horizons of relevance for institutions such as pension funds or life insurance companies. Such apparently mundane differences in the risk premium can therefore radically alter the solvency perspective of pension plans or the ability of life insurers to meet their liabilities.

Even at much shorter timescales (say, five years) trends in most cases still dominate over the "volatility." Suppose that, in 2006, we were considering the "risk" of investing a portfolio in debt instruments. What is riskier: going for long-maturity bonds or for a rolling program of reinvestment in short-maturity bonds? If for the moment we neglect the trend, it is not difficult to generate a profit-and-loss distribution for these two hypothetical portfolios. We just take the daily changes in the relevant rates that happened over the last twenty or thirty years, *after subtracting any trend these data may have*. When we do this, over a five-year horizon the return from the long-bond portfolio will have a much wider spread (see figure 10.1), simply because a long-dated bond will respond to changes in rates much more than a short-dated one.

This suggests that the long-bond portfolio should be much riskier. But let us not forget that we subtracted the trend in the historical rates in carrying out our exercise. In reality the true realized change in the overall level of rates (the *trend* in rates) will cause a shift in the two distributions that will, most likely, more than compensate for the original difference in their widths (see figure 10.2). If in 2006 we were really contemplating a five-year investment proposition, the really relevant risk question would be, "Are we about to enter a period during which central banks will manage to keep inflation in check and rates will remain subdued, or were the last ten-or-so years of low rates and low inflation

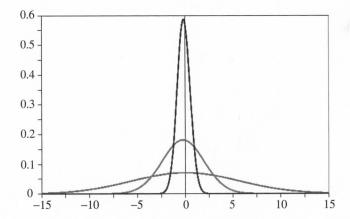

Figure 10.1. The return distributions from a position in two-year, five-year, and ten-year bonds after thousands of simulations of the interest rates over five years. (The position in two-year bonds was rolled over.) In these simulations the trend from the interest rate data has been subtracted.

the exception rather than the norm, and are we going to revert to the higher level of rates of the decade before?" The answer to this question does not come from a frequentist application of statistics to our data set. Our subjective input will dominate by far what the raw data by themselves can tell us.

The other side of the coin is that over very short time horizons even a strong trend is easily overwhelmed by the noise component of price moves. If a stock has a trend of 12% per annum and a volatility of 20%, the price move over the average single day will be affected forty times more by the volatility than by the deterministic term. I have covered this in chapter 8, and I will not repeat the argument here.

So, paradoxically, when carrying out risk analyses purely statistical (frequentist) information about expected returns should often be neglected for either of two opposite reasons: over very short horizons because returns do not matter; and over long horizons because they matter too much.

The fact that return information cannot be readily gleaned from standard statistical techniques does not mean, of course,

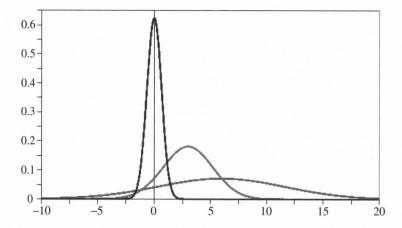

Figure 10.2. The return distributions for the same bonds as in figure 10.1, but now *without subtracting the trend from the interest rate data*. The two-year distribution is still the narrowest, but it is now displaced to the left because during the five-year period covered by the simulation rates by and large declined. (As rates fall, all bonds rise in value, but long-dated ones do so more strongly.) Note how, even over a relatively short horizon, the information coming from the trend totally overwhelms the information from the dispersion.

that return considerations should not enter an investment analysis. What the discussion above *does* imply, however, is that return assumptions are often exogenously applied to (superimposed on) the analysis of the risk-and-return profile of a prospective business activity. Simplifying greatly, we often want to enter a "trade" because information that is not purely based on data makes us believe that its return will be attractive: rates are poised to rise; equity markets will do well; the dollar will outperform the euro; etc. But we employ (rather, *we graft on top*) a statistical risk analysis to make sure that we do not get carried away by our enthusiasm and we do not expose ourselves to unacceptable losses.[6] Not an elegant solution, perhaps, but a pragmatically useful one.

Finally, if we are using a statistical model to carry out our risk analysis, and if this model incorporates internal or exogenous assumptions about returns, it is extremely important to carry out what is called a sensitivity analysis: would our conclusions differ dramatically if the (often exogenous) estimated return were 10% instead of 12%? If so, how confident are we that our decisions would be robust to this degree of uncertainty? By how much can I be wrong in my return assumption for my decision not to change?

Looking at the Risk Part of the Equation

So much for the expected-return part of the equation. What about risk? How should we carry out our risk analysis? What do we mean by "risk"?

I propose that first we should try to understand in a quantitative and qualitative manner the overall risk nature of the project (e.g., its typical and exceptional range of variability, its sold-insurance or long-lottery-tickets features, etc.). This is where judiciously applied frequentist statistical analysis can best help us. All the caveats about relevant data, frequency of sampling, length of holding periods, and the time homogeneity of the phenomenon at hand are obviously relevant here.

When this analysis has been carried out, we can move on to addressing a few specific questions, designed to tease out in a cognitively resonant manner the risk aspects that we are likely to find relevant in reaching our decision. We are moving, as we make this step, from gathering information to making decisions. I cannot stress strongly enough that this is not a small step. There is a well-established science that teaches us how to extract the best information from the data. It is called statistics, and its use in risk management is well-known. There is, however, another science that deals with how actual human beings reach financial decisions once the data have been gathered. It is a branch of experimental psychology, and it is also well-established. Unfortunately, its use in risk management is nowhere near as widespread as that of statistics. I will therefore have to rely, in presenting the following recommendations, on my experience and intuition, but I am well aware that what I propose could be readily improved upon by a more systematic and "scientific" approach. This is therefore a call to arms for experimental psychologists to do more work in this area (and to make their results available to a wider audience).[7]

So, here are some of the questions that can complement the more traditional statistical analysis. The first has to do with survivability. Can we afford to embark on this initiative or trade if things do not pan out according to plan A? Can we survive a failure? What is our ultimate loss tolerance? How does the risky prospect look in this light?

A more unusual but, in my opinion, very useful question is, if everything *does* work out in the best plausible manner, how much better can I realistically hope to fare than if I entered a riskless investment? In other words, is the potential upside in the rosiest scenario worth the risk I am taking?

Finally, I find it useful to ask the following question: "By how much would things have to go wrong before the risky initiative performed no better and no worse than putting the money in a safe deposit account?"

I will explain why these three types of questions (survivability, best outcome, and breakeven analysis) are useful in reaching a decision in the rest of this chapter.

It may all sound rather vague and abstract at this stage. The following subsections show how this program can be carried out in practice. Let us start from the quantitative analysis of the return distribution.

Risk: What Is the Dispersion in the Distribution?

After expected return, the second-best-known statistic for analyzing a risky prospect is variance (or standard deviation). At a qualitative level, the information it conveys is about the dispersion of outcomes under relatively "normal" circumstances. It has an illustrious pedigree in classic asset allocation and investment theory, where, together with returns, it constitutes *the* cornerstone of decision theory under uncertainty. Probably because of this association, it has become synonymous with "risk," but this identification is clearly unsatisfactory. We can construct distributions that have identical variance but with which we would associate very different degrees of "riskiness"—and risk, as the saying goes, is one word but is not one number. The most-quoted example for showing the shortcomings of variance as a risk indicator is the case of a "trade" when there is a great variability of *positive* outcomes, but a very limited downside. Variance does not distinguish this situation from its toxic mirror image (when you have sold not bought insurance). However, if the information it conveys is complemented with an understanding of the finer features of a distribution (its higher moments), then variance does become a very useful indicator of risk. For this reason I quickly turn to statistics that can shed light on these finer, but for risk assessment essential, distributional features.

Risk: Is My Distribution Symmetric?

We begin to deal with more interesting characterizations of the risk–return profiles of a distribution when we ask ourselves whether we are "selling lottery tickets," "buying insurance," or "throwing dice." As we move beyond expected return and variance, the first important task of a risk indicator is therefore to discriminate between these fundamental types of risky activities. Let us look at how this can be achieved in some detail.

Bought-insurance trades create distributions populated by many small losses (the cost of the lottery tickets) and (hopefully) a few large gains. We therefore expect the right tail of the distribution to extend farther out than the left one. Swap "small" for "large" and "left" for "right," and the same applies to selling lottery tickets. The standard statistical tool to detect this feature of a distribution is, of course, its skewness (related to its third moment). The problem with the estimation of moments higher than two is that the value obtained from a finite sample can be very noisy—the higher the moment we are trying to estimate, the noisier it gets. Generalizing greatly, for the typical amount of relevant data available for financial applications,* skewness tends to be just at the boundary of robust "estimability." Kurtosis (the measure of how "fat" the tails are, i.e., of how much we are exposed to very large losses or gains), which we will encounter below, is often past this robust-estimability boundary. The reliable estimation of moments higher than four for daily time series or those gathered less frequently almost always belongs to the Christmas wish list. (And, by the way, the higher the moment, the less confident we can be that such a high moment is well-defined at all for the true underlying distribution.)

So, going back to our measure of the asymmetry of the distribution, my recommendation is to use some more robust proxy measures for the skewness. To do so, you should determine first how far out in the tail, given your data set, you can reliably push your gaze. How much do you trust your 25th and 75th percentiles? Your 10th and 90th? Your 5th and 95th? Note that these pairs of points are symmetrically positioned with respect to the center of the distribution, because these are the points we want to use in order to assess the sold- or bought-insurance nature of a given trade.[†]

Once we have settled on a couple of reliable percentiles, what we want to do next is measure the distance from the center of the distribution of these two symmetrically positioned points and take the difference. Clearly, if the distance from the center is (close to) zero, the distribution is (nearly) symmetric. If the difference is positive, your distribution has bought-insurance features. If negative, it belongs to the sold-lottery-ticket type.

---

*As usual, high-frequency foreign exchange data are plentiful enough to detect possible asymmetries in the distribution. Credit data are nowhere near as plentiful, but they can also be sufficient because of the extremely asymmetric nature of the distribution.

[†]There are many ways to get a feel for the degree of confidence we can have in these estimates. To begin with, do we get similar numbers if we calculate them using the first half of the data and then the second half? A bit more cleverly, since these percentiles are independent of the order of the observations, we can sample, say, half of the observed points many, many times and calculate the associated percentiles. How stable are they?

By the way, there are worse things that you could do than plotting this difference as a function of the distance from the center. As well as being intrinsically interesting, this plot will quickly give you an idea of how far out in the tails you can reliably go (see figure 10.3). This figure was obtained by using the most benign distribution of all: the well-domesticated bell (Gaussian) curve. Five hundred points were randomly drawn, and the differences of the distances from the center were taken for all the symmetrically arranged percentiles. Apart from the vagaries of the particular random draw, all these differences should be exactly zero. Indeed, most of the values hover around zero, but the curse of the high percentile again becomes evident for the last points. In this case, of course, we know what the answer *should* be (zero everywhere). If we did not, and these were real data, a casual inspection of this graph suggests that we would do well stopping not far beyond the 95th percentile.

Risk: Should I Be Throwing Dice Instead?

Variance gives us an insight into the typical range of variability of returns. Skewness tells us whether, *given an overall degree of variability*, the most frequent source of this variability comes from good or bad events. The next step is to look at whether we are taking more or less risk than if we were throwing dice (again, *given an overall degree of variability*). In other words, we want to look at whether we are exposed to more or fewer extreme events than a normal distribution *with the same variance* would have.

There is, of course, a well-known statistical tool to answer this question: it is called kurtosis, and an Excel spreadsheet will calculate it for you in a microsecond for any reasonable data set you may have. The problem is that this statistic can be very strongly influenced by a few large outliers (this is because deviations from the mean are raised to the fourth power). For this reason a few bad apples can totally spoil the meaningfulness of your number. You must be careful, though, in labeling points as "bad apples" (erroneous data points, for instance) as they may be exactly the large events you were interested in.

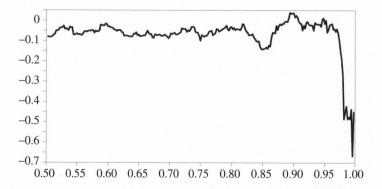

Figure 10.3. Getting a feel for how far out in the tails we can reliably estimate skewness. Each point on this curve has been obtained by taking the differences of the distances from the center taken for all the symmetrically arranged empirical percentiles. The percentile is on the *x*-axis. The empirical percentiles were obtained by simulating 500 random variables from a standard Gaussian distribution. In the absence of noise all the differences should be exactly zero. In this case, i.e., when we know the answer beforehand, the deviation from zero therefore gives an indication of the error in our statistical estimate. In a real-life situation, when we do not know what the answer should be, the tell-tale sign that we are just looking at noise is the type of erratic and jagged behavior we observe in this figure after the 95th percentile.

Another reason why the kurtosis statistic may fall short of your expectations is that it is often expressed as "excess kurtosis," i.e., as the *extra* fatness a given distribution may have over and above the fatness of a Gaussian distribution (the one you would obtain in the limit by throwing a fair coin). Kurtosis is therefore expressed as a number above or below 3. This is all well and good, but how do you interpret the number of, say, 4.2 returned by your Excel function? Granted, they are fatter than the tails of a normal distribution, but how "fat" are they really? Should you worry or not?

A simple and stable alternative that allows you to gain a more intuitive feel for the degree of tail fatness of your distribution can be arrived at as follows. First you should "standardize" the hypothetical profit-and-loss values that you produced. This means that you should subtract the mean from each value and divide this difference by the standard deviation of all the values. This puts data with different trends and different variances on the same footing. As a next step you should rank these standardized profit-and-loss values from the smallest to the largest. Once we have produced this list of numbers, you can then look, say, at the standardized value such that only 15% of the values are higher (i.e., at the 85th percentile). If this standardized value is significantly greater than 1,* your real distribution is likely to have "fatter tails" than a Gaussian one in the tail of area 0.15. There is nothing magic about the value of 1. Table 10.1 gives the critical standardized values at different percentile levels that correspond to the bell (Gaussian) curve. You can then easily use these values for comparison.

This table also tells you a bit more than the usual kurtosis value. So, if the standardized 85th percentile we obtain from our real data set were 1.28 instead of 1, the table tells us something more interesting than that the tails are fat: it also shows us that if your real data had been drawn from a Gaussian distribution, only 10% of the occurrences should be larger than the value you obtained. In our real data set there are instead more very large occurrences: 15% of the real losses will be larger than the loss corresponding to the 85th percentile. So, *for the same variance*, with your real distribution you are likely to draw one time in six returns of such magnitude that you should see them only one time in ten if you were dealing with a Gaussian distribution. Are *you* comfortable with this level of tail risk?

Why focus on the Gaussian distribution? Again, there is no fundamental reason for this choice. It is simply the distribution that in the limit results when you toss a fair coin many times. If you think (as I do) that such a coin-tossing example is a relevant reference point, the Gaussian is a plausible choice.

*The exact value would be 1.036. For our purposes a value of 1 is good enough.

Table 10.1. The right column gives the area above the standardized percentile in the left column (see the text for a fuller description).

Standardized percentile	Probability
4.26	0.999 99
1.64	0.95
1.28	0.9
1.03	0.85
0.84	0.8
0.67	0.75
0.52	0.7
0.38	0.65
0.25	0.6
0.12	0.55
0.00	0.5
−0.12	0.45
−0.25	0.4
−0.38	0.35
−0.52	0.3
−0.67	0.25
−0.84	0.2
−1.03	0.15
−1.28	0.1
−1.64	0.05
−4.26	0.000 01

How was the 85th percentile chosen? There is nothing special about this value either. For typical financial data sets, collected daily or at higher frequency, this is likely to be a percentile that can be reliably and robustly estimated. If you trust your data (and their relevance given the current market conditions!) to the 90th or the 95th percentile, by all means do make use of these values as well, or instead. But please make sure, perhaps with a simple plot of your percentiles, that you are not just looking at statistical noise. If you begin to talk to me about the relative fatness of your tails with respect to the Gaussian distribution at the 99.9th percentile,

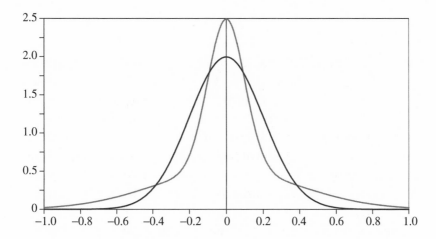

Figure 10.4.   Two distributions with the same variance but different degrees of tail fatness (kurtosis).

I will probably think that you are up to no good. And even if you could estimate such a high percentile reliably, are you sure that you are truly interested in making your risk choices based on such a rare (albeit probably catastrophic) event?

It is easy to understand why we should care about the symmetry of the distribution. But why should we care about the fatness of the tails? This is a behavioral statement that I can only hope will find resonance with you. Look, for instance, at figure 10.4. The two distributions are perfectly symmetric and have the same variance. Suppose that the numbers on the *x*-axis represents profits or losses *for you, now*, in tens of thousands of pounds. Would you prefer to receive a random outcome from the sharply peaked gray curve with long tails, or from the black curve? To help you in your decision let me tell you that with the first distribution you have a 5% chance of losing (or making) at least $6,500. With the normal distribution, at the same probability level you could lose (or make) at least $3,500. Which one do you prefer? What if losing $6,000 would make the cheque you wrote yesterday bounce—a pertinent analogy to the prudential capital held by a bank?

Risk: Scenario Analysis—The Good, the Bad, and the Breakeven

With these simple diagnostics we have hopefully put together a synthetic statistical description of our "trade." We are now ready to move from these key indicators of how much risk our trade has and about the nature of this risk to the choice we ultimately want to make. As I said, I strive in this respect for a cognitively resonant set of decisional crutches. "Cognitively resonant" means that these decisional tools should use the risk dialect that speaks most directly to the way human beings understand, perceive, and constructively interact with risk.

An important step in achieving these goals is defining the "worst plausible" and the "best plausible" scenarios. The terms immediately suggest that we are firmly in subjective-probability land: a worst plausible scenario, for instance, is the set of events that both the risk manager and the "trader" agree could indeed occur with sufficient probability *that they are worth worrying about.* It is the action (the "worrying," the setting of a limit, the buying of some protection insurance) that determines the critical level of probability, not the other way round. It is the amount of insurance paid, or of profit foregone, to avoid a negative event that shows its implied subjective probability.

This is where the checks and balances, and the different compensation structures, for risk managers and "traders" that exist in a bank show their usefulness: if a party (the "trader") gains too much from the upside and loses too little on the downside, he will be naturally inclined to skew his subjective probabilities toward the positive scenarios and to downplay the plausibility of negative outcomes (sometimes even when similar or identical occurrences have already happened in the past: "This time it's different!"). Risk managers, of course, are not unbiased and impartial forecasters either. Playing it safe is a good way of safeguarding their jobs.* In real-life situations, achieving convergence between

---

*Although playing it *too* safe is the safest way for a risk manager to lose his job with near certainty!

traders' and risk managers' views is therefore extremely important: many studies have shown that "expert advice" is far from correctly calibrated, and can be strongly affected by the risk aversion, incentives, and mental make-up of the expert. Philip Tetlock has written a beautiful book on expert judgement that touches on many of these issues (and much more besides).*

So, in the following we will assume that, perhaps after a long discussion between the head trader and the head risk manager, the worst and best plausible scenarios have been agreed upon. What are we going to do with them?

Can I Survive the Worst Plausible Outcome? Given the discussion above, we can safely assume that we already have an estimate of the return from the project we are looking at. The next question to ask, then, is whether we can "survive" the worst plausible scenario. "Surviving" does not just mean "remaining solvent," and it can mean different things to different people: for a risk manager it may simply mean holding on to his job; for a desk-level trader, not hitting his stop-loss limit for the year; for the head of a trading desk, not losing with one large trade, say, half of his yearly budget (and with that, probably, control over his book); for the CEO of a bank it may mean not having to stand in front of a quickly assembled gathering of analysts and journalists at the Stock Exchange to announce a profit warning due to trading losses. In general, survival means avoiding whatever set of outcomes are considered unacceptable *for a given system of assessing performance.*

The last qualifier in italics is important. It highlights that the definition of loss is often not unambiguous but can depend, for instance, on the accountancy regime under which performance is assessed: accrual-accounted managers will, in general, behave very differently in their investment choices and in their definition of what is unacceptable (i.e., of what constitutes "survival") than mark-to-market traders. In the end, of course, there should be just economic value, but in the end we are all dead—or, at least,

---

*Tetlock, *Expert Political Judgement*.

retired. Between now and then there are *incentives* designed for *agents*.

Beyond assessing the worst plausible outcome associated with any proposed strategy, this type of scenario analysis can help in a subtler task: determining the "staying power" of a given strategy. Even if the ultimate view that inspires a trade or a strategy is correct, is the size of the investment or position so large that a temporary divergence from the possibly correctly guessed final target will force the unwinding of the strategy at a loss? This consideration is particularly pertinent for the "negative carry" trades discussed in chapter 4.

How Much Do I Gain in the Best Plausible Scenario?   The mirror image of the worst plausible scenario is, unsurprisingly, the best plausible scenario. Identifying the worst plausible scenario is intuitive enough. But why would we want to look at the best plausible scenario as well? When we undertake a best-scenario analysis we already have in the back of our minds how much "risk" (variance, skewness, fat-tailedness, etc.) the trade has. What is all this risk for? There is no single answer, but we can try to estimate how much better than the expected return we can hope to fare if everything turns out in the best (plausible) way. If we find that such a best plausible outcome is worryingly close to what we have assumed for our expected return, we may want to pause for thought. If it is *worse than* our expected outcome, we certainly have a problem.

Note that if the best outcome is rather close to the expected return this does not necessarily mean trouble: perhaps we are just dealing with a sold-insurance business, from which we expect to make frequent small gains and to suffer rare but large losses. In this case expected return and best plausible scenario may indeed be very close to each other. However, discovering that the best outcome is not too different from the expected one should at the very least send us back to the statistical analysis described in one of the previous sections ("Is My Distribution Symmetric?"). Of course, if we believed that we were entering a bought-insurance strategy—which should, by definition, have small frequent losses and large rare gains—and our best scenario suggests that the best and expected outcomes are very similar, then we *do* have a problem.

What Is My Breakeven? Another pertinent question when analyzing a risky prospect is how badly things have to go for it to yield a return no better than the riskless one (say, depositing the same money in a bank or investing it in Treasury Bills). For instance, if we intend to buy 100 risky loans that pay, say, three percentage points above government debt and hold these loans to maturity, how many of these loans have to default for our return to be the same as from the safe Treasury paper? In general, the extra return earned by risky investments is there to compensate the investor for a number of possible sources of risk: credit risk (the risk that the borrowers we lent money to may not pay us back); liquidity risk (the risk that the demand for what we want to sell may be very low when we do decide to sell); prepayment risk (the risk that the same borrowers may pay us back when we do not want to receive the repayment of the loan); etc. It is almost always possible, and, in my opinion, always useful, to ask the question, "To what extent do these sources of risk have to materialize for the extra return that we were hoping to make to be wiped out?"

Why is it better to phrase this analysis in terms of breakeven events rather than in terms of probabilities? Because, in my experience, this is a much more cognitively resonant way of looking at risk. If I tell you that it only takes two defaults in a given basket of bonds for your supercharged collateralized debt obligation to yield no more than putting your money under the mattress, I have you worried in a manner difficult to achieve if I had recited to you tables of probabilities. The two types of statement may be logically equivalent, but there is a lot more to risk perception than cold logic.

These observations about the breakeven event can be generalized. The three "decisional crutches" I have suggested have one feature in common: they do not (directly) make reference to probabilities, but point to events (say, the best or worst plausible scenario) and to the consequences of their occurrence. They start from what is for us, say, unacceptable, and work out what has to happen for this ultimate pain threshold to be reached. In the abstract there is nothing special or magical about looking at a risky prospect from the perspective I suggest. In theory, one could equivalently say, for instance, that the probability of six loans defaulting is 0.3%. Or that the probability of our chosen worst plausible scenario is 1.2%. But such a framing of the problem has, in my opinion, two obvious shortcomings: first, it is likely to make use (implicitly or explicitly) of a frequentist concept of probability that I often consider inappropriate in this context—the more so, the more remote the probabilities; second, it speaks a language to which we, as human beings, cognitively react poorly—again, the more so, the lower the probability.* Perhaps the human mind can be trained to overcome these cognitive difficulties, but I do not see a good reason why we should swim against the current. Ultimately, risk tolerance is the *description* of (not the *prescription* for) our behavioral response to uncertain events. And if this behavioral response is affected by the framing of a problem, a good description should squarely reflect this.†

The usual criticism leveled against my proposal is that it lacks "scientificity" or "objectivity." I believe that this picture of "objectivity" is, in most cases, misguided. Using subjective probabilities forces us to recognize the limits of our statistical understanding of a complex problem, and to state honestly the assumptions we are using (perhaps simply "the future looks exactly like the past") rather than sweeping them under the carpet. Linking probabilities

---

*In addition to the references quoted in chapter 2, further studies on the cognitive difficulties and biases experienced when dealing with low probabilities can be found, for instance, in D. Kahneman and A. Tversky (1992), *Judgement Under Uncertainty—Heuristics and Biases* (Cambridge University Press), or T. Glovich and D. Kahneman (2002), *Heuristics and Biases: The Psychology of Intuitive Judgement* (Cambridge University Press).

†The interested reader can pursue some of these topics (and in particular the importance of framing) further in M. Bacharach (2006), *Beyond Individual Choice: Teams and Frames in Game Theory* (Princeton University Press).

to actions does not mean failing to make use of "good and solid" empirical information. Quite the opposite. If we truly believed this empirical information to be so good, solid, and relevant to the problem at hand, why would we not make use of it in arriving at our metaphorical advertised odds? Conversely, if it is truly the case that nothing else, apart from the collected data, matters in reaching our prediction, why would we make our life more difficult by contaminating our best estimate with irrelevant information? And finally, by requiring that all the parties in the exercise (the risk manager, the trader, the CEO) should have something important at stake in the exercise (job, reputation, bonus), we make sure that the implied probabilities are not vacuous utterances but truly reflect the best estimate the involved parties can collectively arrive at.

WHAT CAN THE REGULATORS DO?

The discussion at the beginning of this chapter was centered around the contention that, if the risk-management goals of regulators and private firms are different, so should be the tools that they employ. I argued that ensuring the survival of a bank is a minimal goal for a private-bank risk manager, but the first and foremost task of a regulator. This is because the regulators' concern should be control and containment of systemic risk, not the efficient running of a bank viewed as any other private firm. Greenspan's quote in the first footnote on p. xvii was in this respect even clearer: "The management of systemic risk is properly the job of the central banks."

If such systemic concerns are the domain of central banks and regulators, it would seem that, in drafting their rule books, they would be well justified in including rules and criteria based on the probability of very rare events. In short, it would seem that it would be perfectly acceptable for regulators to ask for the estimation and the monitoring of very high percentiles. And indeed this appears to be the case, as current prudential rules refer to losses incurred over a year at the 99.9th percentile (losses, that is, that should only be exceeded once every thousand years!).

Matters, unfortunately, are not so simple. The rules that the international banking supervisory bodies draft need to have other qualities as well in order to be effective and truly accepted rather than "swallowed" by the banks upon which they are imposed. These qualities are simplicity, transparency, or absence of regulatory arbitrage. Simplicity and transparency are simple to understand. But what does regulatory arbitrage mean? Regulatory arbitrage occurs when institutions are able to exploit loopholes to carry out actions that are within the letter of a given piece of legislation or regulation but run against its grain. The old capital rules, for instance, prescribed capital to be held against all risky loans. It did so by requiring more capital for riskier borrowers and less capital for safer ones. These rules were so coarse, however, that they failed to differentiate, as far as capital went, between lending to Microsoft or BP and lending to the mom-and-pop corner store. Unsurprisingly, under this set of rules banks found it much more capital-effective to lend to riskier borrowers than to safer ones (if the regulatory capital set aside was the same, the *return* on capital would be much higher for lending to the corner store). Clearly, this was not what the regulators had in mind when they drafted their rules.

The regulators learned from this experience and, with the revised capital rules called Basel II, they devised a much more nuanced (and vastly more complex) set of regulations. It may seem that such complexity is the required tool to clamp down on regulatory arbitrage. Unfortunately, experience from other areas of regulation and public law show that over-prescriptive and complex regulation does not eliminate the ability to find legal but "perverse" courses of action that still go against the spirit that informed the rules. Many countries, for instance, have come to the realization that, to avoid tax avoidance, the effective route is not ever more complex fiscal laws but a streamlining and simplification of the tax rules. By and large, highly prescriptive and complex rules do not eliminate regulatory arbitrage, they tend to make it less visible, less easy to control, and often more insidious. Very complex rules tend to divert substantial resources from productive tasks toward the "management" of regulation via complex structures, financial engineering, or Byzantine transactions with dubious economic justification. So, I would offer to regulators this first piece of advice. It may be better to leave some sources of risk imperfectly covered but to keep the rule book simple (and slim) than to try to cover every conceivable risk angle but to create an overly complex (and so insidious-arbitrage-prone) set of rules.

Another temptation that regulators should, in my opinion, strongly resist is to be over-conservative in their prescriptions. It may seem that requiring that a bank should be able to survive the default of 20% of its loans would be systemically safer than requiring solvency after the default of, say, 5% of its loans. Similarly, asking that losses from trading should not topple a bank in the event of a simultaneous increase in all rates by 2% *and* an equity market crash by 30% *and* a doubling of all credit spreads may seem a very "safe" measure to impose. The problem is that the bank itself will perceive such scenarios as capricious, unrealistic, and irrelevant to the true risks it runs. Therefore, the bank may well be forced to calculate the scary hypothetical losses associated with these Armageddon scenarios. Unfortunately, it will inevitably feel that these numbers are wholly irrelevant to its true risks, and will pay little attention to them. As soon as numbers are nodded through at an audit or board meeting, as soon as minuting the reporting of these figures becomes more important than studying them, as soon, in short, as risk management turns into compliance and box-ticking, the true control of financial risk in a bank has taken a heavy blow.

The first set of rules (devised for market risk) that improved the crude Basel I prescription had most of the positive features of good regulation. They were more realistic and nuanced than the coarse and overprudent regulation that preceded them. By using the concept of VaR they appealed to the intuition of virtually anybody in a bank. Requiring the calculation of a reasonable percentile (the 99th for a ten-day holding period, i.e., roughly a once-in-four-years event) faced banks with a demanding but not impossible or meaningless task. Regulators recognized well that they could not allow banks to go bust once every four years, but instead of requiring the calculation of an impossibly high percentile, they chose a laudably simple and commonsensical solution: they multiplied the capital estimated for a once-in-four-years event by a large but reasonable "safety factor." They were in good company in doing so, as lift engineers, for instance, have always multiplied the thickness of their cables, arrived at at the end of precise calculations, by the famous lift factor of ten: just in case.*

As the attention of the Basel II regulators moved from market to credit risk, many of these positive features of the earlier rules were lost. The capital calculations have became not just more complex but more opaque, and their meaning less intuitive. It is a safe bet that regulatory arbitrage will not disappear but will become more ingenious, less easy to spot, and probably more insidious. The simple safety factors have by and large been abandoned, and much higher percentiles have come to the fore. I have expended enough ink in this book arguing why I believe that a 99.9th, one-year percentile (i.e., a once-in-a-thousand-years event) is a meaningless concept both from a statistical and from a cognitive point of view that, hopefully, I do not need to repeat myself. Yet this has become one of the statistical cornerstones of the new rules.

The unfortunate truth is that regulators have been pointing at private banks, and at their economic-capital projects in particular, to justify their requests: if you, the banks, claim to calculate these percentiles (and, for that matter, even much higher ones) for your own internal purposes, why should we, the regulators, not require that you do so for prudential reasons as well? The flaw in this argument is that, as I explained above, banks did not really want to set aside enough capital to be more resilient than the Mycenaean civilization. Rather, they wanted to send to bondholders and shareholders signals that had become linked to the granting

---

*You may want to ponder, when you are about to land at the end of your next flight, that the analogous safety factor for the landing wheels of a passenger aircraft is 1.1: airplanes have to be safe, but they have to be able to take off too.

of credit ratings. Recall that agencies such as Moody's and S&P do *not* grant their ratings using only statistical estimates of probability of default. Rather, they use a variety of quantitative and qualitative criteria on the basis of which firms can be grouped into credit-similar cohorts. The frequency of default of these cohorts are then separately observed. For the very high rating bands to which most banks belong these frequencies are extremely low, and despite the decades of data and the thousands of companies monitored, only a small handful happen to default *in any one year*. Banks unfortunately reasoned that, if they somehow calculated an amount of capital that was linked to such remote frequencies (now understood as probabilities), external observers would associate them with the rating club they wanted to belong to. A tortuous line of reasoning, no doubt, but also a line of reasoning that had very little to do with what the regulators believed banks were up to: banks were not battening down the hatches against the perfect storm. Rather, much as a peacock parading its beautiful but ultimately useless tail, they were engaging in a signaling exercise.

I have had long discussions with many bank regulators. I have been lucky enough to engage with some of the brightest minds in their ranks. One of the architects of the Basel II framework agreed with many of the points above, and admitted that he had always meant that the 99.9th percentile should be given a "metaphorical" meaning (his words). This is all well and good, but very few of the national regulators that sat down to write specific rules made such an enlightened metaphorical interpretation of these guiding principles. When, down in the regulatory trenches, a bank supervisor has to tick a box that requires the 99.9th, one-year percentile to be calculated, metaphors quickly evaporate.

Finally, the last thing regulators should do is impose pseudo-scientific requirements. The myth of quantification is a pernicious (and expensive) one. Nobody's interests are well served when a great part of the finite risk-management resources of a bank are devoted to calculating numbers of dubious meaning, and when these numbers are interpreted using a flawed (frequentist) concept of probability—flawed, that is, given the context. It would be glib and presumptuous of me to say that "the regulators should learn Bayesian statistics." I am sure that many very knowledgeable analysts in the regulators' ranks understand Bayesian analysis and subjective probability extremely well. The real question is, "Why has it not been used more widely?" I admit that prior information, being intrinsically subjective, does not lend itself readily to prescriptive black-and-white regulation. But the caveats and the whole conceptual framework that Bayesian analysis naturally brings to the fore *can* inspire naturally and profitably the structure of the prudential rules. The width of a posterior distribution, for instance, can give useful guidance as to the reasonable size of an effective safety factor. The important thing is not to get a single number right, it is to know by how much we can be wrong and to act accordingly.

My recommendations, in short, would be to keep it simple, keep it believable, and *truly* speak the same language that banks employ. If banks tend to care about adverse events too "mild" for the systemic concerns of the regulators, apply a safety factor. The illustrious mechanical engineering history of safety factors could provide some guidance. And please read the last footnote about the safety factors that apply to the landing wheels of airplanes. Let us all ensure, that is, that the airplane is still light enough to fly after all the safety has been taken care of.

WHERE DOES THIS LEAVE US?

I have presented in this book a critical view of much of current financial risk management. This is not to say that all the recent developments, both on the regulatory and on the private-sector sides, have been bad. The intentions have by and large been laudable. The goal of linking (regulatory or "economic") capital to the financial risk that a bank actually runs makes sense. The sensible use of quantitative techniques can also benefit banking. And it is true that the most sophisticated models are only as good as the data we put into them, but banks have been goaded by regulators to collect better and more abundant data than ever before. They have been doing so with a lot of sighing and rolling of eyes, but, in the end, high-quality data *can* improve and make more robust the practice of banking. All of this is good.

The first cloud on this benign landscape comes in the form of a sense of missed opportunity. For instance, if the terabytes of data collected by banks are only used to estimate a very high percentile in the framework of an economic-capital calculation, we would indeed be spending our resources very unwisely. The same applies if the only use of a painfully and expensively constructed profit-and-loss distribution is to look up one single percentile.

The sky unfortunately gets darker. Some of the supposedly all-informative risk indicators of the new school of risk management (say, the 99.97th percentiles) are virtually impossible to estimate in a meaningful manner. Yet the senior management who are supposed to use these numbers as decisional tools rarely have the technical knowledge to appreciate this. There is more to this than a sense of missed opportunity. When numbers of dubious meaning are supposed to be used in anger in the decisional trenches, the situation can quickly become downright dangerous.

How did we get to this stage? There are "sociological" explanations aplenty to be found in the interaction between quants, their bosses, the bosses of their bosses, software vendors, etc. The root causes are, however, deep and diverse. To begin with, it did not help that modern risk-management thinking seems to be anchored to a singularly unproductive view of probability—a view, by the way, that has been superseded in those areas of scientific enquiry where sophisticated data handling really makes a difference. Applications where Bayesian analysis is now routinely used and has brought above improvements "in parameter estimates by orders of magnitude"* range from astrophysics to information theory to spectral line analysis. It is not necessary to go so far afield to find currently successful applications of Bayesian inference. In what is probably the most germane

---

*P. Gregory (2005), *Bayesian Logical Data Analysis for the Physical Sciences* (Cambridge University Press).

financial discipline to risk management, asset allocation, Bayesian analysis is not just a reality, it is a multimillion-dollar industry. Unfortunately, the Bayesian view of statistics has almost completely bypassed the world of risk management. It is ironic that this should be case just when risk management believes it has finally become "scientific."

A second cause of the current unsatisfactory state is the disconnect between the statistical quantities (painfully if naively estimated) and the decisions they are supposed to inform. Unidimensional, simplistic, cognitively artificial, and difficult-to-justify rules that link a single number (often a percentile) to a decision abound. The desire to have a "magic formula," a single number capable of encapsulating and resolving the complexity of financial decision making, is understandable but does not improve the practice of risk management. Additionally, there are interesting developments in this area (in prospect theory, say) that could be of use in clarifying the thought process underlying a financial decision under uncertainty. These disciplines are by no means newfangled areas of experimentation: their proponents are so much part of the scientific "establishment" that they have been awarded Nobel prizes. I have to admit that the successes reaped by these discipline are nowhere near the advances brought about by Bayesian analysis. It is premature, however, to write them off as theoretical niceties of limited practical importance, especially because the current prescriptions (often cloaked under the grand term of "best industry practice") in risk management are so poor. This area of research could be profitably linked to the currently burgeoning field of financial experimental psychology. Articles about how real human beings (as opposed to hyperrational, quadratic-utility-function-maximizing agents) react to risk have been written in their thousands. What is missing, again, is a constructive overlap with the theory and practice of risk management.

What would the consequences of missing these opportunities and plodding along as we are doing at the moment be? Devoting resources to impossible tasks, making poor use of the data that banks have collected, falling into the trap of "infinite precision"—all of this is bad enough as it is. But two much greater twin dangers are only a small step away. The first is the cynical use of these risk indicators: this occurs when the requirements of the regulators are perceived to be capricious and removed from the actual practice of risk management, and the computationally heavy calculations required by the regulators become an exercise in box-ticking. The second is the naive and uncritical use of the same risk indicators: those banks who naively believe that they have set aside enough capital to safeguard against once-in-three-thousand-years events are likely to be the first to regale the financial press with the next story about "inexplicable losses."

It is not too late to change the current thinking in financial risk management. Both practice and regulation are still evolving, albeit not quite as fluidly as they were only ten years ago. If this book gives pause for thought and serves as a call to arms for related disciplines (Bayesian analysis, decision theory, experimental psychology) to take a look at what is happening in the field of risk management, it will have more than fulfilled its purpose.

ENDNOTES

Chapter 1
Why This Book Matters

1. That is, for readers familiar with Markowitz's theory, unless the mix of businesses of a bank already lies on a point of the efficient frontier. See J. H. Cochrane and C. L. Culp (2003), Equilibrium asset pricing and discount factors: overview and implications for derivatives valuation and risk management, in *Modern Risk Management—A History* (ed. P. Field), chapter 5 (London: Risk Books).

Chapter 2
Thinking about Risk

1. For an intelligent and fascinating discussion of the shortcomings of pundits and experts at predicting political events, see P. Tetlock (2005), *Expert Political Judgement* (Princeton University Press).

2. To make the story simpler, I have changed the number of ships and ducats from Bernoulli's story. This example (with yet another combination of ships and ducats) is quoted in C. Gollier (2004), *The Economics of Risk and Time* (Princeton University Press). The treatment in that book gave me the idea to use it for this discussion.

3. It might be tempting to look at the social backgrounds of Bernoulli on the one hand, and of Pascal and Fermat on the other, and wonder whether their different solutions to a problem that involved risk might have a psychological "explanation" in their different social extractions. Bernoulli's father was after all a merchant, and one who traded in spices. The problem of how to transport such precious wares from

distant countries over perilous seas therefore was, to the Bernoulli family, not an abstract exercise in decision making, but a concrete problem that affected their livelihood. Can we speculate that Pascal, the son of a judge, and de Fermat, an aristocrat judging by the "de," may have been more drawn to abstract and less practical reasoning, and therefore may have found Bernoulli's solution less convincing? Perhaps. Before we get carried away with cheap risk sociology, however, let us not forget that despite the aristocratic-sounding "de," Pierre de Fermat's father was a merchant as well (of leather, in his case). And as for judges, they may have enjoyed at the time a somewhat higher status, but both merchants (of spice or leather) and judges were, after all, of solidly bourgeois extraction. It is perhaps the dodgy "de" for the son of a leather merchant that causes us to raise an eyebrow. If anything, a quirky parallel comes to mind: a few centuries later another extremely gifted mathematician (von Neumann) was to become famous for his infallible logic and the rather otherworldly nature of his solutions to decision problems. Like de Fermat, the name of this exceptionally gifted man also had an aristocratic prefix. However, in his case too, the "von" had simply been bought by John's banker father, presumably to give respectability to the Jewish family that was moving back and forth at the time between Hungary and Germany. Isn't it annoying that reality always turns out to be a bit more complicated than our pat explanations would like it to be?

4. An important and closely related field of study goes under the name of "bounded rationality." See, for instance, G. Gigerenzer and R. Selten (2002), *Bounded Rationality—The Adaptive Toolbox* (Cambridge, MA: MIT Press).

5. See, for example, J. P. Forgas, K. D. Williams, and W. Von Hippel (eds) (2003), *Social Judgements* (Cambridge University Press), and references therein. The terms System I and System II are commonly, but not universally, used. For instance, the terms "intuitive mode" and "controlled mode" are used by Kahneman (see, for example, D. Kahneman (2002), "Maps of bounded rationality: a perspective on intuitive judgement and choice," Nobel Prize Lecture (December 2002)).

6. See, for example, J. LeDoux (1996), *The Emotional Brain* (New York: Simon & Schuster). See also on a related topic work by G. Lowenstein, B. Knutson, and D. Prelec, recently published in *Neuron*, about the activity of different parts of the cortex involved in assessing trade-offs between pleasurable and adverse outcomes when evaluating a purchase (quoted in *The Economist*, January 13, 2007, p. 73).

7. For a simple discussion of the evolutionary advantage conferred by decisional heuristics, see, for example, P. M. Todd (2002), Fast and frugal heuristics for environmentally bounded minds, in *Bounded*

Rationality—The Adaptive Toolbox (ed. G. Gigerenzer and R. Selten), chapter 4 (Cambridge, MA: MIT Press).

8. For a modern discussion of the importance of salience, see, for example, M. Bacharach (2006), *Beyond Individual Choice: Teams and Frames in Game Theory* (Princeton University Press).

Chapter 3
Thinking about Probabilities

1. In some (rare) cases we may know virtually nothing about a phenomenon before we begin collecting the evidence. In these situations our prior belief is said to be "diffuse." Diffuse priors are not without conceptual problems (see, for example, P. Gregory (2005), *Bayesian Logical Data Analysis for the Physical Sciences* (Cambridge University Press), for a good discussion), but I cannot deal with this topic here. In practical applications I tend to find that, if too much is made of these logically valid objections, the troublemaker is, statistically speaking, often up to no good.

2. This does not necessarily mean that this is the "right" choice. What I have presented is a variation on the theme of an old paper by Paul Samuelson (P. Samuelson (1963), Risk and uncertainty: a fallacy of large numbers, *Scientia* 98:108–13). Samuelson, an economics professor, offered a colleague a fifty–fifty bet to win $200 or lose $100. The colleague (who became known in the large subsequent literature as "SC," for "Samuelson's colleague"), turned down the bet, but said that he would have accepted the same bet if repeated 100 times. Samuelson went on to prove that SC acted "irrationally" within the normative framework of utility theory. The point here is that turning down the one-shot bet and accepting the series of identical repeated bets seems natural and commonsensical (and, for what it is worth, it would be my choice as well), but it is not uncontroversial. True diversification, on the other hand, *is* uncontroversial. See also the discussion of Rabin's critique of utility theory in chapter 4 on this topic.

3. More precisely, in frequentist statistics, parameters, such as the tail probability of the coin, are fixed and not random. So either the coin is fair or it is not.

4. As I said, most, but not all, of the newspapers behaved this way. Indeed, the *Financial Times* and the *Economist* were two of the few sober exceptions in the British press and provided a rare example of self-restraint and responsibility in their reporting at the time. Five to ten years later, when their more balanced assessments proved much closer to the mark than those of their competitors, they unfortunately failed to reap any direct advantage from their self-restraint. Presumably, they

had simply sold fewer copies at the time of the hype than they could have. The tools at the disposal of the more sober newspapers to reap an advantage by calling the scaremongers' bluff were too blunt.

5. Operational risk is the risk of losses arising from factors such as fraud, human error, terrorist acts, disruptions to the business, etc. An inelegant definition of operational risk used to be "all risk that is left after trading and credit risk."

Chapter 4
Making Choices

1. I will show in chapter 10 that, when it comes to decision making, a "division of labor" of sorts takes place in many institutions. For the moment let us neglect this more realistic but more complex dynamics, and let us just call the decision maker "the risk manager."

2. The astute reader will have noticed that the distribution associated with trade B crosses the A distribution in figure 4.2 (the "no-brainer") only once, but twice in figure 4.3 (the "ambiguous" case). This observation is actually general: if a distribution with a higher mean only crosses another distribution of profits and losses once, then it "stochastically dominates" the latter. This means that *any* utility-maximizing investor would prefer the distribution to the right. See, for example, W. T. Ziemba (2003), *The Stochastic Programming Approach to Asset Liability Management* (Charlottesville, VA: Association for Investment Management and Research).

3. Economists explain that this is the reason why we pay a lot for assets that covary negatively with our consumption. See, for example, J. Cochrane (2001), *Asset Pricing*, chapter 1 (Princeton University Press).

4. For a discussion of this separation between "brawn and brains," see, for example, A. Shleifer (2000), *Inefficient Markets*, chapters 1 and 4 (in particular), Clarendon Lectures in Economics (Oxford University Press).

5. It is difficult, but not impossible. Very smart traders, especially using options, can sometimes put together strategies that display these positive features. As usual, they are likely to destroy the opportunities just by exploiting them. Bad for the traders, but good for the market, which has become a bit more efficient.

6. We are neglecting in this discussion the positive expected drift from investing in equities. Over a short horizon this matters little.

7. Some large fund managers who offer their services to the general public currently only charge (when all expenses are included) as little as one-third of a percentage point per annum for the service. If you happen

to be an institutional investor you will be able to negotiate even better terms.

8. Even if you are a hardcore efficient marketeer, market efficiency does not come about by divine intervention. Prices can only incorporate all the publicly available information about the various stocks because someone has done all the necessary homework. The process by means of which new information becomes translated into prices may be fast—very, very fast, even—but it cannot be *infinitely* fast. It is almost certainly far too rapid for a day trader sitting at home with his laptop computer to exploit. But an army of professional, sophisticated managers equipped with the latest state-of-the-art software and hardware *can* be just a bit ahead of the pack. Indeed, it is just by their actions that market can remain efficient.

9. Explanations along these lines belong to the "limit-to-arbitrage" school of thought.

10. Traders become very averse to losses because they can be "stopped out." Different traders whose losses are reckoned from the beginning of the financial year or on a twelve-month rolling basis are observed to display different risk-taking behavior.

11. Perhaps this is because financial firms are managed not by the ultimate shareholders (who may well care about *their* consumption pattern), but by their agents (the board, the CEO, the CFO, etc.) and it is much easier to incentivize these agents in terms of their profits and losses. The ultimate owners of a firm may well therefore be motivated in their choices by the absolute level of their wealth, but in designing the incentives for their agents, they end up making choices on the basis of profits or losses.

Chapter 5
What Is Risk Management For?

1. We should distinguish here between diversifiable and undiversifiable risk. For a discussion of this point see, for example, C. L. Culp (2003), The Modigliani–Miller propositions, in *Modern Risk Management: A History*, chapter 6 (London: Risk Books). My statement and the ensuing discussion refer to undiversifiable risk.

Chapter 7
Looking Beneath the Surface: Hidden Problems

1. VaR, for instance, lacks sub-additivity (i.e., I can increase the total VaR of two portfolios by putting them together, contrary to intuitive notions of diversification and risk). This problem can be fixed by using

a germane measure (conditional expected shortfall): roughly speaking, this is an average of the losses past the desired percentile.

2. Since the historical-simulation method appears to make use of no free parameters, it is often referred to as a nonparametric approach. Yet an extremely important parameter *is* used in the historical-simulation method, i.e., the length of the statistical record (that is, the length of the so-called "statistical window") to be used in the analysis. This implicitly tells us what constitutes the relevant past and does so in a binary manner (fully relevant—and included in the data set—or totally irrelevant—outside the boundaries of our data set).

3. "Financial crashes are 'outliers' " is indeed the title of chapter 3 of Sornette's book *Why Stock Markets Crash*, devoted to the study of extreme events in a variety of financial markets. An "outlier" in this context is an occurrence that does not belong to the population of normal events. It is one of the "Errors of Nature, Sports and Monsters" referred to in the quote that opens this section.

Chapter 8
Which Type of Probability Matters in Risk Management?

1. I am making the assumption here that the nature of the phenomenon is timescale invariant. So, having monthly data about corporate defaults is better, from a frequentist point of view, than having yearly data. This is because the underlying phenomenon does not change as a function of our sampling interval. The same may not be true, however, for tic-by-tic price moves and yearly price moves. See the discussion in chapter 7.

2. Establishing this correspondence between market price and fundamental value is essential if one wants to argue that securities held for the long term (say, in an investment portfolio) should also be marked-to-market daily. This observation may seem of rather narrow interest, but it can have a major impact on the risk regulation imposed on pension fund managers. Since this is a multitrillion-dollar industry, even mundane accountancy niceties can have seismic effects.

3. D. Poirier (1995), *Intermediate Statistics and Econometrics* (Cambridge, MA: MIT Press), reaches strikingly similar conclusions as he discusses the use of past data in assessing the probability of catastrophic failure before the fateful launch of the *Challenger* space shuttle in 1986. In his words, "we note that because there had been previously no catastrophic failures, it is difficult to think of an empirically based relative frequency interpretation of this concept. Rather, a 'degree of belief' interpretation seems necessary."

Chapter 9
The Promise of Economic Capital

1. Before we get started, we must keep in mind that the economic-capital view of the world presupposes that it makes sense for the firm (i.e., in our context, the bank) to engage in diversification. This means that the bank managers should not consider investments in isolation, but should look at how they fit into the overall portfolio. Diversification is *not* left wholly to the investor. If this seems too obvious even to state, let us remind ourselves that this is not how finance theory views diversification. If you have never lost any sleep over this, you can read on with abandon, innocent of any doubts that the idea of engaging in diversification may be conceptually flawed—personally, I do not think it is, for the reasons discussed in chapter 5. For the sake of honesty, though, I thought I should place the disclaimer right at the beginning of the discussion.

2. Raising and holding equity capital is more costly due to a combination of taxation rules and agency and information costs. See, for example, K. Froot and J. Stein (1996), Risk management, capital budgeting and capital structure, National Bureau of Economic Research Working Paper 5403 (Cambridge, MA), or R. C. Merton and A. F. Perold (1993), The theory of risk capital in financial firms, *Journal of Applied Corporate Finance* 5:16–32.

3. In a similar vein, readers familiar with asset allocation will know very well that Markowitz portfolios (which assume perfect knowledge of probabilities and correlations) can be radically, not marginally, different from Black–Litterman portfolios (which assume more diffuse beliefs about the same quantities).

Chapter 10
What Can We Do Instead?

1. Perhaps one could push the argument even further, as Chairman Greenspan did in 1998 when he wrote:

> The management of systemic risk is properly the job of the central banks. Individual banks should not be required to hold capital against the possibility of overall financial breakdown. Indeed, central banks, by their existence, appropriately offer banks a form of catastrophe insurance against such events.
>
> A. Greenspan (1998), *The Role of Capital in Optimal Banking Supervision and Regulation*, FRBNY Economic Policy Review (October 1998)

This may be a deregulation bridge too far, especially because a "normal" (i.e., nonsystemic) default of a large bank has the ability to have much wider (and possibly systemic) repercussions. As a consequence, when it comes to banks the boundaries between systemic and nonsystemic events can quickly become rather blurred. Again, it all goes back, in the end, to the fact that a bank is a "resiliently fragile" institution.

2. No one has stated this more clearly than Culp and Miller, who entitled the introductory article of a book they edited: "*Why* a firm hedges affects *how* a firm hedges" (their italics). See C. L. Culp and M. H. Miller (1999), Introduction: *why* a firm hedges affects *how* a firm hedges, in *Corporate Hedging in Theory and Practice: Lessons from Metallgeschaft* (ed. C. L. Culp and M. H. Miller), pp. xix–xxiii (London: Risk Books).

3. Indeed, we have seen in chapter 5 that, according to academia, the reason why private-firm risk managers should continue to draw a salary is not self-evident at all. By enriching the Finance 101 view about risk management within firms ("there should be none"), we did find a role for judicious control of risk in a private bank. Ultimately, we argued, risk management plays an important role in allowing the shareholders (and the bondholders) to discern more clearly, through the fog of financial noise, information about the bank itself.

4. We will consider *profits and losses*, despite the theoretical problems already discussed in chapter 4, simply because we would not even know how to begin to think in terms of "total consumption" (or its proxies) when it comes to the practical decisions the agents who run a financial institution have to make.

5. For a discussion see, for example, B. Cornell (1999), *The Equity Risk Premium* (Chichester: John Wiley & Sons), or E. Dimson, P. Marsh, and M. Staunton (2002), *Triumph of the Optimists* (Princeton University Press).

6. It may seem that this is where risk management and asset allocation differ most. Actually, this is not the case. There is a strong similarity between the "grafting" procedure just described and the Black–Litterman approach, which explicitly solicits from the investor his personal (nondata) views about returns, and directly incorporates them into the investment decision.

7. I do not want to give the impression that experimental financial psychology is virgin territory. Far from it. What is mainly lacking is cross-disciplinary fertilization and a link between the useful research that does exist and risk-management practitioners (and regulators).

INDEX

reinforcing, 120
framing, 95–96, 99–100, 248
Frederick, Prince, 2–3
frequentist probability approach,
18–19, 40, 53; actions and
probabilities, 65–66; belief in
the uniqueness of the "true"
value, 194–96; competitive
advantage in estimating
returns, 228–30; factors
favourable to, 185; long-term
portfolio, 193, 198; market
risk, 191–92; overall risk
nature of project, 235; rare
events and low probabil-
ity, 219; repeatability, 50;
as a special case of the all-
encompassing subjective
probability approach, 50,
182; statements, 48–50; uncertainty, 57–58
fundamental fitting approach,
152–55, 166
"fuzzy" probabilities, 66

"gambler's ruin," 172
Gaussian distribution, 153
Goethe, J. W. von, 2
Goldman Sachs, 115
Greenspan, A., 80, 249
Griffiths, T., 32–34

Hamlet, 107
Harvard University Press, 25
historical-simulation method,
148–49, 166

insurance payments: peace of
mind, 36; willingness to pay
when perceived probability
of risk is low, 35–36

Johnson, B., 139
Johnson, E., 30
joint probability distribution of
risk factors, 127–31, 171

kurtosis, 238–43

Laplace, P. S., 23–24, 91
large proportional differences in
small probabilities, 36–37
law of large numbers, 12
Leibniz, G. W., 2–3
liquidity, 9
long-term portfolio, 192–93; frequentist techniques, 193, 198;
mark-to-market valuation,
192–93, 196; profit-and-loss
distributions, 193; subjective
probability approach, 193–94,
197–98; trends, 197

"magic formula," 68, 105–6
market risk, 186–87; applicability
of Bayesian approach, 190;
frequency of data collection,
188; frequentist techniques,
191–92; relevant data, 188–90;
statistical properties of price
changes, 188
Markowitz, H., 24, 43, 57, 195
mathematics and social issues:
knowledge of, 138
maturity transformation, 12
maximum expected return: recommended investment, 25
Merton, R., 112
Miller, J., 140
modern finance: "no one is
in charge" concept, 10–11;
resourcefulness, reach and
intricacies of, 6–10
modern portfolio theory, 15–16